D1611218

Issues in Pharmaceutical Economics

Edited by

Robert I. Chien
Institute of Health Economics
   and Social Studies
and Roosevelt University

Lexington Books
D.C. Heath and Company
Lexington, Massachusetts
Toronto

Library of Congress Cataloging in Publication Data

Main entry under title:

Issues in pharmaceutical economics.

    1. Drug trade—United States—Addresses, essays, lectures. 2. Drugs—
Prices—United States—Addresses, essays, lectures. I. Chien, Robert I.
[DNLM: 1. Drug industry—United States—Congresses. 2. Economics—
United States—Congresses. QV736.3 I86 1976-77]
HD9666.4.I77   338.4'7'61510973   78-19726
ISBN 0-669-02729-4

Published simultaneously in Canada

Printed in the United States of America

International Standard Book Number: 0-669-02729-4

Library of Congress Catalog Card Number: 78-19726

Contents

Preface

The idea of establishing the Institute of Health Economics and Social Studies (IHESS, a "General Not for Profit Corporation" certified by the state of Illinois) to provide the public, academics, and public policymakers with a credible source of information and analysis dates back to the late sixties.

By 1975 public interest in health care in general and the pharmaceutical industry in particular reached such a height that the Center for Health Policy Research had already been established at the American Enterprise Institute and the Center for the Study of Drug Development at the University of Rochester. In addition, several symposia on the drug industry had been held under the auspices of American University. These conferences on drugs and the research supporting them focused on issues relating to the performance of the drug industry and the social benefits and costs of pharmaceutical innovations and government regulations. The results were useful to the public, the regulatory agencies, and Congress.

But the information needed by university faculties and students was another matter. Information about the drug industry in standard textbooks was badly outdated; it was based for the most part on congressional hearings held in the late fifties and early sixties. The methodology of evaluation was based on the conventional structure-conduct-performance paradigm despite the existence of a large number of newer studies that clearly showed the deficiencies of this approach. These newer studies examined specific features of the pharmaceutical industry (high growth rate based on technological breakthroughs, high risks, long gestation period for new products, and an unusually high proportion of investment in intangible assets such as research and development and promotional expenditures). Intense competition for the discovery of innovative drugs (and protective patents) and a new form of price competition that differed from the traditional pattern of short-run, partial equilibrium between cost and price seemed to call for a search for a new common ground in the application of economic theory and the formation of new public policy.

It seemed sensible to expect that new applications of economic theory would most likely come from the dispassionate sphere of academia. Thus IHESS began to look to the campuses to develop seminars on this fascinating industry. As we had hoped they would be, these seminars have been well received.

This volume is based on papers delivered by experts at seminars held at Northwestern University in 1976 and at UCLA in 1977. In addition to several pieces of original and thought-provoking work, this volume contains a collection of reviews of major literature in the field.

There are four sections in this book. The first part discusses facts and measurements of the pharmaceutical market, concentration, supply, entry, and promotion in an attempt to answer questions regarding the competitiveness and market power of the industry.

The second part deals with pricing and profitability issues. Have drug prices been flexible or excessive? Are returns to investment in the pharmaceutical industry comparable to industries in general? Issues concerning the proper treatment of intangible assets such as research and development and promotion expenditures as well as increased risks associated with new drug development are dealt with.

The third and fourth parts of this volume focus on the impact of government regulations on the pharmaceutical industry. Two papers and one commentary are devoted to the impact of regulation on the research process itself in part III while three papers and one commentary deal with the economic impact of regulations in part IV. Of the three economic impact papers, one deals with measures to control drug prices by government fiat, the second contains general comments on the economic impact of regulations designed without regard to such consequences, and the third paper attempts to summarize the future of and the effect of national health insurance on the vitality of the drug industry.

The main implication of the entire volume is that the drug industry has been competitive in the sense that the research-intensive drug companies are competing for dominance in different therapeutic areas. Government policies requiring excessive proof of efficacy and safety have raised the cost and uncertainties of research to such an extent that participation by smaller companies has been inhibited; government policies also appear to have reduced the rate of return for such investment below its opportunity costs. While the first effect has brought reduced competition in research, the second effect has likely impaired medical progress and perhaps reduced rather than improved social welfare.

We hope that this book will be used on the campuses by professors of industrial organization, of business strategy and policy, and of government regulation of business and pharmacy administration. We also believe that government regulators, legislators and their staffs, and corporate public and governmental affairs experts will find it a useful reference. In general, this book should be of particular interest to those interested in the dynamics of the free-market system. This system relies primarily on the provision of incentives such as the patent and trade secret protection for private businesses to achieve the desired allocation of resources for the society rather than on direct intervention by government in the form of price controls and interference with medical practice and with the research and development processes. The dynamics now inherent in the pharmaceutical industry, I believe, are quite clear in this volume and certainly indicate that important public policy decisions must be made in the years ahead.

I would like to express my appreciation to all the contributors, whose cooperation was essential to this volume. My gratitude also goes to financial supporters of the Northwestern University and UCLA seminars and to Lexington Books for its interest in publishing the work. Finally, without the efforts of Erol Caglarcan of Hoffmann-La Roche, Kurt Landgraf of the Upjohn Company, Charles Fry of Pfizer, James Riley of Merck and John Virts and Douglas Cocks of Eli Lilly and Company, it is unlikely that these seminars and consequently this proceedings would have become reality.

Robert I. Chien

**Part I
The History of Medicine and
Application of Economic Theory**

1

The History of Drug Discovery, Development, and Regulation

William M. Wardell

Overview: *At the beginning of this century there was essentially no scientific basis for therapeutics or, for that matter, medicine. The following four major developments led to what we now know as scientific therapeutics.*

1. *The growth of synthetic organic chemistry and the emergence of the synthetic drug molecule.*
2. *The rise of the sciences of physiology and pathology, and the emergence, on the basis of these, of pharmacology as an academic discipline.*
3. *The refinement of pharmacologic methods of examining natural substances for biological activity, and for quantitating the activity thus discovered (biological preparations and bioassay methods).*
4. *The development of scientific methodologies for studying drugs in man for efficacy and toxicity (controlled clinical trials).*

    The modern era begins in the mid 1930s with sulfanilamide, and experiences both with this drug and a later drug, thalidomide, led to the drug laws of 1938 and 1962, respectively.

    As a result of conservative practices, while the basic knowledge base has been increasing greatly, therapeutic progress has slowed. These constraints are particularly marked in the U.S., and current regulatory and legislative proposals would increase the constraints on the clinical application of biomedical knowledge in both the U.S. and the other major drug developing countries.

At the beginning of this century there were very few drugs that could be called safe and effective, and most of them were derived from plants. They were synthesized by nature and had been known for a long time, some back to medieval times and some to antiquity: morphine and its derivatives, digitalis (an eighteenth century discovery), and drugs for treating fever. Fever was thought to be a disease in its own right, not simply a sign of something wrong. There were drugs for treating "the fevers." One was the Peruvian bark that contained quinine. In the eighteenth century when the Jesuits cut off the supply of Peruvian bark to Europe, it was discovered that the bark of another tree—the willow—growing in a swamp (where fevers were thought to originate) had the

3

same effect of lowering fever. Because it came from the bark of the willow tree (genus Salix), it was called salicin. When it was synthesized, a derivative became aspirin.

No one knew much about disease, and therapy was crude. There were treatments that would today be called hazardous and ineffective, such as heavy metals. Mercury and bismuth, for example, were tried on sick people. Until the middle of the last century, mercury was virtually the only substance that was even slightly effective in treating syphilis. Artificially induced malaria was also used, because the high fevers caused by malaria kill the spirochetes of syphilis a little faster than they kill people. This was a useful, if hazardous, therapeutic margin. Hence the expression, "one night with Venus, a lifetime with Mercury."

There were many drugs whose efficacy (that is, effectiveness as therapy) was untested and unknown, and whose safety had never been examined. There were secret remedies (patent medicines or nostrums) such as snake oil and other "cures" proffered for cancer and tuberculosis. The obvious problems surrounding these secret remedies helped to stimulate passage of the 1906 Pure Food and Drugs Act, which primarily addressed the adulteration of foods and then medicines. One of its main achievements was to eliminate patent, secret remedies and to require truthful labeling.

This regulatory heritage makes the Federal Food and Drug Administration (FDA) justifiably nervous about drugs like Laetrile which have never been through the current regulatory process and on which there are no good scientific data. The popular movement to legitimize a drug like Laetrile threatens some of the safeguards that have taken the FDA and society a long time to achieve. It is this spectre of what might happen if Laetrile and other such drugs bypass the scientific pathways that is upsetting. We must distinguish clearly between substances like Laetrile, and the newer synthetic drugs that have been through the legitimate pathways of investigation and are judged on scientific data.

What led to the changes that brought us where we are today? Four major developments began in the middle of the last century; some of them are still happening.

One was the rise of the science of physiology and the emergence of the science of pharmacology. Physiology is the study of how the body works. Pharmacology is the study of how drugs act. Knowing the physiology and being able to integrate the actions of drugs with how the body works is the beginning of understanding how drugs affect living tissues. It is the rise of these two as academic disciplines and their merging with the sciences of pathology and experimental medicine that started the changes. The work of Claude Bernard around 1850 is rightly regarded as a landmark in this development.

Another landmark in this regard was Oliver and Schafer's discovery in 1895 that a ground-up adrenal gland injected into cats greatly increased the blood pressure; hence, adrenaline, a hormone of the body that acts potently on many physiological systems. In 1905 Henry Dale, a famous English pharmacologist, took this purified hormone (now called adrenaline in Europe and epinephrine in this country because "Adrenalin" had been taken as a trademark in the U.S. by Parke-Davis) and showed that adrenaline had different types of actions on different tissues, and paved the way for demonstrating its role as a neuro-effector transmitter. In part as a result of this work, he won a Nobel Prize.

In 1947 Raymond Ahlquist, a U.S. pharmacologist, clarified adrenaline's different actions on different tissues and postulated two types of adrenergic receptors: alpha and beta. Modification of the molecule of adrenaline led to different degrees of activity on the alpha versus the beta receptors (including pure alpha and pure beta stimulants), and further modifications even led not only to drugs that would mimic the actions of these two aspects of adrenaline, but to drugs that would block them. As a result of this chemical modification of the adrenaline molecule (perjoratively termed by people who don't like it, "molecular manipulation" or "molecular roulette"), by the 1940s there was an array of stimulant drugs for asthma and for maintaining blood pressure and by the 1960s an array of drugs that would block either the alpha actions or the beta actions of adrenaline selectively.

The beta blockers are a classic example of how advances in pharmacologic knowledge are harnessed by the pharmaceutical industry to produce drugs of therapeutic value. The discoverer of the beta receptors (Ahlquist) and the industrial developer of the first usable beta blocking drug (James Black) were awarded the 1976 Lasker Prize for medicine and therapeutics for what was described as one of the most important findings of this century, the discovery of beta blockers and their action in cardiovascular disease.

The second major development that led to today's state of knowledge is the refinement of pharmacologic methods for examining substances with biological activity: qualitative and quantitative bioassay. In this procedure, pieces of tissue are used to define the actions of substances, either synthetic or natural. Most of the hormones we know were assayed and standardized in this manner. Among the earliest were thyroid hormone, the estrogens (female sex hormones), and (in the early twenties) insulin. Bioassays are still used today, although as the analytical methods have become better, substances can be synthesized and characterized by physical techniques such as mass spectroscopy, and the molecule can be identified by its chemistry rather than its biologic activity. A phase that still persists in the pharmacology of any substance, however, is the need to characterize its actions on body systems.

The third major development consists of techniques for examining compounds for toxicity and efficacy: in particular, formal experimental designs for, and statistical procedures for analyzing the results of, toxicity and efficacy studies in both animals and man. Generally the human studies present the greatest methodological challenge, hence the importance of the controlled clinical trial.

The first such controlled clinical trial of modern times is probably that by

James Lind, a naval physician in Britain who was seeking ways to combat scurvy. The British navy was experimenting with boiled fresh vegetables of different types and beer brewed from fresh plants. The results of Lind's clinical trials were used by Captain James Cook, the success of whose voyages in 1769 was probably due to the fact that these were the first large-scale expeditions in which a large proportion of the crew did not die of scurvy. In his clinical trial Lind took twelve sailors sick with scurvy and divided them into two groups of six each. One was a control group and the other the test group. He selected the ones nearest death for the active (fresh vegetable) treatment, so it was not a randomized study. Today we would probably have to reject this study because it was not "well controlled" in the regulatory sense: the two treatment groups were biased by selecting the worse people for the drug. The sickest people who got the treatment all improved, and those who didn't get the treatment got worse. Today we know the active principle of this treatment as vitamin C.

Modern history was heavily influenced by the agricultural statisticians of the 1920s, especially R.A. Fisher and Fisherian statistics. Most of the designs that we use today in clinical testing originated in this discipline. Plots, randomized blocks, Latin squares, and the analysis of parametric data depend heavily on agricultural methods. I believe that some of our present problems have come about because physicians in the 1950s seized on these methods which then become virtually written into the law, or at least into the regulations, beginning with the Kefauver-Harris Amendments of 1962 with their rigid, controlled clinical trials. At present the pendulum is probably still swinging towards the direction of too-rigid requirements.

Today we rely considerably on what are termed double-blind, randomized, controlled, clinical trials. "Controlled" means that there must be a comparison group of some type. The control may turn out to be good or bad, and this is sometimes a matter of vigorous scientific debate. The law calls for trials to be "adequate and well-controlled" and the regulations define what FDA believes is meant by "well-controlled." "Blind" means that the patient does not know whether he is receiving the treatment or the control medication. "Double-blind" means that the physician does not know either; that is, the medication is decoded afterward to avoid the problem of subjective bias by the evaluating physician.

The fourth major development has been the growth of organic chemistry from about the seventeenth century to the present—very important as a scientific discipline and as an industry. Progress in organic chemistry has made it possible to synthesize molecules unknown in nature and to pass these to the newly developing disciplines of physiology, pharmacology, and experimental medicine. This process began in the Swiss and German dyestuff industries where they were manipulating the molecules to get different colors as well as substances that would stick more permanently to textiles. Much expertise developed there from the earliest stages.

Then around 1850 we had developments that led to theories of how drugs interact with biological material, based on the newly developed science of histology in which tissues were stained with dyes for viewing under the microscope. Researchers noticed that different dyes affixed themselves to different parts of cells. From this came the theory that "a magic bullet" that could lock onto infecting organisms, especially parasites, would make it possible to stain parasites selectively and perhaps wipe out the parasites selectively without affecting the human they were in. (This development was due to Paul Ehrlich around 1900.)

Many disciplines converged to bring this about. Key events include the synthesis of aspirin in about 1880; synthesis of barbituric acid in 1903, leading to all the barbiturates; and the synthesis of organic compounds of heavy metals (the organic forms of arsenicals and mercurials being safer for man than the hazardous metallic salts previously used). (Today, of course, even most of these are considered too hazardous to give to man.) One of the early landmarks was a compound of arsenic called Salvarsan for syphilis.

All the foregoing developments bring us up to the 1920s, and form a prelude to the extraordinary developments of the modern era of pharmacotherapy.

The recent era of the research-based pharmaceutical industry probably begins in the mid-1930s when a substance—again a dye—called prontosil rubrum was tested by French scientists and found to kill streptococci bacterial in test tubes. What made this exciting was that it did not kill mice. Thus the possibility of a large therapeutic ratio was realized—the power of the drug to kill an unwanted organism without killing the person.

This led to sulfanilamide, the first drug of the sulfanomide series, in 1936. Sulfanilamide was found as a hydrolysis product of prontosil rubrum. Once the antibacterial properties of the basic sulphonamide structure had been established, an enormous number of different sulphonamide molecules were synthesized by molecular modification. About 5,000 sulfanomides were synthesized and studied by different companies. Very soon, by serendipitous clinical observation of patients on sulfanomide therapy, it was found that these drugs increased passage of urine. From this, by further molecular modification of the sulphonamide structure, arose the whole family of oral diuretics that we now have available to treat heart failure and hypertension. In a similar serendipitous fashion it was found that in some patients the sulphonamides lowered blood sugar, and so the whole family of sulfonylurea oral hypoglycemic agents was discovered. Other patients developed certain abnormalities of thyroid function while taking the early sulfonamides and this led to the discovery of another class of molecular variants, anti-thyroid drugs for treating hyperthyroidism. Further theoretical and empirical observations led to the use of diazoxide for lowering blood pressure acutely.

The early history of the sulfonamide series illustrates the importance to drug development of serendipitous clinical observations of drug actions—a major pathway of drug discovery whose key importance is not generally appreciated. Many

new therapeutic discoveries about drugs can only be made *after* the drug has
been given to man—in some cases only after years of marketed use for an
unrelated purpose. The implications of serendipitous discovery are that preventing molecules from getting into man—for whatever reason—will prevent new
discoveries from being made, and we will never know what is being missed.

Sulfanilamide, the first therapeutic discovery of the modern era, also was
responsible for the first modern drug disaster and for passage of landmark
legislation concerning drugs. An American company, seeking a way to make
a liquid form of sulfanilamide for children, dissolved it in ethylene glycol
(antifreeze). Although ethylene glycol was known to be very toxic for man,
the company was not aware of this and did not test the resulting "elixir sulfanilamide" in animals. Over 100 children died and this led to the 1938 U.S.
Food, Drug and Cosmetic Act which contained the first specific regulation of
pharmaceuticals, and introduced the requirement for premarket approval, via
an approved New Drug Application (NDA) before a new drug could be introduced into interstate commerce.

The chemotherapeutic advance of the sulfonamides was soon overshadowed
by the isolation of penicillin from cultures of fungi, beginning in 1938 and
leading to its first human use in 1941. By 1960 the molecular structure of
penicillin nucleus had been characterized and the molecule could be modified
structurally. There are now several thousand penicillin-type compounds with
different spectra of activities. Penicillin itself came in 1945 and ampicillin, the
first gram-negative acting penicillin, in 1961. The first penicillin active against
penicillinase-resistant organisms came in 1962 (methicillin) and a number of
similar compounds followed.

How is the system organized today? Basic research leading to the production of new knowledge is largely funded from the public sector, particularly
the U.S. National Institutes of Health, whose budget has gone from zero before
its inception in 1953 to between $1 billion and $2 billion a year today. This
support of basic research is probably responsible for most of the new biological
knowledge in the world at present. Such knowledge becomes common property
because it is published.

The exploitation of this new knowledge to develop usable drug candidates
for man is mainly a function of the private sector. This is, the synthesis of new
drug molecule candidates, the testing of these in animals for pharmacologic
activity and toxicity, and the testing in man for safety and efficacy are done
largely by the pharmaceutical industry which in the United States has a research
budget approximately the size of the government's—between $1 billion and $2
billion annually.

The pace of discovery of new knowledge has increased at an impressive rate.
By any count—the funding, the number of papers—the rate is increasing probably
exponentially. However, the translation of this knowledge into applied therapies
has slowed down over the past two decades.

The reasons for this are complex.[a] One is that the scientific standards of proof have gone up, raising the expenses and making it harder and more expensive to satisfy both current scientific standards and regulatory demands. These rising standards have potential for both good and harm. Obviously, the more we can know about something, the better. On the other hand, the more you have to find out about a compound before it can be tested in man, the more expensive the product will be and the less chance it will have of being developed at all. Small companies will be prevented from testing marginal compounds; and compounds for small markets—even if medically needed—might not make it to the market because of unattractive return on investment.

A second major reason for the slowdown is that research has become increasingly regulated. Regulation is coming from two sources: first, specific regulation under the Food, Drug and Cosmetic Act, both for drugs and more recently for devices; and second, constraints due to concern about human experimentation (societal constraints on human research). Institutional review committees are now required at every hospital for any kind of clinical study. Voluntary prisoner research, which used to be the major locus of phase I drug studies, has just about disappeared in the last two years.

Clinical research on drugs and devices is one of the very few scientific and industrial endeavors where the actual research process is itself subject to regulation, and the regulation in this field has been present longer than anywhere else. In other fields, regulation applies once a product is on the market, but here the process of studying the compound is itself regulated. While regulation exists in some areas of atomic research and has recently appeared for recombinant DNA research, clinical pharmacological research is much more encompassing. Pharmaceutical research has been regulated since 1938 and the regulation gets more detailed by the year.

The essential details of the present system of drug development and regulation in the U.S. are shown in figure 1. The requirement of an approved NDA before a drug could be marketed came in 1938. The Investigational New Drug (IND) requirement which controls clinical investigation was added in 1963 as a result of the 1962 Kefauver-Harris Amendments. At present a preclinical phase of chemical, pharmacological, and animal testing leads to the point of an IND filing. Three phases of clinical studies under the IND lead to submission of an application to FDA by the drug's sponsor for NDA approval. Then the NDA

---

[a]In attempting to explain why the appearance of new therapeutic drugs has declined over the past two decades, the FDA has espoused what can be termed a "knowledge depletion" hypothesis—that is, the previous reserves of basic knowledge on which new drugs are based has been "mined out" and that more basic knowledge is needed to enable us to make applied advances in therapeutics. This view runs counter to the experience of pharmacologists and most other informed people and FDA cannot document it. FDA's hypothesis is that it is not compatible with the existence of a knowledge explosion, and appears to be spurious.

phase begins: the FDA reviews the data and determines whether the evidence presented on the drug satisfies the law's (and regulation's) requirements for proof of acceptable safety and efficacy. If this phase is successful, marketing approval is given and the process enters phase IV (postmarketing) which is not formally regulated at present but which is the subject of the current Drug Regulation Reform bill (1978). The animal toxicology runs parallel to the early clinical investigation and is complete at the point before NDA approval is given.

The process of clinical investigation and NDA approval is quite lengthy (see figure 1-1). Our own studies show that successful new molecules require about three years at the IND stage and two years for the NDA review. Prior to that the time required is uncertain because the events occur inside industrial firms, but a reasonable estimate is that preclinical pharmacology and toxicology and the chemical aspects take anything from one to three years on average. All this diminishes the amount of patent protection remaining at the point of NDA approval for the market; although the nominal patent life is seventeen years, the effective patent life for those new molecules approved in 1977 in the U.S. was just under nine years.

There is a considerable attrition of compounds at each stage of the development process. Attrition at the earliest stages is a matter of conjecture because this is all proprietary information. However, it is reasonable to estimate that about 10,000 potential drug candidates are synthesized for every one that gets to market and that about 1,000 of these undergo some animal testing to determine whether they have any activity. From this point on, the rates of attrition are very well defined. For every ten that reach the stage of an IND filing in the U.S., five are dropped by the firm by fifteen months into human testing. Nine out of the ten have been dropped by the stage of NDA submission, but the one survivor that reaches an NDA submission has ninety percent chance of being approved by the FDA, given five years for review at FDA.

The costs are quite formidable, because of the large amount of work that has to be done on compounds that are subsequently dropped and the long time period involved before even the successful ones can give returns on investments. Ronald Hansen's work with us on cost estimates in the U.S. shows that in capitalized 1976 dollars, each successful new chemical entity that reaches the U.S. market represents an investment of $30 million in pre-IND studies and $24 million in post-IND studies, a total of $54 million.

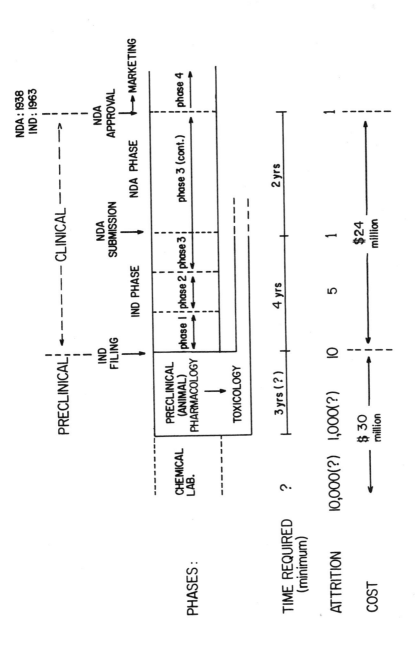

Figure 1-1. Drug Development (U.S.A.)

2

A Summary and Critique of Economic Studies of the Ethical Drug Industry: 1962–1968

Joseph M. Jadlow

Overview: *Economic analyses of the U.S. pharmaceutical industry published from 1962 to 1968 (including studies by Henry Steele, Leonard G. Schifrin, Peter M. Costello, and William S. Comanor) relied heavily on evidence from the Kefauver hearings and tended to be critical of industry behavior and performance. All the studies identified drug patents as the principal cause of this poor performance. Three of the authors advocated compulsory patent licensing, predicting that it would increase price competition in this industry and reduce spending on wasteful research and advertising, while the fourth author called for the elimination of all drug patents. A recent study by Jadlow provides statistical results suggesting that compulsory patent licensing could have a depressing effect on drug innovation.*

Prior to 1962 no studies of the ethical drug industry appeared in any of the major economic journals, probably because the industry was relatively small and because drug industry data were unavailable to economists. Economists began to take an active research interest in this industry as a result of hearings on the drug industry held by the Subcommittee on Antitrust and Monopoly of the Senate Committee on the Judiciary [21, 22, 24] between 1959 and 1962. These hearings, chaired by Senator Estes Kefauver, attracted public attention because of allegations by witnesses about excessive prices and profits for drugs. In addition to the Kefauver hearings that began in December 1959 and the Nelson hearings [23] which got underway in early 1967, at least nine other series of congressional investigations and hearings concerning the drug industry were held over the same eight-year period [18, p. 894].

This paper describes the economic analysis in several studies of the economics of the U.S. pharmaceutical industry which were published from 1962 to 1968. Like many of the congressional hearings during that period, most of these economic studies tended to be critical of various aspects of the behavior and performance of the drug industry. This is not surprising since the sources of much of the data for these articles were those hearings. Brief descriptions of the analysis and public policy proposals of these papers are presented in the sections that follow. The discussion of each investigator's work is followed by a brief critique of his analysis.

13

Henry Steele's Analysis

The first study of the ethical drug market published in a leading economics journal seems to have been one by Henry Steele [19] in 1962. The principal sources employed by Steele in writing this article, as well as a similar paper which he published two years later [20], were the written record of the Kefauver hearings [21, 22] and a 1958 Federal Trade Commission report [8] on the economics of antibiotics manufacture.

Steele's investigation of the production and marketing of ethical drug products convinced him that behavior in this industry was resulting in a misallocation of economic resources. He asserted that his resource misallocation had been

> made possible by the existence and abuse of the patent privilege for ethical drug products and processes and by a number of measures which the industry has taken to foster and exploit the remarkable degree of imperfection of market information which the structure of the ethical drugs market permits [19, p. 132].

Before describing these behavioral abuses in detail, Steele listed several features of the economic framework of the ethical drug market which he considered important in determining behavior. One of these is "the separation of the authority to prescribe from the responsibility to pay" [19, p. 132]. Steele pointed out that prescribing physicians have little economic motivation to prescribe the lowest-priced brands for their patients and that in most states patients cannot substitute lower-priced brands for those prescribed by their physicians. As a result, he suggested, the demand curves for individual drugs or for groups of related drugs are likely to be "extremely inelastic" [19, p. 133].

A second feature of the drug market's framework that Steele discussed was that firms in the United States can obtain both drug "product" patents and drug "process" patents, while only twenty-eight of seventy-seven countries studied by the Kefauver subcommittee grant pharmaceutical "product" patents, and twenty-five of these twenty-eight have provisions for "compulsory licenses" [19, p. 135]. Moreover, it has become easier in recent years to obtain drug patents in the United States because of a broadening of the definition of a patentable drug [19, p. 136].

The third characteristic of the drug market's framework emphasized by Steele is the high concentration in the production of most of the important ethical drugs, even though there seem to be "few, if any, notable economies of scale in the production process" [19, p. 134]. Concentration may therefore be higher than is necessary for production efficiency.

Steele contended that the response of the ethical drug industry to this economic framework may be interpreted as a successful strategy to exploit the monopolistic potentialities inherent in trademarks, the patent privilege, and the great inelasticity of market [demand], in such a way as to overcome the potential for competition implicit in the absence of economies of scale and, to a lesser extent, in the presence of governmental inspection to insure the safety of all drugs placed on the market [19, pp. 136-137].

He argued that the patent privilege is the "most prominent monopoly element in the market" [19, p. 137] and has accounted for much of the high concentration. In addition, he suggested that most price competition has been eliminated from ethical drug markets because generic drug names are complicated and producers' selling efforts have succeeded in getting physicians to prescribe by brand names, most states have antisubstitution laws that prevent pharmacists from substituting lower-priced drugs for prescribed brands, pharmacists have no economic incentive to sell the lowest-priced drugs, drug advertising seldom mentions drug prices, physicians are not price conscious, and large firms disparage the quality of smaller firms' products [19, pp. 140-143]. According to Steele, "product competition" rather than price competition predominates in the ethical drug market and frequently involves only slight modifications of existing products [19, p. 148]. At the same time, he observed, competition based on "product differentiation" also occurs as different firms sell identical drugs under different brand names and heavily promote them as different. Steele provided some evidence that the lack of price competition leads to prices that are much higher than costs for many drug products [19, pp. 159 and 161].

Thus Steele concluded that performance in ethical drug markets has been poor as a result of the use of the patent privilege and the promotion of brand names to reduce price competition. Furthermore he questioned the usefulness of much of the research in this industry on the grounds that its main purpose is to find patentable therapeutic agents which usually turn out to be only slight modifications of products that are already available.

Steele offered several remedies designed to increase price competition for drug products. The most important called for "the abolition of the patent privilege as it applies to drug products" and the introduction of "compulsory licensing, at reasonable royalty rates, of drug process patents" [19, p. 162]. He predicted that these measures would result in the entry of large numbers of firms into individual drug markets. He acknowledged that the incentive of drug firms to do research would be reduced; but, he reasoned, this reduced incentive might improve the use of resources because the most important drug research is the basic research done outside the industry, and industry research is often wasteful.

In addition, he advocated an increase in the Food and Drug Administration's inspection of drug production facilities so that physicians would have confidence in the quality of the products of both large and small producers. He also suggested that in drug labeling and advertising "all ethical drugs be identified solely by the generic name, in conjunction with the name of the seller employed as an adjectival modifier" [19, p. 162] and that all advertising should include "suggested retail prices" [19, p. 163]. He expected these steps—increased inspection, elimination of trade names, and requiring price advertising—to increase the degree of price competition in drug markets.

In summary, Steele expected his proposals, if enacted, to reduce drug profits, prices, and wasteful R&D and advertising. He even thought that the ethical drug industry "might be highly competitive, perhaps almost purely competitive, in the absence of patent protection and the brand name monopoly or oligopoly it makes possible" [19, p. 161].

Most of the characteristics of market structure and behavior that Steele attributes to ethical drug markets seem accurate. Seller concentration is high in most therapeutic drug markets, competition based on the introduction of new products has probably tended to be more important than price competition, and physicians usually do prescribe by brand name rather than generic name. Steele's conclusion, however, that these aspects of market structure and behavior have resulted in a serious "misallocation of resources" [19, p. 132] in drug markets is not proved by his analysis. He reached this conclusion in part because of his view that drug firms carry out "duplicative research and product development programs" [19, p. 163] and thus waste some resources employed for R&D. Over the years many new drug products that have been patented and marketed have been similar to drugs already on the market. Contrary to the impression conveyed by Steele, however, these new drugs provide some obvious social benefits. For example, they provide price competition for established drugs and thus prevent some deadweight welfare losses by keeping drug prices lower than they would be in the absence of the new drugs. (This is clearly demonstrated by some of the findings of Sam Peltzman [16].) In addition, many of these new drugs are different enough from established drugs to benefit some patients who are not able to take advantage of the older products (say, because of adverse reactions to the older products). Therefore the mere fact that many new drugs that have been introduced on the market are "me-too" products does not necessarily imply that resources are being misallocated.

There seems to be little doubt that adoption of the policy proposals advocated by Steele would increase price competition for drugs, but this would be accompanied by a decline in the incentive for private drug firms to do research. Whether the social benefits of the increased price competition would outweigh the social costs of a reduced flow of new drugs is not clear. Given his views that drug firms waste resources on R&D, Steele argues that a "major shift of pharmaceutical research . . . from private firms to public, university, and foundation channels could scarcely avoid resulting in gains" [19, p. 162]. Even if much drug research is wasteful, however, Steele's proposals provide no mechanism for producing a "major shift" of drug research "from private firms to public, university, and foundation channels" [19, p. 162]. In other words, his proposals seem likely to reduce R&D by pharmaceutical firms without providing any means for bringing about a compensating increase in research by outside organizations.

Steele was critical of the types of research carried on by drug firms and many of the new products that they introduce. We now have evidence that the attempt to guarantee the quality of new drug products by a proof of efficacy requirement contained in the Drug Amendments of 1962 may have contributed to a misallocation of resources rather than to improved resource allocation. Empirical work by Sam Peltzman [16] suggests that this increased regulation of drug quality is resulting in an annual social welfare loss of several hundred million dollars because of the forgone opportunities caused by the slow introduction of new products. (For an alternative view, see the critical comment on Peltzman's study by McGuire, Nelson, and Spavins [11]).

Leonard G. Schifrin's Analysis

Leonard G. Schifrin [18] continued the theme presented by Steele in his two articles [19, 20]. According to Schifrin, the U.S. ethical drug industry shifted from a period of great price competition in the 1940s to market behavior since then that has been dominated by the production of differentiated specialty products that are patentable and are promoted under trade names [18, p. 897]. He reported that congressional investigations and hearings on the industry in the 1950s and 1960s revealed, "wasteful use of resources in promotion and research, the dubious contribution of some of its output, and the uneconomic relationship between the costs and prices of its products" [18, p. 894].

Much of Schifrin's discussion of market structure and behavior for ethical drugs is similar to that presented by Steele. Therefore, rather than repeat those points, this section focuses on Schifrin's evaluation of "product performance" [18, p. 903] and "market performance" [18, p. 906] for drug products.

Schifrin praised the industry for the many new drug products that it has introduced. At the same time, however, he complained that much of the industry's R&D is "imitative" [18, p. 905] and that the resulting products do not represent important therapeutic advances. He suggested that the structure of the industry had much to do with creating this behavior pattern.

He listed a number of criticisms concerning the performance of ethical drug markets in terms of the efficiency of the allocation of resources. He speculated that R&D outlays in this industry might be too high and directed more toward obtaining patents than toward developing therapeutically significant products. Similarly he suggested that promotional expenditures were probably too high; and while he agreed that some of the promotion provides useful information to physicians, he expressed misgivings about the quality of some of this information [18, pp. 907-908]. He noted that profits in this industry are consistently higher

than those of other industries and said that this difference suggests that prices
are well above costs. Furthermore he pointed out that high rates of return are
typical for the largest firms in the industry, and he argued that this implies
"low risks" [18, p. 908]. At the same time, he rejected the contention that
high profits are necessary to finance drug R&D because R&D costs have
already been subtracted before profits are calculated [18, p. 910] and because
some firms reap high profits on sales of products that are produced by license
from other firms and are thus not the result of the selling firm's own research
[18, p. 911].

In formulating public policy suggestions for this industry, Schifrin indicated that he was seeking ways to reduce "wasteful outlays" by firms and
"excessive profit margins" without eliminating the "availability of rewards
sufficient to promote the discovery and development of new and better
products" [18, p. 912]. He proposed two principal policy recommendations
that he predicted would greatly increase price competition and eliminate
"wasteful and uneconomic practices" [18, p. 912].

First, he argued that entry barriers created by patents had to be reduced,
and he suggested that this could be done by requiring "compulsory patent
licensing" at a "fair royalty rate" after a "realistic" period (say, three years)
of exclusive patent use for the patent holder [18, p. 914]. Unlike Steele, he
made no distinction between the treatment of product patents and process
patents. Although Schifrin believed that compulsory licensing would result
in entry and increased price competition, he contended that it would also
allow sufficient profits to induce drug firms to continue to do research and
develop new products—in fact, he suggested that "it might generate even
greater effort by inducing swifter turnover" [18, p. 915].

Second, he recommended prohibiting the use of trade names in prescription writing [18, p. 913]. He expected this provision to result in an increase
in generic prescribing and the selection of drugs "on the basis of price rather
than company identification" [18, p. 913].

Clearly the policy proposals of Schifrin and Steele are about the same.
However, they differ somewhat in the effects that they expect these policies
to have on industry R&D behavior. Steele anticipated a sharp cutback in R&D
activity by the industry, but he considered this desirable since much industry
R&D activity is development work rather than basic research. In contrast,
Schifrin foresaw little or no reduction in R&D by the industry, and he seemed to
consider this fortunate because, while much of the industry's R&D is applied
research and development work, he believed that the product improvements that
result are often valuable to society.

Many of the criticisms of Steele's analysis also apply to Schifrin's paper. Two
additional points will be made.

First, Schifrin emphasized that profit rates in the drug industry are consistently higher than those of other industries and that this difference implies a misallocation of resources. This inference is not necessarily the case, however, since the profit rates that he referred to are accounting rates of return. As a number of authors have pointed out, most of the expenditures on R&D made by drug firms are actually investment outlays, but these are usually treated as current expenses rather than capitalized, thus making it likely that accounting profit rates are different from the true economic rates of return [1, 9]. Therefore, the relatively high accounting rates of return in this industry do not necessarily indicate allocative inefficiency.

Second, some of Schifrin's arguments seem contradictory. For example, he is critical of "wasteful outlays" [18, pp. 907 and 912] on R&D and promotion, and he predicts that his policy proposals would reduce these wasted expenditures. Yet in defending his proposal for compulsory licensing, he seems to argue that the proposed policy "might generate even greater [R&D] effort by inducing swifter turnover" [18, p. 915] of products. Thus at one point he contends that his proposal will reduce wasteful R&D spending, while at another point he suggests that the policy may actually increase R&D effort and cause an increase in new product competition. He cannot have it both ways.

Peter M. Costello's Analysis

A 1968 paper by Peter M. Costello [7] argued, as did the articles by Steele and Schifrin, that drug patents have undesirable effects on market behavior and performance. Employing information from Federal Trade Commission and Justice Department antitrust cases involving five major antibiotic producers, Costello described behavior in the "broad spectrum" antibiotic market which causes him to conclude:

> Where product discovery threatens to weaken or lessen a few firms' market dominance, patent and license agreements can serve as conspiratorial devices to suppress certain socially desirable forms of competition [7, p. 13].

Costello began his study with a description of the circumstances that generated effective competition in the "narrow-spectrum" antibiotics market. No "product" patent was available for penicillin because it was a "product of nature" and domestic rights to "process" patents were held by the United States Department of Agriculture which licensed all qualified applicants [7, p. 15]. As a result, entry was easy in both the production and packaging of penicillin, and prices for this drug fell throughout the 1940s and 1950s. Similarly Costello indicated that price competition developed for streptomycin, another narrow-spectrum antibiotic, because the developing firm (Merck) was not vertically integrated forward and sold the drug in bulk to many packagers [7, p. 18]. Costello asserted that experience with these two innovations "indicated that the suppression of price competition could be accomplished only by a combination of an innovation protected by a product patent and forward integration to eliminate the packagers" [7, p. 18].

Two important broad-spectrum antibiotics were innovated by firms in the late 1940s: chlortetracycline (Lederle) and chloramphenicol (Parke, Davis). Costello suggested that price competition did not develop for these drugs because each of the two innovating firms was able to obtain a product patent for its innovation and each firm was vertically integrated forward and so did not have to sell to packagers [7, p. 21]. According to Costello, these two drugs and subsequently introduced broad-spectrum drugs were priced under a price-leadership pattern from 1948 to 1967, with Lederle usually the price leader [7, p. 22].

Most of Costello's article is devoted to describing the maneuvering by various firms attempting to obtain a product patent, process patent, or license to produce or sell the broad-spectrum antibiotic known as tetracycline. Costello prefaced this chronology of events by noting that

> up to the discovery of tetracycline, the product patent did serve to prevent imitation, but some firms nonetheless managed to invent *around* those patents, gain entry, and thus force some reductions in price. There is nothing here to suggest that, in the absence of a conspiracy, this process would not have continued, ultimately transforming the market from one of tight oligopoly to a structure approaching that of perfect competition [7, p. 25].

The details of the maneuvering for patents and licenses for this drug will not be recounted here, but by the middle 1950s, according to Costello, license agreements existed among three domestic drug firms (Pfizer, Lederle, and Bristol) which permitted each of them to produce tetracycline. At the same time these agreements prohibited bulk sales of tetracycline to packagers except for the sales to two bulk customers (Squibb and Upjohn) that one producer (Bristol) already had [7, p. 35]. Costello thus concluded that "the license agreements formally tied these firms together in a common effort to prevent entry from the source that historically had produced price competition, namely, the bulk packagers" [7, p. 35].

In addition to the maneuvering that resulted in these agreements, Costello reported "evidence of conspiracy" [7, p. 35] in the marketing practices of these firms, for example, evidence of identical pricing by firms for tetracycline in both domestic and foreign markets [7, pp. 36-37].

In a section of his paper concerned with market performance, Costello showed that in the late 1950s prices for tetracycline tended to be ten to twenty times the manufacturing cost of the drug [7, p. 40]. He noted that only two minor product modifications in the broad-spectrum antibiotics market reached the market from 1954 to 1966, and he concluded that "*monopoly power, once established, is a deterrent to innovation from within the industry and an impairment to entry from without*" [7, p. 41].

Thus Costello seemed to reach two principal conclusions in this case study: (1) there was "a collusive agreement for the orderly marketing of tetracycline" and (2) the "effect of the patent was . . . not the stimulation of invention but, in combination with forward vertical integration, a suppression of competitive forces" [7, pp. 42-43]. His solution for the future was to eliminate all drug patents. He expected this to allow quicker entry by generic producers and more price competition, especially in institutional markets. At the same time he predicted that "technological progress" would be rapid because rewards from innovating and being the first to establish a brand name in a prescription market would remain high and would provide "more than sufficient incentives for research" [7, p. 44].

While Steele and Schifrin were critical of the development and introduction of "me-too" drugs, Costello considered it socially desirable for drug firms "to invent *around* those patents, gain entry, and thus force some reductions in price" [7, p. 25]. According to Costello, in the absence of conspiracy this new product rivalry would ultimately transform the structure of drug markets into something "approaching that of perfect competition" [7, p. 25].

Costello places great emphasis on forward vertical integration as a method by which firms in the broad-spectrum market kept prices and profits high [7, pp. 42-43]. His view seems to be at odds with the generally accepted theory of vertical integration which indicates that a firm that has a monopoly at one stage of the production process (because of a patent) could (under conditions of fixed proportions production) fully exploit that monopoly position regardless of how much price competition there is at a succeeding stage of production or distribution [2, p. 66; 13, pp. 117-120]. Therefore it is not clear why Costello thought that the elimination of drug packagers was essential in order for producers to take advantage of a monopoly for tetracycline.[1]

Costello's policy proposal of eliminating all drug patents is even more drastic than compulsory patent licensing. Most of the criticisms of compulsory patent licensing mentioned earlier also pertain to Costello's proposal.

William S. Comanor's Analysis

In the mid 1960s, William S. Comanor published three papers [4, 5, 6] based on the research findings of his doctoral dissertation on the U.S. pharmaceutical industry. To a large extent these papers are concerned with analyzing the function that research and development plays in this industry.

According to Comanor in a 1964 paper [5], ethical drug markets were easy to enter and highly price competitive through the 1940s. He suggested that this experience convinced leading drug firms that their profits could be increased only by establishing "more protected market positions . . . through some form of product differentiation" [5, p. 373]. The method that they used for accomplishing this differentiation, he said, was an accelerated pattern of R&D expenditures designed to produce an increased flow of new drug products. Thus price competition has been replaced in this industry by "a vigorous form of rivalry . . . which has taken the form of . . . 'competition in creativity'" [5, p. 375] and a rapid rate of product turnover has resulted.

Comanor contended that this form of new product rivalry has been encouraged by the availability of both product and process patents in the United States; consequently "entry into a specific therapeutic market requires, in most cases, some form of scientific or chemical product differentiation" [5, p. 379]. He concluded that drug patents and the "high selling expenditures" [5, p. 380] used to promote products have raised entry barriers, increased market power and market concentration, and raised drug industry profits.

In this paper and in a 1966 article [4] Comanor discussed the nature of the drug R&D that this product rivalry engenders. For example, he described much of this research as imitative and designed "to invent around existing patents" [5, p. 381]; despite its imitative character, however, he agreed that some of this research results in significant product modifications. He also noted that product rivalry has been socially beneficial; it has caused drug firms to pay close attention to research results in nonindustry laboratories, and as a result, new scientific knowledge from these sources is rapidly translated into marketable products.

One of Comanor's most interesting observations was that most of the research undertaken by the drug industry is "complementary" rather than an "alternative" to the drug research done outside the industry [4, p. 15]. He argued that the differences between these two areas of research "may well constitute a necessary and desirable division of labor" and that the "peculiar attributes of each probably create for it a comparative advantage for the specific activities which it, in fact, undertakes" [4, p. 16]. For example, he indicated that "basic or fundamental research" is probably facilitated more by the "freedom" present in a government or university laboratory than a commercial one, while the setting of a profit-oriented firm where goals are well defined is probably most conducive to "applied research" [4, p. 16]. From this perspective, he contended, the industry should not be criticized for not providing dramatic new scientific breakthroughs.

With regard to public policy toward the pharmaceutical industry, Comanor made the one major recommendation that compulsory patent licensing be adopted [4, p. 18]. He believed that this would result in lower prices and profits. He agreed that it would also lead to less R&D spending in this industry, but he argued that the main effects would be to eliminate "projects of limited medical value" and to reduce product differentiation [4, p. 18].

> Nevertheless, it is not at all certain that compulsory licensing would sig-nificantly lower the rate of introduction of the most important new products. The largest proportion of these come originally from non-industry laboratories [4, p. 18].

Even with the introduction of compulsory licensing, however, he predicted that the industry would continue to do much R&D that would result in product modification and differentiation.

The main empirical results of Comanor's research on the pharmaceutical industry were presented in a 1965 article [6] in which he examined the relation-ship between R&D output and R&D input for different-sized drug firms. One of the ways that he measured a firm's research output for this study was by calculating the first two calendar years of dollar sales of new chemical entities first marketed in the United States during the period 1955-1960. One of the methods that he employed to measure the scale of each firm's R&D input activity was to compute the average number of professional R&D personnel employed between 1955 and 1960. Firm size was determined by the mean value of annual hospital and prescription drug sales between 1955 and 1960.

One of Comanor's findings was that "the marginal productivity of profes-sional research personnel is inversely related to size of firm" [6, p. 187]. However, his most frequently cited findings concern the elasticity of research output with respect to research input (measured by the percentage change in research output for a unit percentage change in research input when firm size is held constant) for different-sized firms. This elasticity turned out to be above unity for small pharmaceutical firms and below unity for moderate and large companies. He thus concluded that there were "increasing returns to scale in R and D" for small drug firms and "decreasing returns" when firm size became moderately large [6, p. 188]. He went on to suggest: unilinear

> One implication of this finding is that an actively enforced pro-competitive policy in this sector is not likely to dampen the rate of technical change and may well stimulate it [6, p. 190].

Comanor's argument that drug firms' have a comparative advantage in doing applied research and development is very convincing. However, pharmaceutical firms do some basic research and, as Comanor acknowledged [4], much of the applied research and development carried out by drug firms is socially beneficial.[2] Therefore it is not clear that he is correct in asserting that the main effect of compulsory licensing would be to reduce or eliminate R&D spending on "projects of limited medical value" and that this "may well be a small 'price' to pay for a more competitive determination of pharmaceutical prices and profits" [4, p. 18]. It has often been pointed out in the literature on the economics of invention [for example, 15] that it is difficult for private firms to capture the full market value of the social benefits generated by their fundamental research, for example, because new knowledge itself is not patentable. Compulsory licensing might make it even more difficult, and thus the first projects eliminated might very well be ones toward the basic end of the R&D spectrum rather than development projects of limited social value.[3] One would expect that a private firm's decisions about which R&D projects to undertake would depend mainly on the expected profitability of each research project and not on its social value. Because of their inherent uncertainty and the externality problem, basic research projects are already at a disadvantage; compulsory licensing could cause the private funding of such projects to become even less frequent than it already is.

   With respect to Comanor's often cited findings concerning the efficiency (measured in private terms) of different-sized drug firms' research activities, evidence from a 1973 study by Douglas L. Cocks [3] and a 1974 study by John M. Vernon and Peter Gusen [26] suggests that Comanor's findings for the late 1950s may not apply to the drug industry for the years after the enactment of the Drug Amendments of 1962. For example, Vernon and Gusen found that for the period 1965-1970 the elasticity of sales-weighted new product output with respect to firm size was much greater for large drug firms than for small ones, and thus "larger pharmaceutical manufacturers appear to have decided advantages over smaller ones in accomplishing technical change" [26, p. 301].

Summary and Conclusions

The most common view expressed in the papers summarized seems to be that the drug patent is the principal factor that causes rivalry in the U.S. pharmaceutical industry to be based on the introduction of new products rather than on price competition. Steele, Schifrin, and Comanor each advocated some form of compulsory patent licensing as a remedy to increase price competition, while Costello called for the elimination of all drug patents. In addition, Steele and Schifrin recommended that trade names for ethical drug products be prohibited and that only the seller's name and the drug's generic name appear in labeling and advertising.

   All these economists expected their policy proposals, if adopted, to result in increased entry to drug markets and vigorous price competition. To some extent, however, they disagreed about the likely effects of their recommendations on the level of R&D activity and the rate of innovation. Steele expected a decrease in R&D in the industry, but he did not think that this would affect the rate of introduction of important new drugs because he believed that research outside the industry was mainly responsible for originating these. Schifrin predicted that compulsory licensing might result in more R&D and more rapid product turnover. Costello suggested that the elimination of drug patents would not only stimulate greater price competition, but also provide incentives that would result in a greater flow of important drug innovations. Finally Comanor asserted that compulsory licensing would eliminate some R&D of limited social value but would not significantly lower the rate of introduction of the most important new products because the industry does not have a comparative advantage in the development of such products and is thus not the main source of these products.

Everyone seems to agree that compulsory licensing (or the elimination) of drug patents would increase price competition for existing drug products. If there is easy entry to markets for products that do not have significant scale economies in production, a high degree of price competition seems almost certain.

The principal area of uncertainty and disagreement, then, concerns the effects of compulsory licensing (or elimination of patents) on the level of R&D activity, the rate of introduction of new drugs, and social welfare. My view is that compulsory licensing would greatly reduce the incentives for drug firms to do research and that the rate of private R&D activity would decline. The rate of introduction of new drugs would also probably fall. This view is supported somewhat by a study that I recently completed of the effects of market structure on drug innovation in the post-drug amendments period 1963-1973; I found a statistically significant positive relationship between seller concentration and the rate of innovation in therapeutic drug markets [10, p. 152]. This suggests that reductions in seller concentration brought about by compulsory patent licensing could have a depressing effect on drug innovation. The most important question, however, is, What would be the overall effect of compulsory licensing on social welfare? Unfortunately there seems to be no consensus among economists on the answer to this question.

Notes

1. In the case of variable-proportions production, of course, profits could be increased by vertically integrating [2, pp. 80-81; 25]. This argument was not employed by Costello, however, and does not seem to have been the basis for his argument.

2. According to surveys by the National Science Foundation and the Pharmaceutical Manufacturers Association, about 14 percent to 15 percent of

drug firms' company-financed research and development expenditures (within firms) in the United States seems to be for basic research [12, 17].

3. The likelihood of this occurring is suggested by the results of a series of interviews several years ago by the National Science Foundation with top research officials of two hundred companies engaged in research and development. In describing the results of the survey, Richard R. Nelson noted that officials of companies in markets so competitive that the firms were mainly concerned with "staying in business" indicated that their research programs were concerned more with "short-run problem-solving" than with long-term investment in basic research [14, p. 124].

References

1. Bloch, Harry, "True Profitability Measures for Pharmaceutical Firms," in Joseph D. Cooper, ed., *Regulation, Economics, and Pharmaceutical Innovation* (Washington, D.C.: American University, 1976), pp. 147-157.

2. Burstein, M.L., "A Theory of Full-Line Forcing," *Northwestern University Law Review* 55 (March-April 1960): 62-95.

3. Cocks, Douglas L., "The Impact of the 1962 Drug Amendments on R and D Productivity in the Ethical Pharmaceutical Industry," Ph.D. dissertation, Oklahoma State University, July 1973.

4. Comanor, William S., "The Drug Industry and Medical Research: The Economics of the Kefauver Committee Investigations," *Journal of Business* 39 (January 1966): 12-18.

5. _____, "Research and Competitive Product Differentiation in the Pharmaceutical Industry in the United States," *Economica* 31 (November 1964): 372-384.

6. _____, "Research and Technical Change in the Pharmaceutical Industry," *Review of Economic and Statistics* 47 (May 1965): 182-190.

7. Costello, Peter M., "The Tetracycline Conspiracy: Structure, Conduct and Performance in the Drug Industry," *Antitrust Law and Economics Review* 1 (Summer 1968): 13-44. Copyright © 1968 by *Antitrust Law and Economics Review, Inc.,* P.O. Box 6134, Washington, D.C. 20044. Reprinted by permission.

8. Federal Trade Commission, *Economic Report on Antibiotics Manufacture* (Washington, D.C.: U.S. Government Printing Office, 1958).

9. Friedman, Jesse J., and Murray N. Friedman, "Relative Profitability and Monopoly Power," *Conference Board Record* 9 (December 1972): 49-58.

10. Jadlow, Joseph M., "An Empirical Study of the Relationship between Market Structure and Innovation in Therapeutic Drug Markets," final report to the National Science Foundation under grant no. RDA75-21075, June 1976.

11. McGuire, Thomas; Nelson, Richard; and Spavins, Thomas, "'An Evaluation of Consumer Protection Legislation: The 1962 Drug Amendments': A Comment," *Journal of Political Economy* 83 (June 1975: 655-667.
12. National Science Foundation, *Research and Development in Industry* (Washington, D.C.: U.S. Government Printing Office, various years).
13. Needham, Douglas, *Economic Analysis and Industrial Structure* (New York: Holt, Rinehart and Winston, 1969).
14. Nelson, Richard R., "The Economics of Invention: A Survey of the Literature," *Journal of Business* 32 (April 1959): 101-127.
15. _____, "The Simple Economics of Basic Scientific Research," *Journal of Political Economy* 67 (June 1959): 297-306.
16. Peltzman, Sam, "An Evaluation of Consumer Protection Legislation: The 1962 Drug Amendments," *Journal of Political Economy* 81 (September/ October 1973): 1049-1091.
17. Pharmaceutical Manufacturers Association, *Annual Survey Report* (Washington, D.C., various years).
18. Schifrin, Leonard G., "The Ethical Drug Industry: The Case for Compulsory Patent Licensing," *Antitrust Bulletin* 12 (Fall 1967): 893-915.
19. Steele, Henry, "Monopoly and Competition in the Ethical Drugs Market," *Journal of Law and Economics* 5 (October 1962): 131-163. Reprinted with permission.
20. _____, "Patent Restrictions and Price Competition in the Ethical Drugs Industry," *Journal of Industrial Economics* 12 (July 1964): 198-223.
21. U.S. Senate, Committee on the Judiciary, Subcommittee on Antitrust and Monopoly, Hearings on *Administered Prices,* 86th Congress, 1st Session (Washington, D.C.: U.S. Government Printing Office, 1960).
22. U.S. Senate, Committee on the Judiciary, Subcommittee on Antitrust and Monopoly, Senate Report No. 448, *Administered Prices: Drugs,* 87th Congress, 1st Session (Washington, D.C.: U.S. Government Printing Office, 1961).
23. U.S. Senate, Select Committee on Small Business, Subcommittee on Monoply, Hearings on *Competitive Problems in the Drug Industry* (Washington, D.C.: U.S. Government Printing Office, beginning in 1967).
24. U.S. Senate, Committee on the Judiciary, Subcommittee on Antitrust and Monopoly, *Hearings on S. 1552,* 87th Congress, 1st Session (Washington, D.C.: U.S. Government Printing Office, 1962).
25. Vernon, John M.; and Graham, Daniel A., "Profitability of Monopolization by Vertical Integration," *Journal of Political Economy* 79 (July/August 1971): 924-925.
26. Vernon, John M.; and Gusen, Peter, "Technical Change and Firm Size: The Pharmaceutical Industry," *Review of Economics and Statistics* 56 (August 1974): 294-302.

3

New Studies on Market Definition, Concentration, Theory of Supply, Entry, and Promotion

Henry G. Grabowski and
John M. Vernon

Overview: *Recent studies since 1968 point to rapid rate of innovation in the pharmaceutical industry as a key element of competition which positively influences consumer welfare, both by providing therapeutic advances and by introducing a dynamic form of price competition. Promotion activities are a complementary activity to diffusion of innovation and the entry of new firms into particular therapeutic markets.*

The higher costs and risks of drug innovation in the more stringent post-1962 regulatory environment appear to have operated as a barrier to competition through new product introduction. Consequently the supply of new drugs has not only declined but also become more concentrated in large multinational firms better able to deal with this more stringent environment.

A number of studies by economists have in one way or another addressed the competitive structure and overall performance of the drug industry. Many researchers have used the perspective of the traditional structure-conduct-performance model (as developed by Mason, Bain, and others) to analyze this industry. Such studies have frequently concluded that the industry is characterized by considerable market power (in terms of seller concentration and entry barriers) which in turn has allowed it to earn consistently above-average profits (the primary index of resource misallocation in these studies).

At the same time a number of studies have challenged this basic view of the industry's structural characteristics and performance. These studies generally tend to emphasize the importance of Schumpeterian-type competition through new product innovation, as well as the implications of this dynamic competition in innovation for entry, promotion, prices, and profit rates. These studies draw conclusions about the industry's competitive structure and performance that are usually very different from the conclusions drawn by studies employing the traditional structure-conduct-performance approach.

Market Definition, Concentration, and Market Share Turnover

Market Definition: Theoretical Considerations

We need to be explicit about the theoretical definition of an industry or market. (As we shall observe shortly, the problem of delimiting the "ethical drug industry" is difficult: should all ethical drugs be combined into a single market, or are therapeutic categories, such as antibiotics, the correct theoretical markets?) Stigler has suggested the following economic criteria:

> An industry should embrace the maximum geographical area and the maximum variety of productive activities in which there is a strong long-run substitution. If buyers can shift on a large scale from product or area B to A, then the two should be combined. If producers can shift on a large scale from B to A, again they should be combined.
>
> Economists usually state this in an alternative form: All products or enterprises with large long-run cross-elasticities of either supply or demand should be combined into a single industry [Stigler, 1955].

Of course, the adjectives "strong" and "large" necessarily require that judgment be used in setting industry and market boundaries.

Alternative Measures of Seller Concentration

Armed with this theoretical definition of a market, we now precede to examine various measures of seller concentration in the drug industry. These in effect involve different operational constructs of the relevant market for ethical drugs.

We shall begin with the broadest possible definition of the pharmaceutical industry: the Bureau of Census four-digit SIC classification "Pharmaceutical Preparations." This particular industry combines both ethical drugs and proprietary drugs into a single market. Table 3-1 provides data on the four-firm concentration ratios in 1972 using this industry measure. Table 3-1 also provides concentration data for a selected group of other manufacturing industries in the same year. Using the government four-digit Standard Industrial Classification (SIC) measures, we see that the pharmaceutical industry (with a four-firm ratio of 26) is much less concentrated than other important industries, such as passenger cars, steel, aluminum, and petroleum refining.

Of course, one might plausibly argue that a market definition that combines ethical and proprietary drugs is much too broad in scope. While government statistics do not provide concentration figures for ethical drug sales alone, one may use private data sources, Intercontinental Medical Statistics (IMS) data, on firm market shares to calculate such an index. In table 3-2 concentration

Table 3-1
Concentration of Selected Industries, 1972

Industry	Four-Firm Ratio	Number of Firms
Passenger cars	99	n.a.
Flat glass	92	11
Electric lamps	90	103
Cigarettes	84	13
Primary aluminum	79	12
Tires and inner tubes	73	136
Soap and detergents	62	577
Farm machinery	47	1465
Blast furnaces and steel mills	45	241
Textile machinery	31	535
Petroleum refining	31	152
Footwear, except rubber	30	153
Pharmaceutical preparations	26	680
Bottled and canned soft drinks	14	2271
Screw machine products	6	1780

Source: Bureau of Census, *Census of Manufactures 1972. Special Report Series: Concentration Ratios in Manufacturing MC 72 (SR)-2* (Washington, D.C.: U.S. Government Printing Office, 1975).

ratios for the total ethical drug market using this approach are presented. A shortcoming of the data underlying these ratios is that only sales to drug stores and hospitals are included. Sales to the U.S. government and some other governmental agencies, which make up about 20 percent of total ethical drug sales, are excluded. The figures are nevertheless quite consistent with those in table 3-1 and indicate a low level of concentration for the industry as a whole. (for example, a 27.8 four-firm concentration ratio in 1973)

In his leading textbook in industrial organization F.M. Scherer [1970] has stated that "when the leading four firms control 40 percent or more of the total market, it is fair to assume that oligopoly is beginning to rear its head." According to this rule of thumb, the 27.8 concentration ratio for ethical drugs in 1973 would not even place it in the oligopoly category. However, most economists would consider the ethical drug industry oligopolistic, and they would argue that the relevant markets should be therapeutic categories (or combinations of categories) rather than the total ethical drug market. Measday has observed that we should not

> ignore the fact that the overall drug market is fragmented into a number of separate, noncompeting therapeutic markets: antibiotics are

Table 3-2
Concentration of Sales in the U.S. Ethical Drug Industry, 1957-1973

Year	Four-Firm	Eight-Firm	Twenty-Firm
1958	28.8	50.9	79.5
1959	26.8	48.0	75.5
1960	25.8	47.3	75.4
1961	25.8	45.6	75.3
1962	25.4	44.3	74.5
1963	24.5	43.5	74.6
1964	23.7	42.2	74.1
1965	23.4	42.3	73.7
1966	24.4	42.7	74.1
1967	24.5	41.8	72.3
1968	25.4	43.6	74.4
1969	26.1	43.9	74.4
1970	26.3	43.2	73.6
1971	26.5	43.7	76.0
1972	27.6	43.6	75.4
1973	27.8	43.5	75.7

Source: Henry G. Grabowski and John M. Vernon, "Structural Effects of Regulation on Innovation in the Ethical Drug Industry." Reprinted with permission from *Essays on Industrial Organization in Honor of Joe S. Bain,* Robert T. Masson and P. David Qualls eds. (Cambridge, Mass.: Ballinger, 1976), pp. 181-206. Copright 1976, Ballinger Publishing Company.

not substitutes for antidiabetic drugs, and tranquilizers are not substitutes for vitamins. Manufacturers do not compete on an industry-wide basis, and hence concentration must be evaluated within the various therapeutic groups of drugs in which competition does occur [Measday, 1971].

A number of classifications of therapeutic categories as markets have appeared in the literature, usually as part of a study testing some particular hypothesis. For example, Vernon [1971] in a study of the relationship between concentration and promotional intensity in the ethical drugs classified drug products into nineteen therapeutic markets. He constructed these markets after consulting with marketing personnel in the drug industry. His markets, which are shown in table 3-3, are based exclusively on the (estimated) degree of demand side substitutability between drug products. These therapeutic markets have an average unweighted concentration ratio of 68, significantly greater than the concentration ratio for total ethical drug sales given in tables 3-1 and 3-2. Similar measures of therapeutic markets have been used in a number of other studies [for example, Telser, et al., 1975].

Table 3-3
Concentration of Sales in the U.S. Ethical Drug Industry, by
Therapeutic Markets, 1968

Therapeutic Market	Four-Firm Ratio
Anesthetics	69
Antiarthritics	95
Antibiotics-penicillin	55
Antispasmodics	59
Ataractics	79
Bronchial dilators	61
Cardiovascular hypotensives	79
Coronary-peripheral vasodilators	70
Diabetic therapy	93
Diuretics	64
Enzymes-digestants	46
Hematinic preparations	52
Sex hormones	67
Corticoids	55
Muscle relaxants	59
Psychostimulants	78
Sulfonamides	79
Thyroid therapy	69
Unweighted average	68

Source: John M. Vernon, "Concentration, Promotion and Market
Share Stability in Pharmaceutical Industry," *Journal of Industrial
Economics* 19 (July 1971): 246-266. Reprinted with permission.

Two recent studies that arrived at market categories operationally different
from those in table 3-3 are worthy of attention. First, Hornbrook constructed
a classification of sixty-nine therapeutic product markets (see table 3-4) as part
of a recent study of promotional intensity and market domination. Hornbrook
began with the classification used by the *National Prescription Audit* of R.A.
Gosselin and Company. These were then modified as necessary on the basis of
his own evaluation of substitutability within each class. Hornbrook's employed
the following operational definition of therapeutic substitutes:

Therapeutic substitutes: two products will be considered to be substitutes,
and hence to belong in the same market, if they produce essentially the
same primary therapeutic effect in the majority of patients, while at the
same time having generally similar, but not necessarily identical secondary
effects, as conditioned by general medical knowledge and prevailing prescribing patterns [Hornbrook, 1976].

Table 3-4
Therapeutic Product Markets Used by Hornbrook

 1. Amebacides and trichomonacides
 2. Narcotic analgesics
 3. Nonnarcotic analgesics
 4. Antacid-antispasmodic combinations
 5. Anthelminitics
 6. Antiarthritics
 7. General antibacterials
 8. Urinary antibacterials
 9. Tetracyclines
10. Chloramphenicol
11. Medium-spectrum antibiotics
12. Penicillins
13. Antibiotic-sulfa combinations
14. Anticoagulants
15. Anticonvulsants
16. Antidiarrheals
17. Antinauseants
18. Antihistamines
19. Amphetamines
20. Nonamphetamine antiobesity preparations
21. Antispasmodics
22. Ataraxics
23. Bile therapy preparations
24. Bronchial dilators
25. Hypotensives
26. Coronary vasodilators
27. Peripheral vasodilators
28. Digitalis preparations
29. Narcotic antitussives
30. Nonnarcotic antitussives
31. Cough and cold preparations
32. Antihistamine cold preparations
33. Nasal decongestants
35. Fungicides
36. Oral antidiabetics

37. Diuretics
38. Digestant enzymes
39. Proteolytic enzymes
40. Hematinics
41. Hemorrhoidal preparations
42. Hemostatic preparations
43. Hormones: Corticoids, plain
44. Hormones: Corticoids, analgesic combination
45. Hormones: Corticoid, antiinfective combinations
46. Harmones: Androgens
47. Hormones: Estrogens
48. Hormones: Androgen-estrogen combinations
49. Hormones: Oral contraceptives
50. Hormones: Other progestogens
51. Hormones: Anabolic
52. Lipotropics and cholesterol reducers
53. Oral muscle relaxants
54. Psychostimulants
55. Sedatives: Barbiturates
56. Sedatives: Nonbarbiturate
57. Sulfonamides
58. Thyroid therapy preparations
59. Prenatal multivitamins
60. Geriatric multivitamins
61. Pediatric multivitamins
62. Antineoplastics
63. Miotics and glaucoma preparations
64. Mydriatics
65. Ophthalmic decongestants
66. Ophthalmic antiinfectives
67. Ophthalmic corticoid, antiinfective combinations
68. Antiarrhythmics
69. Otic antiinfective preparations

Source: Mark C. Hornbrook, "Market Domination and Promotional Intensity in the Whole-sale-Retail Sector of the U.S. Pharmaceutical Industry," National Center for Health Services Research, Technical Paper Series Number 5, 1976. Reprinted with permission.

He used the *Physician's Desk Reference,* the *American Drug Index,* and other pharmacology reference books to determine the chemical composition, principal therapeutic action, and side effects of each product, and he consulted with medical experts where necessary.

This classification procedure, which is based on similarities of therapeutic effects, yielded a much more disaggregate market measure than Vernon's measure in table 3-3. For example, tetracyclines and chloramphenicol are separate markets in the Hornbrook analysis, while they are part of the antibiotics market in Vernon's analysis.

In another recent study Cocks and Virts [1974] have attempted to define therapeutic markets by systematically evaluating physicians' prescribing habits using data from the *National Disease and Therapeutic Index.* Their final classification, which is presented in table 3-5, yields a class of ten "economic"

Table 3-5
Economic Markets Employed by Cocks and Virts and Corresponding Grouping of Therapeutic Classes

1. Antiinfective market
   a. Broad to medium-spectrum antibiotics
   b. Penicillins
   c. Sulfonamides
   d. Antibiotic-sulfa combinations
   e. Other antibiotics
   f. Urinary antibacterial analgesics
   g. General antibacterial antiseptics
   h. Corticoids with antiinfectives

2. Analgesic and antiinflammatory
   a. Narcotic analgesics
   b. Nonnarcotic analgesics
   c. Antiarthritics
   d. Plain corticoids
   e. Oral muscle relaxants
   f. Corticoids with analgesics
   g. ACTH
   h. Local and topical anesthetics

3. Psychopharmaceutical market
   a. Ataractic tranquilizers
   b. Psychostimulants
   c. Barbiturate sedatives
   d. Nonbarbiturate sedatives

4. Cough and cold market
   a. Cough and cold
   b. Antihistamines

5. Antihypertensive and diuretic market
   a. Rauwolfias
   b. Other hypotensives
   c. Diuretics

6. Vitamin and hematinic market
   a. Vitamins
   b. Hematinics

7. Oral contraceptive market

8. Anticholingeric and antispasmodic market

9. Antiobesity market
   a. Amphetamines
   b. Nonamphetamines

10. Diabetic therapy market

Source: Douglas Cocks and John Virts, "Pricing Behavior of the Ethical Pharmaceutical Industry," *Journal of Business* 47 (July 1974): 349-362. Reprinted with permission of the University of Chicago Press.

Note: These therapeutic class designations are those used in the R.A. Gosselin and Co. *National Prescription Audit.*

markets that are more broadly defined than the therapeutic markets in table 3-3 or 3-4.

Cocks has provided the following description of their approach:

> Previous analyses of the pharmaceutical industry have used the therapeutic class to denote relevant demand-side markets, but it appears that in some cases the products in one therapeutic class may actually be substitutes for products in another therapeutic class. In addition, there are cases in which the products in a given subclass are not substitutes for products in the overall therapeutic class. By measuring how physicians use various kinds of drugs, it is possible to group products into relatively meaningful markets. The method is to align therapeutic classes or subclasses according to their use as alternatives. If there are three therapeutic classes A, B, and C, and it appears that physicians use the products in classes A and B for treating a particular diagnosis and products B and C as alternatives for another diagnosis, then all three therapeutic classes are grouped as a set. In other words, a group of products of one therapeutic class that intersects with a group of another class can be combined to form an overall set of products. Intersection is based on the way physicians use various drugs, and it is the intersection of these groups in use that establishes the boundaries of the particular market [Cocks, 1975].

Given the generally more aggregate character of these markets compared with the therapeutic classes given in table 3-3, one would expect concentration ratios constructed under these market definitions to be considerably lower than the ratios observed in table 3-3.

While it is possible to argue the merits or drawbacks of these alternative classifications of ethical drug markets at considerable length, their wide range suggests that the construction of markets at the present time combines elements of art and science.

A further important qualification to all these attempts to define therapeutic markets, as opposed to a single ethical drug market, is the lack of attention paid to supply-side factors. According to Stigler's definition of a market, producers who can shift on a large scale from product B to A should be combined into a single market. Thus if firms producing antidiabetic drugs can enter the antibiotic market relatively easily, then they should be included as part of a larger combined market. This omission of supply-side substitution possibilities suggests that concentration ratios may be subject to some positive bias on this account, whatever other problems and biases they may contain.

Concentration versus Market Share Turnover

While particular therapeutic markets may be subject to high levels of concentration at any given time, it has also been argued that there is a high rate of turnover in market shares in most of these markets as a consequence of vigorous competition through new product innovation. As a corollary, it also has been suggested that changes in firm market shares provide a more accurate index of the degree of competition for industries like ethical drugs where there is substantial technological change over time.

A dynamic analysis of the pharmaceutical industry along these lines has been undertaken by Doublas Cocks [1975]. As one index of the degree of market share turnover, he computes the Hymer-Pashigian instability index for a group of major firms in the drug industry and compares it to indices calculated for other industries by Hymer and Pashigian. This index of market instability is calculated according to the following formula:

$$I = \sum_{i=1}^{n} \left(\frac{S_{t,i}}{S_t} - \frac{S_{t-1,i}}{S_{t-1}} \right) \tag{3.1}$$

where

I = index of instability

$S_{t,i}$ = sales of the ith firm at time t

S_t = total industry, hospital, and drugstore sales at time t

His findings in this regard are presented in table 3-6. He notes that this table

> presents instability indices calculated by Hymer and Pashigian for nineteen two-digit standard industrial classification (SIC) industries. These cover the changes in shares of assets for these industries between 1946 and 1955. As a means of comparison the drug industry instability index is also presented. Note that there is only one industry's instability index higher than the index for the drug industry. This comparison becomes more significant when it is realized that the two-digit industry classes are probably too broadly defined to represent realistic industries. Thus, the instability indices for these industries will have a tendency to be higher than those for more properly defined industries [Cocks, 1975].

Cocks also performs an analysis of the effects of dynamic turnover of particular ethical drug product shares on product prices and other variables within given pharmaceutical market classes. His findings in this regard are considered in the next section as part of the general discussion of entry and supply in ethical drugs.

Table 3-6
Indices of Market Share Instability

Industry	Instability Index[a]	Number of Firms
Food	10.83	119
Tobacco	9.06	12
Textile mill products	9.30	61
Apparel	1.48	7
Lumber and wood products	4.45	16
Furniture and fixtures	3.86	8
Paper	9.63	49
Printing	14.82	25
Chemicals	17.42	74
Petroleum	−24.38	35
Rubber	9.16	14
Leather	5.69	8
Stone, clay, and glass	13.25	31
Primary metals	14.25	76
Fabricated metals	8.70	51
Machinery (except electrical)	12.71	n.a.
Electrical machinery	17.24	46
Transportation	19.92	70
Professional and scientific	17.19	19
Drug industry	22.80[b]	21

Source: Douglas L. Cocks, "Product Innovation and Dynamic Elements of Competition in the Ethical Drug Industry," in Robert B. Helms, ed., *Drug Development and Marketing* (Washington, D.C.: American Enterprise Institute, 1975). Reprinted with permission.

[a] All indices are computed with mergers excluded. Hymer and Pashigian calculated their indices on the basis of shares of assets; the calculation for the drug industry is based on shares of hospital and drugstore sales.

[b] Calculated by Cocks (see text).

Theory of Supply, Entry, and Promotion

Entry Conditions

The conditions of entry into a market are usually analyzed in terms of the existence of any "entry barriers" or cost disadvantages that deter potential competitors from entering an industry when profits are above competitive yields.

Three factors have been cited in the literature as important sources of entry barriers in the ethical drug industry: patents, brand differentiation, and scale advantages in research and development.

A good indication of the scope of patent coverage in drugs is provided by the so-called master drug list assembled by the Task Force on Prescription Drugs [1969]. The list contains 366 drugs most frequently prescribed in 1966 for elderly patients and accounts for nearly 90 percent of both the number and cost of prescriptions filled by retail pharmacies for these patients. Of these 366 drugs, 293 (or 80 percent) were "still under patent, available only under brand name for a single supplier." William Comanor has argued in this regard:

> Product patents . . . are a relatively strong vehicle of protection from competitive suppliers. Once a product patent has been granted, a rival firm cannot supply the identical compound without fear of legal proceedings. . . . Patent protection in this industry is, moreover, especially significant since a large proportion of individual products are covered. A survey of the industry estimated that over two-thirds of all prescription sales are for patented drugs.
>
> . . . Since a large proportion of pharmaceuticals have some degree of patent protection, entry into a specific therapeutic market requires, in most cases, some form of scientific or chemical product differentiation. . . . The importance of pharmaceutical patents, however, can easily be overstated. While monopoly positions are conferred, patent protection does not normally confer the power to monopolize any of the therapeutic markets. This is borne out by the high turnover among leading firms and the vigorous product competition within these markets [Comanor, 1964].

A second hypothesized source of entry barrier in ethical drugs is product differentiation through the promotion of brand name products. It has been frequently argued that the agency relationship that exists between patient and doctor in the prescription of drugs serves to increase the opportunities for successful product differentiation in this industry. In particular, it is the doctor rather than the patient who decides which product and which brand to prescribe. It is generally maintained that doctors' decisions in this regard are most directly influenced by considerations of product quality and reputation of the manufacturer and only secondarily by a product's price. In many states the pharmacist is prohibited by law from substituting a product different from one prescribed by the doctor. (However, in recent years, many states have repealed these antisubstitution laws and this movement seems to be accelerating.) Drug firms in turn spend a considerable sum to inform physicians about their particular brands.

A 1958 Federal Trade Commission report on antibiotics has described the nature of demand and product differentiation in this industry in the following manner:

> Whether an antibiotic will be used in a particular case is determined by the physician rather than the patient, and the choice is made on con-

siderations of health rather than price. Even if the patient influences the
choice, it would hardly be on a price basis; if he places health considerations
first, he simply follows his doctor's directions. A high price will do less
to discourage demand than in many other industries. On the other hand,
a physician is not likely to select a drug about which he knows little or
whose maker he does not trust. Manufacturers, therefore, try to keep physicians familiar with their own names and the merits of their drugs. Where
antibiotics sold by two or more companies are identical or closely substitutable, however, a lower price charged by one of them may influence
the demand of distributors, hospitals, or even physicians [FTC, 1958].

Advantages of large scale in research and development are a third postulated
source of entry barriers discussed in the literature. These stem in considerable
part from the cost and risk of developing and gaining Food and Drug Administration (FDA) approval of new products. Given the importance of new product
competition in ethical drugs, high cost and risk can be important entry barriers
to small firms with small resource bases or to firms without expertise in some
facet of drug R&D. There is considerable evidence that increased regulation of
the drug innovational process in recent years has increased the importance of
large firm size in the development and marketing of new drug products.

Prior Studies and the Evidence for Entry Barriers

A central focus of economists and policymakers concerned with the competitive
structure and performance of the drug industry has been the persistently high
rate of profits earned by the industry; This concern has been interpreted by
many observers as strong evidence that concentration and entry barriers must be
high in this industry. The nature of data used to support this point of view is
illustrated in table 3-7. The rate of profit for a representative group of drug
firms is compared with the average profit rate for all manufacturing over the
period 1958-1972. That drug industry profits have been persistently above the
average (indeed ranked first or second among all manufacturing industries) provides persuasive evidence to many economists and policymakers that entry
barriers must be very high in this industry. If this were not the case, they argue,
one should observe a tendency for these high profit rates to be eroded over time
by the entry of new firms into this market.

While this line of argument is apparently convincing to many individuals,
several other hypotheses and possible interpretations of this observed high rate
of return have also appeared in the literature. Most recently considerable
attention has been directed to the possibility of significant biases in the accounting rate of return for discovery-intensive industries like ethical drugs. These
biases arise from the fact that R&D and advertising outlays are treated as current
expenses rather than as capital expenditures. These are likely to be particularly

Table 3-7

Rates of Return After Taxes on Average Stockholders' Investment, Twelve Large Companies, 1958-1972

Year	Twelve Large Drug Firms (%)	All Manufacturing (%)
1958	20.3	8.6
1959	20.3	10.4
1960	18.4	9.2
1961	17.6	8.8
1962	17.1	9.8
1963	17.8	10.3
1964	18.9	11.6
1965	21.0	13.0
1966	21.1	13.4
1967	19.0	11.7
1968	18.8	12.1
1969	19.9	11.5
1970	19.6	9.3
1971	19.4	9.7
1972	20.3	10.6

Source: Federal Trade Commission, *Rates of Return for Identical Companies in Selected Manufacturing Industries* (Washington, D.C.: U.S. Government Printing Office, annual).

important in the present situation because the drug industry ranks at the top of all industries with respect to R&D and advertising sales intensities.

Aside from the drug industry's high overall rate of profits, a second perceived symptom of monopoly power and entry barriers that has received considerable attention in congressional hearings is the wide price disparities that frequently exist between brand and generic products. Along these lines, the late Senator Estes Kefauver noted:

In 1961 McKesson & Robbins inaugurated the practice of selling, on a nation-wide basis, ethical drugs under generic names. One of the first drugs selected was prednisone. . . . Their price to the retail druggist, in bottles of 1000, is $20.95. For exactly the same volume, Schering and the other major drug companies charge the retailer $170.00—more than eight times the price charged by McKesson & Robbins. . . . Obviously, this is a tremendous price disparity by any standard [Kefauver, 1965].

Many other examples of brand name products selling at much higher prices than chemically equivalent generic products can be given. For example, Squibb's

Noctec brand of chloralhydrate had more than half the market in the Task Force survey [1969], and at wholesale prices from three to four times the cost of the generic product. These large price disparities for chemically equivalent products have been attributed by Kefauver and others in large part to the high promotional expenditures for new drugs over the initial period in which a drug typically enjoys a patent monopoly. These outlays, it is argued, contribute to effective brand differentiation which can persist in the mind of doctors long after the patent protection has expired and permits a substantial price premium to be earned relative to generic equivalents.

Of course, the extent to which chemically equivalent generic products are also bioequivalent and of comparable quality to branded products has been a source of much controversy and debate between the industry and its critics. Given the importance of this issue to public proposals such as the maximum allowable cost (MAC) reimbursement scheme for Medicare and Medicaid, considerable scientific scrutiny of this question can be expected in the next few years.

The notion that advertising and promotion outlays are a major source of entry barriers in consumer-oriented industries has also been put forth on the basis of interindustry cross-sectional studies of the determinants of profit rates [for example, Camanor and Wilson, 1974]. The drug industry is typically included in the sample of industries used to test this hypothesis, and it generally ranks among the top industries in terms of both advertising intensities and profit rates. The behavior of the drug industry is consistent with the more general findings advanced by Comanor and Wilson, namely that high advertising intensity is positively associated with high profit rates in consumer-oriented industries. They believe that this happens because advertising outlays are a primary source of product differentiation entry barriers.

New Studies of Entry and Supply

The view that the drug industry is characterized by a high degree of entry barriers and monopoly power has been strongly disputed in some recent work. These studies generally emphasize the importance of dynamic competition through new product innovation in the ethical drug industry. They further maintain that the introduction of products that represent therapeutic advances over existing products, directly enhances consumer welfare. Moreover a significant by-product of the entry of new products and firms into existing markets is increased price competition and a strong tendency for the prices of established products to fall.

Cocks [1975] has adopted a model of Clemens to explain competition in the drug industry that embodies these essential features. He summarizes the main elements of this model in the following terms:

(1) The model highlights the idea that a firm in a technological environment can adapt its R&D and manufacturing processes to develop and produce products in several areas of drug therapy. This context emphasizes that the behavior of these firms is determined by profit-maximizing decisions that consider several different kinds of drug products.

(2) When an individual firm is successful in developing innovative new products whose demand curves presumably are favorable relative to costs, resources should flow to that firm as the profit incentive dictates. This implies that the firm that is relatively more successful in the stochastic process of finding new drugs should receive an increased market share and an increased ex post rate of return.

(3) As firms attempt to develop singular new products, they develop, as a by-product of R&D, products that compete with existing ones. From an empirical standpoint this can be expected to result in a substantial amount of entry into drug markets, market shares should be affected, and price pressures should be evident [Cocks, 1975].

Cocks presents a number of empirical points in support of such a model. First, he demonstrates that market share turnover (as measured by the market share instability index) is large in ethical drug compared with other industries. Second, he shows that market share changes of firms in this industry are positively related to their new product innovation. Finally, he demonstrates a positive association between the observed price declines in particular therapeutic markets and the amount of new product innovation and new firm entry into these markets.

Telser et al. [1975] has constructed a more formal model of firm entry and applied it to the pharmaceutical industry. Their basic assumption is that firms will exhibit an optimal supply response to any particular demand changes. In particular, they postulate that inputs will adjust to new demand conditions at least total cost.

Using this model as their theoretical underpinning, Telser et al. perform an empirical analysis of entry and price changes for seventeen ethical therapeutic markets over the period 1962-1972. The basic thrust of this empirical analysis has a number of similarities to Cock's work. However, Telser et al. give particular attention and emphasis to testing whether promotion outlays in fact facilitate or deter entry into this industry.

In the first part of this analysis, Telser et al. regress entry on a number of factors including growth in sales, market size, market stability, and promotional intensity. Entry is measured as the percentage of sales in a given therapeutic category in 1972 accounted for by companies absent from that category in 1964. In the second stage of the analysis, Telser et al. test whether the variables positively influencing entry have a negative effect on prices.

In general, Telser et al. observe a pattern of relationship conforming to this expectation. Their most interesting finding in this regard is that promotional intensity exhibits a positive relation with entry and negative relation with prices, holding other factors constant. Hence, they argue, promotional activities facilitate rather than hinder entry and competition in this industry. Their conclusions are therefore in direct conflict with the inferences of Comanor and Wilson and others who have analyzed this question on the basis of interindustry cross-sectional analysis of profit rates.

One possible explanation for this conflict stems from the omission from these interindustry cross-sectional analyses of any variables related to new product innovation. Hence they also ignore possible interrelationships between the rate of new product innovation and promotional outlays. It is well established that innovating firms must generally be prepared to make much larger promotion expenditures per dollar of sales in the initial stages of a new product's life cycle than those expended for existing products for which a considerable stock of information is already available. For this reason, industries characterized by above-average R&D intensity and rapid product turnover due to technological innovation should also possess above-average promotional intensity. This expectation is consistent with the positive significant correlation between an industry's R&D intensity and its advertising intensity observed by Leonard [1972] for a cross-sectional sample of industries. The drug industry ranks among the top of all industries in both R&D and promotional intensity.

Thus the information diffusion role of promotion outlays may on balance outweigh its entry barrier effects in highly research-intensive and innovative industries like ethical drugs. Of course, this may not be true in other industries such as cigarettes, cereals, beer with high promotional intensities but very different characteristics. This fact could account for the difference between the findings of Telser et al. in their analyses of entry into different therapeutic drug markets and those obtained in the traditional multiindustry analysis of this issue in the industrial organization literature.

Another recently completed study of the effects of promotional intensity on market competition was performed by Mark Hornbrook [1976]. In general, this study (in contrast with those of Telser et al. and Cocks) employs the basic framework of the structure-conduct-performance model rather than the dynamic competition approach. Nevertheless the concept of market dominance that Hornbrook uses as the basic dependent variable in his model is an attempt to measure a dynamic concept of structural power. In particular, market dominance is defined as "the ability of the same group of established firms in a specific product market to occupy a commanding or controlling position with respect to influencing price, quantity, and the nature of the product in that market from one time period to the next" [Hornbrook, 1976]. Empirically market dominance is measured by Hornbrook as the linear regression coefficient of period t market shares on period $t-1$ shares.

Hornbrook constructs a simultaneous equations model in which market dominance and promotional intensity are the endogenous variables. Market dominance is postulated to be positively related to a number of variables determining entry (promotional intensity, patents, innovation) and inversely related to variables making entry attractive (market growth, stability). Promotional intensity in turn is postulated to have either a substitute or complementary relation with all other entry barrier variables. Hence they are included as determinants in this equation (along with other determinant factors such as dummy variables indexing the type of drug therapy).

This model is estimated using the sample of sixty-nine therapeutic markets listed in table 3-4 over the period 1961-1971. In general, the model does not perform well in the sense that many of the estimated coefficients do not conform to the pattern predicted using the entry barrier structural framework. In this respect promotional intensity has a negative estimated (t value of 1.85) coefficient in the market dominance equation. On this basis Hornbrook concludes that "promotion has a procompetitive effect, other things being the same, in that it acts as a means of entry—a market penetration tool—more effectively, on balance, than as a barrier to entry." Thus in this particular respect Hornbrook's findings do not contradict but are consistent with the results of Telser et al.

In his promotion intensity equation Hornbrook finds that promotion intensity is significantly negatively related to innovation and the rate of growth of market sales and related (but not significantly) in a U-shaped manner to concentration (it is larger at high and low concentration levels). All these findings are highly implausible on theoretical grounds and contradict a large body of empirical work, suggesting that Hornbrook's model is subject to some serious misspecification or data measurement problems.

The Effects of Regulation on Innovation

Considerable evidence has now accumulated to support the hypotheses that increased regulatory control in ethical drugs has been a major factor leading to higher costs and risks of pharmaceutical innovation. As a result, the supply of new drug innovation not only has declined, but is also apparently becoming much more concentrated in the larger multinational drug firms.

Recent Regulatory Developments

Since 1938, with the passage of the Food, Drug, and Cosmetic Act, Congress authorized the Food and Drug Administration (FDA) to perform a premarket safety review of all new drug compounds. Despite these new regulatory controls, innovation in ethical drugs flourished over the next two decades. Several notable therapeutic advances were achieved in antibiotics, tranquilizers, and other areas. Furthermore drug industry R&D expenditures increased dramatically along with the annual volume of new chemical entities (NCEs) introduced commerically. While the premarket safety reviews of the FDA obviously resulted in time lags for all drugs and deterred some new drugs from the marketplace, regulatory review times were still quite short (seven months on average) and the annual volume of NCE introductions at record levels (over fifty per year) at the end of the decade of the fifties [Grabowski, 1976, ch. 2].

In the early 1960s, following the thalidomide tragedy, FDA regulation of ethical drugs became more stringent. A major factor in this regard was the passage by Congress in 1962 of the Kefauver-Harris Amendments to the Food, Drug, and Cosmetic Act. This new law required firms to demonstrate the efficacy as well as safety of all new drugs and imposed regulatory controls on the clinical research process and on drug advertising and labeling.

One would expect the more stringent regulatory environment that evolved after 1962 to have some adverse effects on costs, risks, and development times of new drug innovation. In fact, a number of studies have indicated that significant shifts took place in the economics of new product innovation in ethical drugs in the postamendment period. In particular, studies by Mund [1970] and Sarett [1974] and others indicate that development costs and times increased several-fold after 1962. By the early 1970s, Sarett estimated, the introduction of an NCE required more than $10 million in development costs and a gestation period of eight to ten years. In addition, data developed by Lasagna and Wardell [1975] point to a much higher attrition rate on new drug candidates in the postamendment period. Less than 10 percent of the drugs entering clinical testing on humans after 1962 have become commercially available drugs. These adverse developments on the input side have been accompanied by a sizable decline in the annual rate of NCE introductions in the postamendment period (see table 3-8).

While there is little argument that innovational activity in ethical drugs has been characterized by significant adverse structural trends, there has been considerable debate about the role of regulation in explaining this situation. Analytical studies of this question by Baily [1972], Peltzman [1973], Wardell [1973], and Grabowski, Vernon, and Thomas [1978], however, indicate that increased regulation is an important, if not necessarily the only, cause of the increase costs and declining rate of innovation.

Concentration of Innovational Activity

On theoretical grounds one would expect concentration of innovation to occur as the innovational process becomes costly and riskier in nature. This is because the minimum-scale R&D that can be undertaken without exposing a firm to a high variance in earnings will also increase. In effect, a firm must pool a larger number of costlier projects to obtain a balanced total R&D portfolio that provides

Table 3-8
Concentration of Innovational Output in the U.S. Ethical Drug Industry

	Periods		
	1957-1961	*1962-1966*	*1967-1971*
Total number of new chemical entities (NCE's)	233	93	76
Number of firms having an NCE	51	34	23
Total innovational output[a] (millions $)	$1,220.3	$738.6	$726.8
Concentration ratios of innovational output			
Four-firm	46.2	54.6	61.0
Eight-firm	71.2	78.9	81.5
Four largest firms' share of innovational output	24.0	25.0	48.7
Four largest firms' share of total sales	26.5	24.0	26.1

Sources: List of new chemical entities obtained from Paul de Haen, *Annual New Product Parade,* various issues; all data on ethical drug sales from Intercontinental Medical Statistics.

[a]Innovational output is measured as new chemical entity (NCE) sales during the first three full years after product introduction.

security against excessive risks of earnings fluctuations. Small firms with limited resource bases will have particular difficulty adapting to large shifts in costs and risk of R&D projects, unless they are especially confident about their comparative advantage in performing R&D. In addition, firms that are especially risk averse or ones with relatively lower expected returns from R&D activities are also likely to transfer resources out of new drug development.

Some data examining whether innovation has become more concentrated in fewer and larger firms are presented in table 3-8 (see [Grabowski and Vernon, 1976]). The first two rows of this table show the total number of NCEs and the number of firms having at least one NCE over three successive five-year periods, 1957-1961, 1962-1966, and 1967-1971. These data clearly show that the number of independent sources of new drug introduction has declined significantly over time, along with the rate of total introductions.

The third row of table 3-8 gives the dollar value of "innovational output" in each period. This is the total number of NCEs introduced in each period, weighted by their sales during the first three years after introduction. This measure of innovation, like the simple count of NCEs, also shows a significant downward movement over time. Table 3-8 next presents four-firm and eight-firm concentration ratios of innovational ouptut. These data indicate that the leading innovative firms have been accounting for increasing percentages of total innovation in successive periods and reinforce the point that the number of independent sources of innovation is declining.

The final question considered in table 3-8 is whether innovation has become more concentrated in the largest drug firms. The last two rows show the share of innovational output and the share of total drug sales accounted for by the four largest drug firms (ranked by ethical drug sales) for each of these five-year periods. Thus in the preamendment period 1957-1961 and in the first post-amendment period 1962-1966 the four largest firms accounted for a roughly equal amount of innovational output and sales. In the final period, however, the four largest firms accounted for 48.7 percent of innovational output, which was much greater than their share of sales (26.1 percent).

These findings were also consistent with a polynomial regression analysis of innovational output on sales for fifty-one drug firms for the three periods (see [Grabowski and Vernon, 1976]). In the first two periods a linear relationship between innovational output and sales offered the best statistical fit, whereas in the third period a cubic relation offered the best fit, with innovational output increasing at an increasing rate over the upper range of size.

The hypothesis that the largest firms in an industry will be the dominant sources of innovation dates back to Schumpeter's pioneering analysis. However, most empirical studies (including those for the drug industry) have not provided much support for the Schumpeterian hypothesis. Nevertheless the results reported here are quite consistent with the trends in pharmaceutical innovation. Given the much higher costs and risks of drug innovation in the postamendment period, it is plausible that the structure of innovation would shift in the direction of the Schumpeterian hypothesis.

Innovation and the Multinational Activities

The most innovative firms in the ethical drug industry are relatively large in terms of domestic sales and tend to have a strong multinational character. For example, the eight leading innovative firms in the 1967-1971 subperiod in table 3-7 (which accounted for over 80 percent of innovative output in that period) have a strong multinational orientation. Each of these firms had manufacturing plants in at least eight foreign countries, and seven of them had foreign sales in excess of $100 million in 1970. While past studies of the Schumpeterian hypothesis have not considered this aspect of firm structure, it appears to be highly relevant in the current context.

Multinational firms have some significant advantages in their ability to respond to the more stringent regulatory conditions that have evolved in this country. First, they can introduce new drug products in foreign markets (where regulatory conditions are less stringent) prior to (or in lieu of) introduction in the United States. This allows them to gain knowledge and realize sales revenues while a new drug compound remains under regulatory review and development in this country. While a firm with no foreign operations could in principle do the same thing through licensing, the significant information and transaction costs of licensing reduce the gains from such an arrangement.

In addition, multinational firms also can perform R&D activities in foreign countries in order to reduce time delays and the overall costs of developing new products. Some important institutional barriers to this strategy do exist, however. Historically the FDA has been unwilling to accept data from foreign clinical trials or patient experiences. Thus U.S. firms have incentives to perform their R&D in this country, even if they choose to introduce their new drugs first and in greater numbers abroad. Nevertheless only a small fraction of compounds entering clinical testing in the United States ever become commercial products (Wardell and Lasagna indicate that this fraction is now less than 10 percent). Multinational firms therefore have the option of screening new drugs abroad and performing duplicate U.S. trials on the relatively small fraction of drugs for which new drug applications (NDAs) are submitted to the FDA. They can also perform different phases of development alternatively here and abroad in order to reduce regulatory lags and bottlenecks.

In a 1976 paper we show that extensive shifts have occurred in the foreign introductions of multinational firms over the postamendment period [Vernon and Grabowski, 1976]. In an analysis of U.S.-discovered introductions into the United Kingdom we found that in the early sixties (the preamendment period) the vast majority of U.S.-discovered NCEs introduced in the United Kingdom became available there only after they were introduced in the United States. However, a rather dramatic shift in this situation has occurred over time. By the final subperiod analyzed (1972-1974) approximately two-thirds of the U.S.-discovered NCE introductions in the United Kingdom either were introduced later or have yet to become available in the United States. Preliminary analysis of data on France and Germany suggest similar patterns.

Data recently developed by Lasagna and Wardell also suggest that some significant shifts have taken place in the location of clinical testing by U.S. firms. They have recently completed a study of the new drug compounds clinically tested by fifteen large U.S. ethical drug firms over the period 1960-1974. (These firms accounted for 80 percent of R&D expenditures in the United States) Their results suggest an increasing tendency for U.S. firms to perform clinical testing of new drug compounds first in foreign locations. Specifically they found that in 1974 these firms clinically tested approximately one-half of all their new drug compounds abroad first, whereas before 1966 they performed virtually all their clinical testing first in the United States. Although industry R&D expenditure data indicate that the percentage of total R&D outlays expended in foreign countries by U.S. firms is still small (15.4 percent in 1974), foreign outlays are growing much more rapidly than domestic expenditures and this percentage has doubled in the space of a few years [Grabowski, 1976, ch. 3].

In summary, there is strong evidence that U.S.-based multinational firms are increasingly testing and marketing new chemical entities abroad before doing so in the United States. The option to engage in such foreign activities offers multinational firms significant advantages in dealing with the more stringent regulatory situation that has evolved in this country. It is therefore perhaps not surprising that the large multinational firms now account for such a disproportionately large share of innovation in the U.S. ethical drug industry.

Summary

A number of studies using the structure-conduct-performance paradigm have pointed to the high profit rates and wide price disparities between closely substitutable products as strong evidence for high entry barriers and market power in the ethical drug industry. Some recent studies, using a much more microeconomic and dynamic methodological approach, have directly challenged this conclusion. In particular they point to rapid rate of innovation in the industry as a key element of dynamic competition that positively influences consumer welfare, both by providing therapeutic advance over existing products and by introducing a dynamic form of price competition to this industry. Furthermore they offer evidence to support the position that promotional activities are a complementary activity to diffusion of innovation and the entry of new firms into particular therapeutic markets and therefore "facilitate" rather than erect barriers to entry.

At the same time considerable evidence is accumulating from other recent studies that more stringent regulatory controls by the FDA have had significant adverse effects on the structure of pharmaceutical innovation. In particular the higher costs and risks of drug innovation in the more stringent post-1962 regulatory environment appear to have operated as a barrier to competition through new product introduction. Consequently the supply of new drugs has not only declined, but also become more concentrated over time in the larger multinational firms better able to deal with this more stringent environment.

References

Baily, Martin N. "Research and Development Costs and Returns: The U.S. Pharmaceutical Industry," *Journal of Political Economy,* January/February 1972.

Bain, Joe S. *Industrial Organization,* 2nd ed. (New York: John Wiley and Sons, 1968).

Cocks, Douglas L. "Product Innovation and the Dynamic Elements of Competition in the Ethical Pharmaceutical Industry," in Robert B. Helms, ed., *Drug Development and Marketing* (Washington, D.C.: American Enterprise Institute, 1975), pp. 225-254.

Cocks, Douglas L., and Virts, John R. "Market Definition and Concentration in the Ethical Pharmaceutical Industry," 1974.

Comanor, William S. "Research and Competitive Product Differentiation in the Pharmaceutical Industry in the United States," *Economica,* November 1964.

Comanor, William S., and Wilson, Thomas A. *Advertising and Market Power* (Cambridge, Mass.: Harvard University Press, 1974).

Grabowski, Henry G. *Drug Regulation and Innovation: Empirical Evidence and Policy Options,* (Washington, D.C.: American Enterprise Institute for Public Policy Research, 1976).

Grabowski, Henry G., and Vernon, John M. "Structural Effects of Regulation on Innovation in the Ethical Drug Industry" in R.T. Masson and P.T. Qualls, ed., *Essays on Industrial Organization in Honor of Joe Bain* (Cambridge, Mass.: Ballinger, 1976), pp. 181-206.

Grabowski, Henry G., Vernon, John M., and Thomas, Lacy G. "Estimating the Effects of Regulation on Innovation: An International Comparative Analysis of the Pharmaceutical Industry," *Journal of Law and Economics,* April 1978, pp. 133-163.

Grabowski, Henry G., and Vernon, John M. "Consumer Protection Regulation in Ethical Drugs" in *American Economic Review,* May 1977.

Hornbrook, Mark C. "Market Domination and Promotional Intensity in the Wholesale-Retail Sector of the U.S. Pharmaceutical Industry," National Center for Health Services Research, Technical Paper Series Number 5, 1976.

Kefauver, Estes. *In a Few Hands—Monopoly Power in America* (Baltimore, Md.: Penguin, 1965).

Lasagna, Louis, and Wardell, William. "An Analysis of Drug Development Involving New Chemical Entities Sponsored by U.S.-Owned Companies, 1962-1974," in Helms, ed., *Drug Development and Marketing,* pp. 155-181.

Landau, Richard L., ed. *Regulating New Drugs* (Chicago: University of Chicago Press, 1973).

Leonard, William N. "Research and Development, Product Differentiation and Market Performance," 1972.

Measday, Walter S. "The Pharmaceutical Industry" in Walter Adams, ed., *The Structure of American Industry,* 4th ed. (New York: Macmillan Company, 1971).

Mund, Vernon A. "The Return on Investment of the Innovative Pharmaceutical Firm," in J.D. Cooper, ed, *The Economics of Drug Innovation* (Washington, D.C.: The American University, 1970).

Peltzman, Sam. "The Benefits and Costs of New Drug Regulation," in Landau, ed., *Regulating New Drugs,* 1973.

Sarett, L.H. "FDA Regulations and Their Influence on Future R&D," *Research Management,* March 1974.

Scherer, F.M. *Industrial Market Structure and Economic Performance,* (Chicago: Rand McNally, 1970).

Schumpeter, J.A. *Capitalism, Socialism, and Democracy* (New York: Harper, 1942).

Stigler, Geroge J. "Introduction" in NBER *Business Concentration and Price Policy* (Princeton, N.J.: Princeton University Press, 1955).

Task Force on Prescription Drugs. *Background Papers* (Washington, D.C.: U.S. Government Printing Office, 1969).

Telser, Lester G., Best, William, Egan, John W., and Higinbotham, H.N. "The Theory of Supply with Applications to the Ethical Pharmaceutical Industry," *Journal of Law and Economics,* October 1975.

U.S. Federal Trade Commission. *Economic Report on Antibiotics Manufacture* (Washington, D.C.: U.S. Government Printing Office, 1958).

Vernon, John M. "Concentration, Promotion, and Market Share Stability in the in the Pharmaceutical Industry," *Journal of Industrial Economics,* July 1971.

Wardell, William. "Introduction to New Therapeutic Drugs in the United States and Great Britain: An International Comparison," *Clinical Pharmacology and Therapeutics,* September/October 1973.

Commentary

Douglas L. Cocks

Overview: *The model employed by Hornbrook and summarized by Grabowski and Vernon has more of a dynamic orientation than the structure–conduct– performance orientation claimed by Hornbrook. If Hornbrook's model is explicitly placed in a dynamic context, it may yield different competitive implications. A preliminary measurement of the degree of difficulty of achieving oligopolistic coordination among pharmaceutical firms relating to some of the more recent literature summarized by Grabowski and Vernon is given. A previous analysis of market turnover among pharmaceutical firms is refined.*

This discussion of Grabowski and Vernon's paper will be confined to three areas. The first is the Hornbrook paper, for which an alternative explanation of his results is presented. In addition, a couple of comments on specific elements of the Hornbrook paper that could at least be subject to additional research are offered. The second area of comment involves aspects of the theory of oligopoly that may be relevant to the pharmaceutical industry. Finally rough index-of-instability data that compare the pharmaceutical industry with a group of selected industries are presented as a revision to earlier analyses.

In their summary of Hornbrook's paper Grabowski and Vernon conclude by stating: "All these findings are highly implausible on theoretical grounds and contradict a large body of empirical work, suggesting that Hornbrook's model is subject to some serious misspecification or data measurement problems." It may be that the pharmaceutical industry provides an excellent example of a Schumpeterian-like competitive process.[1] In this process innovation generates progressiveness through an industry stock of research and development that also forces price competition. This is possible because the R&D stock is distributed over a significant number of pharmaceutical firms.

Thus as an alternative the Hornbrook results may be considered consistent with this competitive process. Removing the Hornbrook model from the structure-conduct-performance framework and putting it in a Schumpeterian context may render the results consistent with a theoretical foundation.

In the market domination equation Hornbrook found the following variables to be statistically significant:

1. Promotional intensity, affecting market domination inversely
2. Concentration, affecting domination directly
3. New product innovation, negative impact on domination
4. New product imitation, negative impact on market domination
5. Patent X innovation interaction, negative impact on market domination

53

6. Brand name X innovation interaction, negative impact on market domination
7. Market growth rate, positive impact on market domination
8. Market share instability, negative impact on market domination

These results may at first indicate the existence of a dynamic form of competition consistent with the notion of workable competition. Hornbrook's model did include a price fluctuation variable that had a negative sign, but it was found to be statistically insignificant. It appears that Hornbrook's measurement of this variable suffers from a significant error-in-variables problem. Price fluctuation is measured as "the average squared percentage in average new prescription price per product between year $t-1$ and year t." It is necessary to adjust prescription prices for the size of the prescription in order to get the per unit price of product.[2] Not making this adjustment would seemingly bias the results that use this variable, since it is a characteristic of many drug products to have the average prescription size grow over time. This bias occurs because not adjusting for size dampens the true variability that would be associated with the price variable. It may well be that a revised price fluctuation variable would become statistically significant and would have a negative sign. This would indicate that the competitive structure of the industry is resulting in price competition.

The positive significance of the concentration variable has a possible alternative explanation. The contribution to market domination that comes from this variable may be explained in the context that has recently been developed by Mancke.[3] That is, stochastic market success through new production innovation by a firm automatically leads to further success that is not a result of overt or tacit collusion. This would be consistent with the signs of the other significant variables in the regression.

Another question about the Hornbrook analysis concerns the use of the therapeutic category as the definition of the relevant economic market. It is not clear that this is appropriate for the demand side, and Hornbrook acknowledges that is not very applicable for supply-side aspects.[4] It seems that further research on the definition of the relevant market for ethical pharmaceuticals is necessary in order to perform studies of competition.[5]

One final comment on the Hornbrook analysis. The empirical results of this paper appear to support a Schumpeterian-like competitive process in the pharmaceutical industry. This process generates progressiveness through new product innovation but at the same time may generate the means and results of price competition. As such, this indicates the industry may be workably competitive. In an earlier version of his research Hornbrook concluded that the industry is workably competitive.[6] If Hornbrook's results do indicate that the industry is workably competitive, then further regulation of the industry would be counterproductive. Thus there is no apparent relationship between his empirical results and the public policy conclusions that are drawn from these results.

The second issue is the application of certain aspects of the theory of oligopoly. One of the more general theories of oligopoly has been given by Stigler. Stigler views the costs of development and adherence to consistent patterns of activity among firms, where these patterns have been labeled tacit agreements, as being significant in determining the probability of the success of these agreements. The higher these costs the less likely there will be such agreements. These costs are most likely a function of the number of firms plus the complexity of the industry's product structure including the differences among buyers in demand elasticities.[7] From the data available there appear to be a minimum of twenty-two R&D-intensive drug firms, a number that indicates that tacit coordination would be very costly. In addition, collusion in the pharmaceutical industry would require the firms to tacitly agree on scientific matters and the inherent complexity of the R&D process would seem to make the costs of collusion very high.[8]

To further elaborate on this notion of the theory of oligopoly it is possible to utilize and expand a concept that has been developed by Scherer in his well-known text on industrial organization. In his discussion of oligopolistic coordination Scherer points out that the difficulty of achieving coordination increases with the number of firms. The significance of this point is highlighted by observing the number of two-way communication flows that would be required among the firms. This number can be expressed by the following combinatorial formula:

$$C = \frac{N(N-1)}{2} \qquad (1)$$

where C is the number of two-way communication flows and N is the number of firms.[9] Scherer points out: "Breakdown of any single channel can touch off independent actions threatening industry discipline."[10] If the coordination took place just among the leading R&D-intensive firms, there would have to be 231 two-way communications.

This communication problem can be expanded by considering the spectrum of activities that would have to be coordinated with the two-way communication process among the firms. This can be expressed by the combinatorial formula that sums the number of combinations of firm activities. These activities would have to be monitored and "policed" if the amount of cheating is to be held to a minimum. Thus the summed combinations of activities times the number of necessary two-way communication yields an indicator of the degree of difficulty of coordination. This can be expressed as

$$C_a = \left[\frac{N(N-2)}{2} \right] (2^a - 1) \qquad (2)$$

where

C_a = number of two-way communications over all alternative firm
activities

N = number of firms

a = number of activities that would have to be coordinated

These activities can be thought of as elements that, to use another of
Scherer's concepts, would require the establishment of focal points in order to
establish mutual understandings.[11] The greater the number of these focal points
and the more complicated they are, the higher the cost of establishing agreement.
If these activities are viewed as broad policy areas, then there could be several
alternative strategies for each policy category and these would simply add to the
sum of the number of activities that would have to be coordinated. Using a
game theory approach, Sherman found that with a greater number of pricing
strategies a given set of competitors is less able to establish coordination.[12]

If it is assumed that there are five activities that would have to be coordinated
among twenty-two drug firms, then the communication equation (2) can be
applied to get an indicator of the degree of coordination difficulty. These five
activities might include

1. Pricing
2. Product heterogenity
3. Research and development
4. Promotion
5. Costs of production, productivity, and full costs including R&D

Thus we get C_a = 7161. In essence this would be the two-way communication
network that prevails on the supply side, and it has been asserted that in order to
understand the realm of rivalry among drug firms it is necessary to consider the
relevant demand-side markets.[13] There are at least two ways of defining relevant drug markets. The way that has been accepted by several economists is
having the therapeutic category serve as a valid representation of demand-side
markets. In these therapeutic categories there would be an average number of
companies with a significant amount of activity in all therapeutic categories, and
if all companies have a given average representation in all therapeutic categories
the two-way communication indicator would generally become

$$C_{am} = \overline{m}\left[\frac{\overline{N}(\overline{N}-1)}{2}\right](2^a - 1) \qquad (3)$$

where

C_{am} = number of two-way communications for average of m demand-side markets over all alternative firm activities

$\bar{m}$ = average number of markets in which all firms have significant representation

$\bar{N}$ = average number of firms in all demand-side markets

a = number of activities that would have to be coordinated.

If it is assumed that on average at least five companies are significant within each therapeutic category, $\bar{N}$ = 5, that on average each company is important in five therapeutic categories, $\bar{m}$ =5, and that there are five activities to be coordinated, then we can use equation 3 to get an indicator of the amount of communication that would have to take place.[14] This result is shown in table 1.

In an earlier work ten important demand-side markets that account for approximately 80 percent of all retail prescriptions were identified.[15] Various aspects of the leading products in these ten markets were tracked and it was found that on the average there were at least seven significant firms in each market.[16]

If it is assumed that on the average a firm has a significant amount of activity in five of these markets, the values for the communication model become $\bar{m}$ = 5 and $\bar{N}$ = 7. Table 1 provides the estimate of the number of two-way communications that would be required for coordination for three markets.

The use of equation 3 as representing the communication process that would

Table 1
Two-Way Communication Flows for Drug Firms under Supply and Alternative Demand Assumptions

	Supply, Major R&D Intensive Firms	Demand	
		Therapeutic Categories	Ten Major Markets
Number of firms, N	22	5	7
Number of activities to be coordinated, a	5	5	5
Degree of coordination difficulty, C_a, C_{am}	7161	1550	6510

have to take place among drug firms within demand-side markets implicitly assumes that the communication and thus the degree of coordination difficulty is additive for the whole industry. This assumption is considered valid because it implicitly recognizes the supply-side characteristics of these demand markets. The main aspect of these supply-side characteristics is that with a significant stock of R&D existing in a substantial number of firms it is relatively easy for any one R&D intensive firm to develop a product in any one of the markets.[17]

The preceding exercise is offered merely as additional support of some of the findings that Grabowski and Vernon have summarized in their paper. There are indications that effective price competition operates in the drug industry and that the usual theory of oligopoly as it appears in structure-conduct-performance analysis is not appropriate for the industry. These two-way communication combinations may be a rough measure of the degree of difficulty of coordination among drug firms and may thus indicate the cost of that coordination. Applying the Stigler approach to oligopoly would indicate that coordination is too costly and thus will not be viable. If the evidence on the competitive nature of the industry is valid, then these two conclusions reinforce each other.

The last comment of this discussion is not really a comment on Grabowski and Vernon's paper, but rather a revision of some of the work that has been done by this writer that they summarize in their paper. This revision concerns the Hymer and Pashigian index of instability.[18] In an earlier paper an index of instability was calculated for the pharmaceutical industry and was compared with instability indexes for several two-digit SIC industries as calculated by Hymer and Pashigian.[19] The main difficulty with this comparison is that the pharmaceutical industry was calculated on the basis of sales while the Hymer and Pashigian indexes were calculated on the basis of reported assets. These different bases would not necessarily make the comparisons valid. Thus I have attempted an extremely rough index calculation for a selection of the very broad industry groupings that were used by Hymer and Pashigian on a sales basis. There calculations were made from Fortune 500 data for the period 1963-1972. Table 2 presents these data as well as the previously reported drug industry index. With the exception of the rubber industry these indexes are fairly consistent.

Table 2
Indexes of Market Share Instability

Industry	Index Based on Sales 1963-1972	Hymer and Pashigian Indexes 1946-1955
Chemicals	16.6	17.42
Petroleum	18.8	24.38
Primary metals	14.2	14.25
Rubber	20.2	9.16
Drugs	22.8	n.a.

Sources: *Fortune Directory*, (1964); *Fortune* (May 1973); Douglas L. Cocks "Product Innovation and the Dynamic Elements of Competition in the Ethical Pharmaceutical Industry," in Robert B. Helms, ed., *Drug Development and Marketing* (Washington, D.C.: American Enterprise Institute, 1975), pp. 225-254; and Stephen Hymer and Peter Pashigian, "Turnover of Firms as a Measure of Market Behavior," *Review of Economics and Statistics* 44 (1962): 82-87.

Notes

1. Douglas L. Cocks, "Product Innovation and the Dynamic Elements of Competition in the Pharmaceutical Industry," in *Drug Development and Marketing,* ed. Robert B. Helms (Washington, D.C.: American Enterprise Institute, 1975), pp. 225-254.

2. Douglas L. Cocks and John R. Virts, "Pricing Behavior of the Ethical Pharmaceutical Industry," *Journal of Business* 47 (July 1974): 349-362; John M. Firestone, *Trends in Prescription Drug Prices* (Washington, D.C.: American Enterprise Institute, 1970); and W. Duncan Reekie, "Price and Quality Competition in the United States Drug Industry," *Journal of Industrial Economics* 26 (March 1978): 223-237.

3. Richard A. Mancke, "Causes of Interfirm Profitability Differences: A New Interpretation of the Evidence," *Quarterly Journal of Economics* 88 (May 1974): 181-193.

4. See Douglas L. Cocks and John R. Virts, "Market Definition and Concentration in the Ethical Pharmaceutical Industry"; Cocks and Virts, "Pricing Behavior of the Ethical Pharmaceutical Industry"; and J. Fred Weston, "Pricing in the Pharmaceutical Industry," (Chapter 5 in this volume).

5. For discussion of establishing criteria for market definition see Kelwin J. Lancaster, "A New Approach to Consumer Theory," *Journal of Political Economy* 74 (April 1966): 132-157; and Morton Schnabel, "Defining Product," *Journal of Business* 49 (October 1976): 517-529.

6. Mark C. Hornbrook, "Market Structures and Conduct in the Wholesale-Retail Sector of the Pharmaceutical Industry," paper presented at the Pharmacy Session of the American Public Health Association Meeting, New Orleans, Louisiana, October 20, 1974.

7. George J. Stigler, *The Theory of Price,* 3rd ed. (New York: Macmillan Company, 1966), p. 220.

8. For a discussion of these same points see Robert B. Helms, "Highlights of the Discussion (Part Four: Factors Affecting Drug Industry Structure and Costs)," in *Drug Development and Marketing,* ed. Robert B. Helms (Washington, D.C.: American Enterprise Institute, 1975), p. 293.

9. F.M. Scherer, *Market Structure and Industrial Performance* (Chicago: Rand McNally, 1970), pp. 183-184.

10. Ibid., p. 184.

11. Ibid., p. 179-182.

12. Roger Sherman, *Oligopoly: An Empirical Approach* (Toronto: Lexington Books, D.C. Heath and Company, 1972), pp. 23-33.

13. Mark C. Hornbrook, "Market Domination and Promotional Intensity in the Wholesale-Retail Sector of the U.S. Pharmaceutical Industry," (paper presented at the Western Economic Association Annual Conference, San Francisco, California, June 24-27, 1976), p. 8.

14. For data on the number of firms represented in various therapeutic categories, see David Schwartzman, *Innovation in the Pharmaceutical Industry* (Baltimore, Md.: Johns Hopkins University Press, 1976), pp. 103-135.

15. Cocks and Virts, "Market Definition and Concentration in the Ethical Pharmaceutical Industry."

16. For the definition of leading products see Cocks and Virts, "Pricing Behavior of the Ethical Pharmaceutical Industry," p. 350.

17. A more accurate representation of the two-way communication process which recognizes that the combinations may be different for individual markets is given by

$$
C_{am} = \left(\sum_{i=1}^{n} \left[\frac{N_i\,(N_i - 1)}{2} \right] \right) \; (2^a - 1)
$$

where

C_{am} = number of two-way communications over all alternative firms activities

m = number of demand-side markets

N_i = number of firms in each of m markets

Again the coordination model is additive across all markets to take into account supply-side elements.

18. Stephen Hymer and Peter Pashigian, "Turnover of Firms as a Measure of Market Behavior," *Review of Economics and Statistics* 44 (February 1962): 82-87.

19. Douglas L. Cocks, "Product Innovation and the Dynamic Elements of Competition in the Pharmaceutical Industry," in *Drug Development and Marketing,* Robert B. Helms, ed. (Washington, D.C.: American Enterprise Institute, 1975), pp. 222-254.

4

Competition in the Pharmaceutical Industry

William S. Comanor

Overview: *There is no conflict between the use of market share turnover as a measure of innovative competition and the use of the difference between price and marginal cost as a measure of price competition. Rapid innovation and the exercise of considerable market power may not be inconsistent with each other. Circumstances may exist in which rapid innovation may be at the expense of substantial price competition, and we need to be concerned with the trade-offs that exist between these two sets of objectives.*

Henry Grabowski's review of the recent literature on competition in the pharmaceutical industry provides a useful survey of a number of recent studies. What he adds, and what is the major point of interest in his paper, is the suggestion that there are two ways of appraising the competitive process in the pharmaceutical industry.

Although Grabowski does not say so directly, he implies that one approach is superior to the other. It represents a "newer" set of studies and is concerned more with dynamic than with static considerations. He implies as well that the second approach is more relevant for policy judgments. What seems to be of concern is not so much specific policy actions but rather whether approving or disapproving statements should be made regarding the performance of the pharmaceutical industry. The question at issue appears to be whether one should appraise the industry as competitive, despite indications that the industry is quite competitive in some areas but less so in others.

Grabowski divides these studies into two categories, based essentially on the underlying methodological approach. Of some interest, however, is that the first category includes works that are generally critical of the performance of the industry, while the second contains studies that are generally approving.

The author is grateful to his colleague H.E. Frech for helpful comments in the preparation of this paper. The author is currently director of the Bureau of Economics, Federal Trade Commission, but this paper was written prior to his assuming this position. Moreover, the views expressed are his own, and do not necessarily represent those of the Federal Trade Commission nor of any individual commissioner.

63

Structure, Conduct, Performance

The first of Grabowski's two categories refers to studies that generally follow the conventional industrial organization paradigm of structure, conduct, performance. There is little need to review here this methodological approach.[1] However, there are various dimensions of performance. The traditional paradigm is concerned not only with static efficiency, in all of its various aspects, but also with dynamic efficiency or "progressiveness." The latter is as important a dimension of performance as the former.

Many of these studies call attention to the relatively high prices and profits reported for this industry and seek to provide an explanation. While these observations are important features of industry conduct and have implications for static efficiency, there can be no claim that they provide much evidence on progressiveness.

In this approach to industrial organization there is an element of asymmetry in the relationship between competition and these two dimensions of performance. Recall that competition—or its inverse, the degree of market power in an industry—is defined by the extent to which the behavior of firms is different from that enforced under the purely competitive model although with the same cost and demand conditions.[2] This definition focuses on the extent to which actual market conditions depart from those expected under competitive conditions with the same exogenous factors present.

While the model of pure competition provides a necessary benchmark by which to appraise actual states of competition in the marketplace, its use creates some analytical problems. Foremost among these is that the competitive model, while it is fairly precise regarding certain variables, provides little information on others. For example, it is well known that the competitive price is equal to marginal cost. So fundamental is this equality to the concept of competition that it is the basis of the well-known Lerner index of monopoly, which is the percentage difference between price and marginal cost.[3]

Although the competitive model is relatively precise regarding price and quantity, it is of little assistance in defining competitive levels of advertising or research. There is no apparent way of determining how much competitive firms would spend for these purposes, once we admit that some positive amount is called for. Indeed the difficulty inherent in defining competitive norms for these variables has created numerous problems in the enforcement of antitrust policy.

It is relevant that we can define competitive values for prices and outputs that relate to static efficiency, although there are no corresponding competitive norms for the variables that relate to progressiveness. Since the degree of competition is defined on the same basis as static efficiency, it is evident that the more competition, the better—at least if we ignore problems of the second best. Unfortunately this correspondence is not necessarily present in the case of progressiveness. The possibility therefore exists that competition may be inversely related to that dimension of performance.

This point is not new. Indeed the essence of the Schumpeterian hypothesis is that consumer welfare, influenced by the rate of innovation, may not be served by the maximum degree of competition.[4] As a result, there can be a conflict between static and dynamic efficiency. While we cannot come to any general conclusions on this point here, there is little doubt that this issue is not new to the study of industrial organization and that it falls within the conventional paradigm of structure, conduct, performance.[5]

The New Approach

Grabowski suggests that there is a new group of studies whose approach departs from the conventional paradigm and which lead to substantially different conclusions. Studies that fall into this category "emphasize the importance of Schumpeterian-type competition through new product innovation as well as the implications of this dynamic competition in innovation for entry, promotion, prices, and profit rates." Elsewhere, he refers to this group of studies as those that use "the dynamic competition approach." Similar terms and descriptions are scattered throughout his paper. How different are these studies from those that follow the more traditional approach?

Many of the studies reviewed by Grabowski conclude that the rapid pace of new product introduction in the pharmaceutical industry represents substantial product innovation and has led to much improved consumer welfare. Although there are differences among them, the common theme is that competitive product innovation is a major feature of this industry and has important implications for its performance. While these findings are probably correct, their relation to other features of the pharmaceutical industry is also relevant.

Some of these studies use an index of market share turnover to measure the degree of "dynamic competition." By this measure the pharmaceutical industry appears highly competitive. It is argued that this type of variable is a more accurate index of competition in this industry than the more conventional measures of concentration or profitability.

What seems evident is that market share turnover, which reflects the rate of change of market shares among rival firms, is neither better nor worse than the conventional variables but rather different. This variable measures a different facet of industry behavior, which may bear little relationship to what is reflected by concentration or profitability. *The question is not which is a better measure of competition, but rather what it is that each variable measures.* In the case of the pharmaceutical industry market share turnover is likely to reflect the pace of innovation, for it is the latter factor that is largely responsible for past changes in market shares. New products have replaced older ones, and leading market positions have changed hands.

Note that if the pace of new product introduction is the primary reason for the high level of market share instability in the pharmaceutical industry, then it is quite compatible with substantial degrees of market power, defined by the relation between prices and marginal costs. *Rapid innovation is not inconsistent with the exercise of considerable market power.* Indeed, where rapid innovation is related to the development of product differentiation, it may be a source of the underlying market power.[6] What is evident is that the various indices of market share turnover measure something quite different from the traditional measures of competition, and there is no necessary reason that the two should go together.

While this discussion has focused on alternative measures of competition, it is concerned with more substantive issues and is not merely a problem of measurement. The important point is that competitive product innovation is not the same as price competition. Without more information, one cannot say whether it is more or less important, but one can readily say that it is different and has different consequences.

Although consumer welfare may be improved by the rapid pace of product innovation, it may also be reduced by prices that exceed costs because of limited competitive pressures. In the best of circumstances rapid innovation would not be at the expense of effective price competition. However, such circumstances are not always encountered, and the dilemma posed by the Schumpeterian hypothesis is that rapid innovation may indeed be at the expense of substantial price competition. Whether this is the case is a major question regarding the role of competition in the pharmaceutical industry. Yet the "new" studies contribute little on this issue.

The Effect of Promotional and Advertising Expenditures

An important area where the differences between the two groups of studies is more apparent than real is the role of promotional and advertising expenditures. These expenditures are substantial in the pharmaceutical industry. At one point it was reported that they were approximately four times greater than expenditures on research and development.[7]

Grabowski refers to a recent paper by Telser et al. who find, across a sample of therapeutic markets, a positive relationship between promotional intensity and entry into particular markets. The latter is measured by the proportion of 1972 sales of firms absent from the market in 1963 and is thus closely related to market share turnover. Telser et al. argue that "it is plain from these results that promotional outlays do not constitute a barrier to entry."[8] Grabowski suggests that this represents a further area in which the conclusions of the "new" studies depart from their older counterparts.

Telser's findings suggest that the returns from advertising new products are higher than those from advertising older ones, so that expenditures are greater for the former. This observation, however, indicates little regarding the impact of advertising on entry barriers. Whether or not entry barriers are created, the returns from promoting newer products may well be greater than from older ones.

Using either the definitions of entry barriers proposed by Bain or Stigler, such barriers must rest on advantages, cost or otherwise, that established firms have relative to new entrants for the same product.[9] Entry restrictions are present when established firms can raise prices over costs without attracting new firms into production of the same products.

In the pharmaceutical industry entry into particular therapeutic markets generally requires new patented products if the products are to command prices comparable to those of the leading established products. To enter a therapeutic market in this manner requires substantial research effort, for there is frequently the need to invent around existing patents. A second vehicle of entry into therapeutic markets is based on generic products which are generally without patent protection. These products, however, frequently cannot command the same price as their established counterparts. Note that there may be physical entry, even though entry barriers exist, as long as price differences remain.

One cannot deal with the question of entry restrictions without paying attention to relative prices, which are largely ignored in the analysis of Telser and his colleagues. For this reason, the simple correlations that are computed indicate little about the presence or absence of barriers to entry due to advertising. What they do provide is information on the process of product innovation. We observe that those therapeutic markets most characterized by new product innovation, and therefore having the highest values of Telser's measure of entry, are also those associated with the heaviest promotional activity. While an interesting observation, and one deserving of further elaboration, there is no necessary conflict between this observation and the inferences regarding advertising and entry barriers reported in our book and referred to by Grabowski.[10]

Conclusion

During the past dozen years or so, a large number of economic studies dealing with various facets of the pharmaceutical industry have appeared. For the most part these studies have examined specific features of this industry. What is particularly needed at this time is a framework to consider how the results offered fit together. What Grabowski's review indicates is that many of these studies point in different directions. Searching for the common ground among them represents a major task before us.

Notes

1. See F.M. Scherer, *Industrial Market Structure and Economic Performance* (Chicago: Rand McNally, 1970).

2. Carl Kaysen and Donald F. Turner, *Antitrust Policy* (Cambridge: Harvard University Press, 1959) p. 75.

3. Abba P. Lerner, "The Concept of Monopoly and the Measurement of Monopoly Power," *Review of Economic Studies* 1 (June 1934): 157-175.

4. Joseph A. Schumpeter, *Capitalism, Socialism, and Democracy* (New York: Harper, 1950), chs. 7-8.

5. For a general discussion of this question and a review of the available evidence, see Scherer, *Industrial Market Structure*, ch. 15.

6. William S. Comanor, "Research and Competitive Product Differentiation in the Pharmaceutical Industry in the United States," *Economica* 31 (November 1964): 372-384. Reprinted with permission.

7. The statistics from which this figure is derived refer to the largest twenty-two pharmaceutical firms in 1958. U.S. Senate, Subcommittee on Antitrust and Monopoly, *Report of the Study of Administered Prices in the Drug Industry*, 87th Congress, 1st Session, 1961, p. 31.

8. Lester G. Telser et al., "The Theory of Supply with Applications to the Ethical Pharmaceutical Industry," *Journal of Law and Economics* 28 (October 1975): 477.

9. Joe S. Bain, *Barriers to New Competition* (Cambridge: Harvard University Press, 1956), p. 3; and George J. Stigler, *The Organization of Industry* (Homewood, Ill.: Richard D. Irwin, Inc., 1968), p. 67.

10. William S. Comanor and Thomas A. Wilson, *Advertising and Market Power* (Cambridge: Harvard University Press, 1974).

**Part II
Pharmaceutical Price and
Profitability Studies**

5 Pricing in the Pharmaceutical Industry

J. Fred Weston

Overview: *The traditional short-run partial equilibrium analysis of standard microeconomic theory represents an oversimplification of the pricing mechanism. In this study, the numerous demand, supply, and environmental factors that influence the pricing of pharmaceuticals are presented. The price of a drug product is its nominal price plus quality factors, and price competition takes place on many dimensions of quality. These dimensions include, for example, efficacy, safety, clinical evidence and experience, information communicated to physicians, and the reputation of the manufacturer. Product competition results in continuous price reductions on older products. Furthermore price competition takes place in the discounts and rebates to wholesalers and other distribution outlets. There are relatively high cross elasticities of demand between drugs in a product group, and there are not likely to be wide departures between long-run marginal cost and price for most drug products. Possible departures from technical pricing tests are more than offset by advances in innovation resulting in substantial benefits to consumers.*

Framework of the Analysis

Unless pricing is placed in the context of industry economics and the total planning and resource allocation processes of firms, a distorted view of the pricing process will be produced. Standard microeconomic theory is especially guilty of unjustifiable overgeneralization of simplified price analysis. It is convenient in developing the theory of the firm in microeconomic theory to *assume* for analysis of some types of problems or decision areas that all other variables are at their optimum values or are assumed to be held constant, while only price and output vary. In this type of partial equilibrium analysis a demand curve and average and marginal cost curves are "given." For an atomistic firm average revenue and marginal revenue are equal, and the pricing rule is to equate marginal costs to (average) price to determine the firm's "output" rate.

Even for short-run analysis assuming that the demand and cost curves are known is a vast oversimplification. Even for a given scale of plant demand and cost factors are subject to uncertainty and change. In a long-run context, in which changes in scale of plant may take place, the assumptions of known and certain demand and cost functions may provide useful exercises but are

71

misleading as guides to industry policy. They fail to capture the strategies, policies, and processes by which firms seek to deal with change and uncertainty. Nevertheless the formal partial equilibrium analysis of standard microeconomic theory will considered next.

The static partial equilibrium model is based on a number of assumptions: (1) absence of economies of scale, (2) a large number of sellers, (3) a large number of buyers, (4) perfect knowledge of factor input prices and qualities by producers, (5) perfect knowledge of product prices and qualities by buyers, (6) perfectly homogeneous products, and (7) instantaneous mobility of factors.

Under these assumptions the demand function facing the individual atomistic firm is horizontal with infinite elasticity, and marginal revenue equals average revenue equals price. If a firm faces a demand function that has a negative slope to some degree, marginal revenue will be less than average revenue. The firm will equate marginal cost to marginal revenue, and part of the difference between price or average revenue and marginal cost is a measure of "consumer welfare loss."

Under the atomistic competitive theory the mechanisms for eliminating above-normal profits are entry, the revaluation of fixed assets, and rebidding on other costs. Exit is the mechanism by which supply conditions are reduced to increase price, and the revaluation of assets downward takes place through reorganization and bankruptcy to eliminate the losses of submarginal firms and to bring their profits up to normal levels.

This theory of atomistic competition may be contrasted with the assumptions and economic processes under the alternative model of oligopolistic competition applicable to the pharmaceutical manufacturing industry. The familiar partial equilibrium ceteris paribus diagrams in textbook presentations give an unnecessarily narrow view of pricing decisions in both large and small firms. In the long-run framework it is not meaningful to hold other factors constant because of their interaction with pricing decisions. Other groups of variables to be considered are (1) product characteristic vectors, (2) relative price vectors in relation to product quality, (3) the nature of the sales or dealer organization vectors involved in marketing the product, (4) advertising and other promotional effort vectors, and (5) the quality of the financing and service organizations to support product sales and use.

Broad environmental influences, combined with the constraints presented by existing products and firms in the market, lead the firm to develop adaptive policies with respect to product, quality, prices, sales methods, promotion efforts, service organization, and financial facilities. These decisions in turn influence the quantity and type of fixed investments and the level and behavior of other costs. Even on new products, constraints are set by the market, since new products substitute in some degree for older products. The price concept itself is extremely complex on durable goods for which maintenance costs and availability of repair and service facilities are important decision variables in the purchase. In addition, the stock of used durable goods represents a multiple of any given year's flow of new output. Hence there is continuous competition between the stock of used durable goods and those newly produced.

Strategies are formulated to offer either breadth or specialization in a range of combinations of product characteristics. Iterated reviews of product quality characteristics, materials characteristics, production methods, and marketing methods seek the optimal product quality, cost levels, and marketing attractiveness. Since administrative discretion is exercised in selecting from alternative combinations of choices under uncertainty involving pricing decisions in relation to the other variables, atomistic firms as well as firms in concentrated industries may be said to have price policies.

A tentative decision may be made with regard to the amount of fixed investment, fixed costs, and the level and behavior of other costs. This produces a range of expected volumes or turnover of investment. These estimates are initiated by making a forecast of industry volume. Next an estimate is made of the firm's expected share of the market. Obviously the firm could simply forecast its expected volume. The share-of-market analysis is particularly useful because an explicit comparison with other firms can be made. In addition, volume estimates that involve a large increase in the firm's share of the market can be expected to result in responses by other firms in the industry. Relating the expected level and behavior of costs to expected prices and volume in relationships to the total investment involved indicates an expected return on investment.

Many uncertainties are involved at each place in the decision process. There are uncertainties with regard to both the present and future behavior of rivals. The broader environmental factors are also subject to change. As a consequence, there are capital investment decisions involving probability distributions and uncertainty at each stage of the process.

Therefore the analysis may be repeated with alternate judgments about the probabilities involved. This may yield another expected return on investment. Repeating the process yields probability distributions of returns on investment. The decision makers in the firm will accept the investment or reject it depending on the level of the expected returns and the degree of dispersion in the probability distribution, particularly the cumulative probability that the investment might earn less than a required return on investment.

Finally the foregoing framework is used to reconsider a generalization with respect to oligopoly theory. This relates to the proposition that various degrees of oligopolistic awareness will lead to spontaneous collusion by firms operating in concentrated industries. The concept of oligopolistic awareness is only plausible in the setting of partial equilibrium analysis. If decision making is limited to output or pricing so that there was only one dimension of interaction, oligopolistic awareness would indeed be facilitated.

However, the reality is great complexity in the decision-making process involving output or pricing decisions. There are a large number of interacting areas, each with numerous vectors. These areas include research and development, product variations, quality of product, style of product, manufacturing processes, management techniques, channels of distribution, advertising methods, and so forth. The dimensions of decision making in the business firm are much too complex, with too many dimensions to permit oligopolistic awareness to have any realistic meaning.

The kind of awareness implied in the concept of oligopolistic spontaneous collusion would be possible only if the dimensions of decision making were as narrow as postulated under conditions of atomistic competition in which all dimensions other than output or price were held constant. Oligopolistic awareness is simply a figment of the assumptions of partial equilibrium analysis under extreme ceteris paribus reasoning. For the complex and multidimensional decision aspects of the real world, even atomistic firms have policies and many types of policies.

Demand and Supply Influences on Drug Prices

Within this complex framework the formulation of policies with respect to price must take a number of economic, political, and social factors into account. Both demand and supply factors influence price. Among the demand factors that influence the prices of pharmaceuticals are the following:

1. Product characteristics defined by (a) acceptability, (b) efficacy, and (c) absence of side effects
2. The therapeutic qualities of a drug in relation to other products
3. Classes of physicians who are the most likely prescribers
4. Price schedules for related products
5. Daily dosage quantity and expected duration of patient therapy
6. Dosage or treatment costs in a health care program
7. Effects on related costs in a health care program
8. Extent and characteristics of probable users, considering age group, income levels, and so forth
9. Elasticity of demand with respect to price
10. Cross elasticities of demand with respect to price and product qualities
11. Elasticity of demand with respect to income
12. Probability and timing of appearance of new competing products
13. Projected volume at various prices
14. Duration and pattern of probable product life cycle
15. Extent of use of prepayment plans, insurance plans, and government programs in paying for health care and drugs

The supply factors that influence price in the pharmaceuticals are also complex and numerous. They include

1. Number and types of competing products
2. Number and types of competing companies
3. Rate of future prospective development of competing products
4. Research, production, and quality control requirements expressed in required investments and cost levels
5. Nature of distribution systems required for effective marketing
6. Size, forms, and strengths of products to be marketed
7. Expected shelf life of products
8. Patent position of the firm in relation to other products and firms
9. Other products produced by the firm and their prospective prices, costs, volume, and returns
10. Ease of imitation or improvements by others
11. Location of production in relation to markets served; domestic versus exports
12. Sources of raw materials
13. Differences in required associated services to the medical profession
14. Tax patterns
15. Government regulations and procedures required for certifying drugs
16. Sources and costs of capital
17. Types of scientific and technical capabilities required
18. Production and quality control supervision by regulatory agencies

In addition, a host of environmental factors also influence drug prices. Environmental variables include

1. Size of the economy
2. Percentage of income spent on health care
3. Nature and expectations toward health care systems
4. Consumption habits and patterns with respect to the use of pharmaceuticals
5. Standard of living in the economy
6. Size and distribution of gross national product
7. Characteristics of the political environment
8. Role of government in payment for health care
9. Role of government as regulator and inspector
10. Rate of growth of the economy
11. Economic instability or stability
12. Patterns of price changes in the economy as a whole
13. Import, export, foreign exchange regulations
14. Antidumping regulations

15. Laws with respect to patents
16. Laws and administrative policies with respect to compulsory licensing
17. Licensing regulations
18. Comparative licensing regulations among different countries

Thus a meaningful discussion of prices and pricing requires that the nature of prices be recognized. Prices of all products, but especially drug products, have a number of dimensions. The main dimensions of drug product prices are the following:

Quality   =   efficacy + safety + clinical evidence + experience + information communicated to doctors and other professionals + reputation of manufacturer based on performance of prior products

Nominal price   =   price to wholesaler − discounts to wholesaler − discounts and rebates to hospital or other distribution outlets

(Actual) price   =   nominal price ÷ quality

Price competition takes place therefore among manufacturers in their competitive striving on all the dimensions of the product's quality, since changes in quality change the actual price. Price competition also takes place in the discounts and rebates to the wholesalers and hospitals and other distribution outlets and users.

The quality characteristics of drug products set boundaries on feasible prices. A drug product cannot be priced above the quality-price relations of other related drugs in the therapeutic product class or related therapeutic product classes. Since subjective elements are to some degree involved in the quality assessment and determination, judgment must be exercised in seeking the appropriate price relation.

In the analysis of the behavior of prices and the price responsiveness of quantity sold to apparent price changes, it is quality-adjusted prices that need to be taken into account and not just the nominal price. Yet critics of drug pricing have ascribed simple rules to pricing. For example, in referring to the use of some of these demand factors, Steele characterizes them as "a sort of value-of-service standard in connection with prescription drug prices, implying that if the price does not exceed what it is worth to the buyer, then it is reasonable. But this is just the monopolistic practice of charging what the traffic will bear."[1] Mr. Rucker states:

> We have assumed that the traditional model for price setting—getting all that the traffic will bear—is inappropriate for guiding pricing decisions in the health care area. We have also assumed that cost-

oriented criteria should serve as the primary basis for prescription pricing. In addition, the new social model would postulate that expenditures designed to give any supplier control over his demand curve are redundant. This interpretation is derived from the premise that such outlays are not likely to enhance the intrinsic value of the prescription, and hence, improve the patient's welfare.[2]

But value in use is only one of a large number of factors influencing prices and price changes. Certainly it is one of the demand influences, but it is a distortion of industry practice to characterize value in use as the sole or main determinant of price.

Nor would it be sound to have prices determined by costs. Unless demand factors are taken into account, some products would be priced so high in relation to user income that consumer health care needs would be met to a much less desirable degree than they are today.

A basic question is whether losses from negatively sloped demand curves exist to any appreciable degree in the pharmaceutical industry with its low degree of concentration overall and the generally temporary leadership of individual products. Hence it is useful to test the foregoing theoretical materials by empirical evidence.

Tests of Dynamically Competitive Prices

The first issue is the question of price flexibility or the frequency of price change. The general argument is made that in oligopolistic industries prices are administered and do not respond to changes in demand and supply conditions. These generalizations have been examined in careful detail and have been found not to be valid.[3]

Some limited evidence has alleged price inflexibility in the pharmaceutical industry. During the Kefauver hearings data were presented on the prices of antibiotic drugs and corticosteroid hormones. In another study Markham computed prices for individual products for the ten-year period 1949-1959. Of the 308 individual drug product prices he observed, more than 50 percent did not change at all during the ten-year period.[4] But these previously published pricing studies were based on stated wholesale prices as reflected in published price lists. It is now generally recognized that price lists represent initial offering prices from which various discounts and deals are frequently made. Different policies in services and returns also have the effect of price changes. In addition, salesmen have varied prices by providing additional units directly from their vehicle "free of charge." Such competitive price changes are not reflected in official pricing documents. One way to reflect such special pricing activity is to observe the resulting retail transactions prices, as an indirect measure of variations in manufacturing prices.

The findings by Cocks and Virts on drug prices in actual transactions are set forth in table 5-1 for individual products for three different therapeutic product classes. In table 5-2 price changes are averaged over the leading products in ten ethical drug product sets.

Next the movements of drug prices over time are considered. Table 5-3 presents the trend in prices of drugs that held a leading market position at the start of the time period for analysis. The data cover ten therapeutic product classes for the period 1962-1971. The average decline for the leading drug was 8.9 percent. Excluding the cough and cold market, the average decline was 11.0 percent for the leading drug and 3.1 percent for the second leading drug. For the leading products, as a group, the average decline was over 8 percent, compared with a rise in the consumer price index of more than 30 percent over the same 1962-1971 period.

Of course, drug prices may have been too high to begin with. But the fact that the leading drugs were subject to substantial price declines with the appearance of substitute drugs is evidence of strong competition between the drugs. It is reasonable to infer that the actual and potential competition between drugs would influence their initial prices at introduction as well as subsequently.

An Empirical Study of Drug Pricing

In the study by W.D. Reekie all new chemical entities introduced in the United Kingdom market between 1962 and 1970 were identified.[5] A sample was drawn from an original list of 470 entities introduced in world markets between 1958 and 1970, compiled for the National Economic Development Office's (NEDO) study "Innovative Activity in the Pharmaceutical Industry" (1973). A sample of 125 compounds sold in thirty-five submarkets (from a possible eighty) which accounted in 1973 for over 80 percent of all National Health Service (NHS) sales. Data for 1958-1961 were excluded because of lack of necessary price and sales data. Submarkets that in no year achieved 1 percent of NHS sales were also excluded.

The 125 entities were ranked on a scale of 1 to 5 during the NEDO study by pharmacological or clinical experts in a relevant discipline. Entities were ranked from 1 to 5 with the lowest number indicating the highest degree of major clinical significance of the new product introduction. The assessments were made on the basis of the situation at the actual date of launch but were made reflecting some degree of hindsight, since the evaluations were made later.

The study emphasizes the price and market share performance of the new chemical entities introduced. Price was measured by daily dosage cost. The modal daily dosage and its form of presentation were selected as "representative" for the product in question. The container that had the largest financial

Table 5-1
Price Flexibility in the Pharmaceutical Industry: Price Changes of the Leading Products

Product No.	No. Possible Price Changes	No. Changes of at Least 1, 2, 4, 8, Index Points			
		1	2	4	8
A. Antiinfective product set					
1	9	7	4	2	0
2	9	6	3	0	0
3	9	8	8	7	4
4	9	6	5	3	1
5	9	7	6	3	0
6	9	7	2	1	0
7	9	5	4	3	2
8	9	6	5	0	0
9	9	8	6	6	3
10	9	5	4	1	1
11	9	9	7	4	1
12	8	8	7	3	1
Total	107	82	61	33	14
B. Analgesic and antiinflammatory product set					
1	9	7	2	0	0
2	9	8	4	2	2
3	9	7	5	3	0
4	9	7	5	2	1
5	9	6	4	1	0
6	9	5	3	2	0
7	9	4	2	0	0
8	9	6	2	1	1
9	9	7	6	2	0
10	9	4	3	1	1
11	6	4	4	0	0
12	4	4	2	1	0
Total	100	69	42	15	5
C. Psychopharmaceutical product set					
1	9	6	6	0	0
2	9	5	4	1	0
3	9	7	6	3	0
4	9	7	4	2	0
5	9	7	5	2	0
6	9	7	5	4	0
7	9	6	3	2	0
8	9	7	5	4	2
9	8	6	4	1	0
10	6	4	4	0	0
Total	86	62	46	19	2

Source: Douglas L. Cocks, and John R. Virts, "Pricing Behavior of the Ethical Pharmaceutical Industry," *Journal of Business* 47 (July 1974): 360. Reprinted with permission of the University of Chicago Press.

Table 5-2
Price Flexibility in Ten Ethical Drug Products: Average Price Changes of the Leading Products

Product Set	Average No. Possible Prices Changes	Average No. Changes of at Least 1, 2, 4, 8, Index Points				No. Different Firms in Product Set in	
		1	2	4	8	1962	1971
1. Antiinfectives	8.9	6.8	5.1	2.8	1.2	7	8
2. Analgesic and anti-inflammatory	8.3	5.8	3.5	1.3	0.4	7	8
3. Psychopharmaceutical	8.6	6.2	4.6	1.9	0.2	7	7
4. Cough and cold	8.8	7.6	4.2	2.6	1.2	7	7
5. Antihypertensive diuretic	8.4	6.1	3.6	0.8	0.1	6	6
6. Vitamin and hematinic	8.7	6.7	4.8	2.6	0.6	9	8
7. Oral contraceptive	4.6	4.0	3.6	2.3	0.3	1	6
8. Anticholinergic and anti-spasmodic	9.0	6.8	4.4	1.9	0.4	8	8
9. Antiobesity	9.0	6.1	4.4	2.5	0.4	6	6
10. Diabetic therapy	8.3	4.8	3.2	1.7	0.3	4	4

Source: Douglas L. Cocks and John R. Virts, "Pricing Behavior of the Ethical Pharmaceutical Industry," *Journal of Business* 47 (July 1974): 360. Reprinted with permission of the University of Chicago Press.

volume of sales was regarded as the modal container. The related price was then obtained.

Indices of relative price were constructed utilizing either an unweighted or weighted average of the prices of the leading three or five products in the relevant therapeutic submarket in the year of introduction, divided by the price of the innovation. Market success was measured by the share achieved in the relevant submarket during either the first two calendar years of a product's life or during the first three years. Sales data and market share information were taken from the *British Pharmaceutical Index* from 1962 through 1972. Approximately one-third of all innovations were introduced at lower prices than the leading available substitutes. However, most of these occurred among the innovations of fourth and fifth rank importance. For innovations of first and second rank importance the ratio of existing product prices to the innovation price was 50 percent or less.

With respect to market performance Reekie shows that most minor innovations obtained a market share of 5 percent or less after two years, or 7.5 percent or less after three years. The innovations of major rank achieved

Table 5-3
Price Trends of Leading Drugs in Ten Therapeutic Product Classes: Changes in Drug Prices, 1962-1971

Product Set	Product 1	Product 2	Leading Products
1. Antiinfective market	(29.7%)	(6.2%)	(31.8%)
2. Analgesic and antiinflammatory market	(11.6)	5.1	(2.0)
3. Psychopharmaceutical market	(15.6)	(6.8)	(8.3)
4. Cough and cold market	10.2	28.2	(2.9)
5. Antihypertensive and diuretic market	(8.2)	(11.0)	(7.2)
6. Vitamin and hematinic market	(3.0)	12.7	(0.3)
7. Oral contraceptive market	(19.6)	(9.1)[a]	(22.0)
8. Anticholinergic-antispasmotic market	11.9	(6.5)	(0.1)
9. Antiobesity market	(1.3)	4.1	5.1
10. Diabetic therapy market[b]	(22.0)	(10.0)	(13.7)
Average	(8.9)	0.05	(8.3)
Average exclusive of set 4	(11.0)	(3.1)	(8.9)

Sources: Douglas L. Cocks, "Product Innovation and the Dynamic Elements of Competition in the Ethical Pharmaceutical Industry," in *Drug Development and Marketing*, Robert B. Helms, ed. (Washington, D.C.: American Enterprise Institute for Public Policy Research, 1975), pp. 225-254; CPI Index, *Economic Report of the President*, 1975.

[a]Series begins in 1963.

[b]Percentage change in U.S. CPI Index, 1966-1971, was 31.7 percent.

market shares of over 20 percent in two years or over 30 percent in three years.

Reekie's data indicate that most of the major innovations were successes as measured by market share penetration. He found that a price-skimming policy was employed more frequently for major innovations than for minor innovations. When a high-value innovation was priced at a relatively low level, this appeared to be related to a high likelihood that a superseding chemical entity would be launched in the near future.

Successes among minor innovations were associated more frequently with low price than high price. However, low price was employed even more predominantly for the minor innovations that failed to succeed in an appreciable market share. Thus low prices alone did not assure market success for minor innovations.

Reekie also analyzed the influence of a number of market structure variables on pricing policy. He was unable to find a significant relationship between the level of price charged for successful innovations and economic variables such as firm size, market size, the level of existing competition, and the degree of risk attached by doctors to adopting an innovation in the relevant therapeutic submarket.

There was some evidence that a product will be low priced if a related new chemical entity was introduced in the period immediately preceding the launch of this particular product. However, this influence was not statistically significant. On the other hand, a low-price policy was adopted if a superseding innovation was expected in either one or two years following its introduction. In four of eight tests the statistical relationship was significant at the 5 percent level.

In his study of the U.S. markets Reekie analyzed the price behavior of all new chemical entities (NCE) introduced into the United States market between 1958 and 1975. The list of NCEs and their FDA ratings were obtained from the Center for the Study of Drug Development, Medical Center, University of Rochester. In addition, data on dollar sales and prescriptions filled were abstracted from the *National Prescription Audit*. In Reekie's table 1 (table 5-4) FDA rating criteria are related to the ratio of prices on the new chemical entity to the prices of competing drugs in the same therapeutic product class. He observes that the more the therapeutic gain, the greater the likelihood of a higher ratio of the price of the new NCEs to the price of the existing competing drugs.

In his table 2 (table 5-5) Reekie analyzes the behavior of prices over time. Both the mean and variance of the ratio of the prices of the new chemical entities to competing drug prices declined over time. This could result from the lowering of high initial prices of the NCEs over time or from the reduction of the prices of existing drugs, to maintain market position in the face of entry.

In addition, Reekie analyzes demand elasticities over time. He regresses Q, the ratio of the number of new prescriptions written for the NCE to all other new prescriptions written in the relevant therapeutic market on P, the ratio P_{NCE}/P_c in log-linear form. The regression coefficient of the log P_{it} is the price elasticity of demand, where i is a particular NCE and t is the year. His results are summarized in table 5-6. The less important the therapeutic gain, the higher the price elasticity. In addition, price elasticities appear to increase over time.

Reekie indicates that his data suggest that each firm or group of firms will have an incentive to invade markets where price exceeds marginal costs. The competition of the new product innovations will increase the elasticity of the demand curve facing the original market occupant tending to drive prices down toward marginal cost, whence a new cycle may begin.

Reekie concludes that new products are priced at a level determined in large part by the degree of competition for the new products introduced. He

Table 5-4
Reekie Table 1: New Chemical Entities, Analyzed by Price and Food and Drug Administration Rating, 1958-1975

Price	FDA Rating Criteria: Therapeutic Gain			Total
	Important	Modest	Little or None	
Low	7	12	53	72
Medium	6	13	44	63
High	16	9	11	36
Total	29	34	108	171

Notes: All data refer to date of product launch.

Low price = price ratios of unity and below; medium price = price ratios of over 1.0 and of 1.5 and below; high price = price ratios over 1.5.

Price = P_{NCE}/P_c,

P_{NCE} = dollar sales of the NCE made through new prescriptions divided by numbers of new prescriptions written for the NCE, that is, the average price of a new prescription for the NCE.

P_c = weighted average price of a new prescription for the relevant leading competitive drugs; given the oligopolistic nature of the markets, the number of competitors examined was either three, four, or five and these products accounted for the bulk of all the remaining turnover in the market not attributable to the NCE; the weights awarded are the relative sales figures of the competing products.

Important therapeutic gain: Drug may provide effective therapy or diagnosis (by virtue of greatly increased efficacy or safety) for a disease not adequately treated or diagnosed by any marketed drug, or provide markedly improved treatment of a disease through improved efficacy or safety (including decreased abuse potential).

Modest therapeutic gain: Drug has a modest, but real advantage of other available marketed drugs: somewhat greater effectiveness, decreased adverse reactions, less frequent dosing in situations where frequent dosage is a problem, and so forth.

Little or no therapeutic gain: Essentially duplicates in medical importance and therapy for one or more already existing drugs.

concludes that there is price competition among pharmaceutical drugs. He observes also that his evidence strongly supports the view that the pharmaceutical firms behave as though physicans who prescribe drugs are in fact price sensitive.

Canberra Hypothesis

Another challenging study of pricing in the pharmaceutical industry has been termed the Canberra hypothesis.[6] The Canberra hypothesis holds that the

Table 5-5
**Reekie Table 2: Price Statistics Relating to All New Chemical Entities
Launched in the U.S. Drug Market, 1958-1975**

Statistic	Year 1	Year	Year 3	Year 4
Mean	1.618	1.519	1.245	1.287
Mode	1.073	0.998	1.061	1.35
Median	1.104	1.119	1.073	1.084
Maximum	15.516	11.969	5.128	5.449
Minimum	0.251	0.368	0.371	0.402
Range	15.265	11.601	4.757	5.047
n	185	175	163	146
Variance	3.577	2.022	0.709	0.500
F. ratio	1.769	2.852	1.418	
	(all significant at the 1 percent level in Snedecor's table for the variance ratio)			
Coefficient of variation	0.169	0.936	0.626	0.549

Notes: Year 1 is generally the first full calendar year of an NCE's life cycle. This could be any year from 1958 to 1975.

Years 2-4 are the relevant years succeeding year of launch. The data series ended in 1975. All NCE's are included in this analysis whether or not the FDA had rated them at the time of study.

Table 5-6
**Reekie Table 5: Demand Elasticities, Analyzed by FDA
Rating and Product Maturity**

Year	FDA Rating: Therapeutic Gain	
	Important	Modest
1	1.03	1.24
2	1.68	2.64
3	1.34	1.83
4	n.s.	2.84

Notes: n.s. = not statistically significant

The negative elasticity signs have been discarded.

Figures are rounded to two decimal places.

market success of a prescription medicine, other things being equal, is affected
by its price relative to alternative products on the market. It challenges the
alternative view that the price of the medicine is a matter of indifference to the
prescriber. A number of pieces of evidence are assembled in support of the
hypothesis.

1. In 1957 Britain adopted the Voluntary Price Regulation Scheme.
Prices to the National Health Service were to be regarded as reasonable if they
were no higher than the prices in export markets where the patient himself
paid for the prescription. Major price reductions did not result. It is argued
that the scheme demonstrated that the prices being paid by the British Health
Service were already generally lower than those in other countries.

2. Chart 10 from the Kefauver report showed the prices of patented broad
spectrum antibiotics to be above and constant over the years 1951-1960 compared
with the generally declining prices of the unpatented streptomycin and penicillin.
An alternative chart presented in the Canberra study covering the longer period
1948-1974 shows that over the longer period of time there was a general
decline in prices of both the patented and unpatented drugs. The discussion
indicates the role of declining prices after an initial policy of price skimming
was adopted. Additional data are presented from the Ph.D. dissertation of
Duncan Reekie in which he shows that large promotion expenditures were
made in the antibiotic therapeutic class in order to stimulate a large volume of
sales and in turn to enable individual companies to achieve major economies
of scale. This overall strategy was adopted because at the large volumes obtained
by individual companies and the economies of production thereby achieved,
entry by rival firms could be achieved only at comparable low levels of prices.
However, small initial shares of the new entrance would have resulted in substantial losses for them at the relatively low level of prices that had been reached.

3. A third piece of evidence is an analysis of the pricing policy followed in
the introduction of the benzodiazepine tranquilizers. The economies of scale
resulting from a large market position apparently resulted from the low introduction prices adopted by Roche for Librium and Valium. They were introduced
at relatively low prices seen by doctors to represent good value in terms of
patient benefits. "They had started life, as it were, at Volkswagen rather than
Rolls Royce prices."[7] The resulting economies of scale represented an effective
"limit entry" price in that prices were so low that other innovators were unable
to introduce alternative compounds at comparably low prices. The resulting
high profits for Roche resulted from the wisdom of its pricing policy rather
than from unreasonably high prices.

If Roche had followed a price-skimming policy that would have made it
possible for competitive compounds to be introduced, the larger number of
firms sharing the same or indeed a smaller share of a larger market is likely to
have resulted in higher prices than those charged for Librium and Valium. The
profits of each of the firms would have been lower than those achieved by

Roche. From the standpoint of consumers, which is better—lower prices that produce "exorbitant" profits that may in turn provide the basis for further innovation of higher prices, or more "competitors" and lower profits? If consumer welfare is the criterion, the lower price test rather than the traditional performance test of profit levels is the relevant criterion.

4. A fourth piece of evidence is an example of pricing policy followed in topical corticosteroids. The data show that the products with considerable advantages over the original hydrocortisone obtained a large market share despite a higher price. However, "between the two closely competing alternatives, the less expensive one held almost three times as large a market share as its more expensive competitor."[8] This is argued to demonstrate that price competition does, in fact, operate in the pharmaceutical market.

5. Evidence from the therapeutic group of antiinflammatories shows that because dosage must be individually related to patient reaction, price comparisons were not as feasible as for identically sized tubes of topical corticosteroids. Nevertheless the data presented demonstrate that product D with the highest average weekly dosage costs had the smallest market share. Product A with the lowest average weekly dosage cost had the highest market share. Products B and C had similar average weekly dosage costs, somewhat higher than for product A. Product B had almost as large a market share, whereas product C whose differential from the price of product A was somewhat greater than that for Product B, had a market share about half that of products A and B.

The study concludes that a major innovation may establish a high price and still be a success. A minor innovation, however, is forced to a low price if it is to have any hope of success. The irony is that a major innovation that adopts a low-price strategy may be accused of achieving "an unreasonable profit."

Cross Elasticity in the Antiinfectives Market

I made an analysis of the antiinfectives market for the years 1960-1974. Data were first gathered on a number of individual antiinfective drugs. My sample consisted of all the antiinfective drugs in the top ten in rank by sales volume in at least one of the years 1964-1974. These in turn were then placed into three groups to abstract from the particular circumstances that might affect an individual drug. The three categories were based on their relative maturity as measured by the time at which they reached sales leadership. The first group represented drugs that had achieved a sales volume of at least $10 million by 1960. The second group reached their sales maturity levels as measured by the $10 million criterion at a somewhat later date, in 1965. The third group represented all the other antiinfectives that satisfied the first criterion of ranking in the top ten in one or more years between 1964 and 1974.[9]

I gathered data on dollar sales volume and on prices of the strength and package size accounting for the largest volume for each of the individual drugs. I deflated by prices to obtain indexes of physical quantities sold. I also calculated weighted price indexes for each group. The regressions run to test for cross elasticity are summaried in table 5-7.

Equation 1 in table 5-7 relates the percentage change in the quantity sold of groups I and II combined to the ratio of prices of the group III drugs to the prices of the groups I and II drugs combined. The correlation coefficient is significant at the 1 percent level, as is the regression coefficient.

In equation 2 the percentage change in the ratio of prices of group I antiinfectives to the prices of group II antiinfectives is related to the percentage change in the ratio of the quantities sold of group II antiinfectives to the quantities sold of group I antiinfectives. The correlation coefficient drops below the 5 percent significance level. The intercept term performs a much more important role reflecting the influence of group III drugs omitted. Apparently the omission of group III drugs which are also in the market reduces the statistical significance of the relationship.

Analysis of the underlying data reveals a number of patterns. While the actual dollar sales of the group I and group II drugs declined with the appearance of the group III drugs, which occurred mostly in the early 1970s, their deflated unit volume of sales merely leveled off for the group I drugs and continued to rise slightly for the group II drugs. This was achieved by the relatively sharper price declines in the group I and II drugs as compared with the price changes in the group III drugs.

Another pattern that suggested itself is that new, improved drugs sometimes achieve a premium in the form of a higher price or trade off the price

Table 5-7
Cross Elasticity of Demand Measures for Antiinfective Drugs

	N	r
1. Change $Q_{(I+II)} = -2.59 + 0.47$ [Change $(P_{III})/(P_{I+II})$] (3.51)	7	0.84[a]
2. Change $(Q_{II}/Q_I) = 30.8 + 1.24$ [Change $(P_I)/(P_{II})$] (0.87)	13	0.25

Source: Dollar volume of purchases from IMS America, Pharmaceutical Market Drugstores and Hospitals, 1960-1974. Prices from *Drug Topics Red Book,* 1960-1974.

Note: t values are in parentheses under the regression coefficents; change is percent change.

[a]Significant at 5 percent level.

differential to some degree with a larger increase in the growth volume of sales. However, the introduction of the new drugs results in an increase in the total market as well as an increase in market share for the new drugs. The impact of the increase in market share of the new drugs is a tendency toward a decline in sales of the older drugs. The older drugs respond to their decline in sales by price cutting. Their price cutting tends to maintain their volume.

The newer drugs then respond to these price cuts in the older drugs by price reductions from the levels at which the new products were introduced. The first impact is that the price reductions in the older drugs reduce the relative price of older drugs compared to the newer drugs. In the second stage of impact, the newer drugs also make price reductions to sustain a high growth in the volume of their sales. This in turn causes the older drugs to institute further price deductions in the effort to maintain their physical volume of sales.

Sam Peltzman found similar results. He observed the following:

> Over a two-year period, if NCEs with a potential market share of 10 percent are kept from the market, the average prescription price in a therapeutic category will increase about 1 1/3 percent more than it would otherwise. This is not a substantial effect, but that it occurs at all is surprising in view of the alleged weakness of price competition between new and old drugs and in view of the price premium for new drugs. In any case, given the extent to which marketing of new drugs has been restricted since 1962, it is possible to conclude that prescription prices have been rising about one-tenth of 1 percent faster each year than they would have in the absence of the amendments.[10]

It is argued that many drugs are "me-too" drugs, not representing true significant new therapeutic agents. We also have evidence that the introduction of new drugs causes the prices of older drugs to decline. The two sets of factors thus describe the processes by which price competition takes place in the drug industry. Product differentiation coupled with price pressure on older drug products results in a process of price competition that places downward pressures on prices in the drug industry over time.

The complaint is often made that even after the patent on a successful drug has expired, it may still continue to command a differentially higher price without substantial loss of market share. The Peltzman findings indicate that this is not generally the case. Where it does occur, it represents another demonstration that drug products are highly complex, involving a range of variables. The experience with a drug and the reputation of a manufacturer do and should influence purchases. An outstanding performance by a particular drug in achieving dependable therapeutic results is certainly going to add differential value to that drug. This differential value will then, in fact, enable it to command a differentially higher price.

Drug Price Trends

There is considerable additional evidence that the price performance of drugs in relation to general price movements has also been favorable. Details are provided in the study by Cocks and Virts.[11] In table 5-8 the price trends of leading products in three therapeutic product sets are shown. The general trends of prices are down from 1962-1971. In the antiinfective product set the price index of leading products declined by almost 32 percent. It is notable also that the leading product at the beginning of the period generally experienced substantial price declines during the nine-year period. In many instances the price declines of products that were the leading products at the beginning of the period were greater than the other products.

In table 5-9 the price indexes of ten ethical drug product sets are summarized. Through 1967, prices in each of the ten product sets had declined from their 1962 levels. With the onset of general inflation in the United States after 1966, some of the price increases resulted in levels above the 1962 base. This was true for only two of the ten product sets, by 5 percent and 8 percent respectively. For two other product sets the price indexes in 1971 were virtually at the same level as in 1962. For three product sets price decreases between 1962 and 1971 were substantial, approximating a 20 percent decline.

In his book, *Innovation in the Pharmaceutical Industry* (Baltimore: Johns Hopkins University Press, 1976), David Schwartzman presents materials on price behavior. He observes: "The models of oligopolistic behavior which have influenced much of the discussion about competition in the drug industry have been wrong, at least when applied to this industry. Such models predict that oligopolists will collude to maintain prices at the very least simply refrain from price competition" (p. 251). He describes a number of factors that stimulate price competition. One is that marginal costs are small in relation to average costs. Thus price cutting will contribute to covering overhead. A second factor is the growth in generic prescribing. Schwartzman presents data from the national prescription audits that show that generic prescriptions as a percentage of all noncompounded new prescriptions rose from 6.4 percent in 1966 to 10.6 percent in 1973. Over the same period generic prescriptions of new prescriptions for leading multiple-source drugs increased from 19.2 percent to 30.7 percent. He also presents data to show that brand substitution takes place: a pharmacist substitutes another brand name product or a generic product for the ones specified in a prescription, providing he obtains permission from the prescriber.

Schwartzman examines the history of prices in antibiotic markets as well as in other markets. Some of the leading manufacturers of antibiotics cut their prices substantially before the expiration of patents and prior to the actual entry of other firms. In some antibiotic markets the new entrants initiated the price cuts and the leading firm delayed their own price cuts. The

Table 5-8

Price Trends in the Drug Industry, Selected Therapeutic Classes, 1962-1971

Product No.	1962	1963	1964	1965	1966	1967	1968	1969	1970	1971
A. Antiinfective Product Set										
1	100	92.5	91.0	90.2	87.3	76.6	74.6	74.0	72.2	70.3
2	100	100.2	99.1	99.5	98.0	97.0	93.6	95.8	95.9	93.8
3	100	93.6	86.3	79.3	73.5	57.8	54.8	54.6	45.6	33.1
4	100	84.1	81.2	78.8	78.9	79.2	80.3	79.9	72.6	65.6
5	100	92.6	87.8	84.7	81.3	75.7	76.7	73.4	72.7	72.6
6	100	92.3	91.5	89.5	88.4	86.8	85.4	84.2	83.8	82.1
7	100	94.2	91.9	91.5	90.8	78.3	69.3	67.7	67.8	67.8
8	100	97.5	97.0	94.4	91.4	91.0	92.9	94.2	90.5	92.5
9	100	89.3	89.9	83.4	72.3	66.8	55.7	50.3	49.1	47.7
10	100	92.0	91.8	89.1	89.8	86.2	86.0	84.5	84.0	80.3
11	100	93.9	84.2	82.0	79.5	53.7	46.2	44.8	43.3	40.5
12	–	100	104.2	99.9	97.4	94.6	81.4	79.0	77.6	79.9
Price index of leading products	100	92.8	90.4	87.9	84.9	77.6	74.8	73.7	71.3	68.2
BLS consumer price index for prescriptions	100	97.6	96.3	95.2	95.1	93.4	91.8	93.0	94.5	94.6
B. Analgesic and Antiinflammatory Product Set										
1	100	100.5	98.9	96.5	95.2	94.2	91.0	89.3	87.8	88.4
2	100	99.5	96.8	122.4	99.1	97.6	98.7	100.3	102.2	105.1
3	100	105.7	104.6	102.0	101.4	94.3	96.4	97.6	97.8	104.5
4	100	98.5	101.4	104.8	103.4	103.9	101.1	109.7	104.4	105.0
5	100	99.5	105.4	103.8	103.7	106.8	104.5	104.9	107.6	109.0
6	100	100.4	102.1	102.1	105.4	106.1	99.1	103.1	101.2	100.8
7	100	99.3	98.2	96.2	93.4	93.2	92.3	91.5	90.4	89.6
8	100	101.1	102.6	101.1	100.8	98.3	97.1	97.6	97.6	108.3
9	100	102.4	98.3	101.2	101.9	99.9	98.7	102.8	106.0	106.5
10	100	102.2	101.7	100.4	98.4	98.7	97.3	98.2	98.0	108.3
11	–	–	–	100	97.8	94.6	92.1	89.5	88.6	88.9
12	–	–	–	–	–	100	97.3	92.0	90.6	92.5
Price index of leading products	100	100.7	100.0	103.0	99.0	97.5	95.7	96.3	95.6	98.0
BLS consumer price index for prescriptions	100	97.6	96.3	95.2	95.1	93.4	91.8	93.0	94.5	94.6
C. Psychopharmaceutical Product Set										
1	100	98.0	94.6	91.5	92.4	89.7	86.7	86.8	83.6	84.4
2	100	98.0	96.3	94.2	94.2	93.5	89.6	94.1	93.3	93.2
3	100	102.3	102.1	106.7	100.5	103.8	100.3	106.9	105.5	106.1
4	100	101.5	101.6	100.2	96.4	97.9	95.2	99.4	106.0	105.4
5	100	100.4	99.9	101.6	97.2	100.9	96.3	99.2	102.9	104.2
6	100	104.3	108.9	110.3	103.9	103.2	102.2	106.7	107.6	105.5
7	100	102.9	104.7	105.5	104.0	105.1	105.1	104.4	109.1	113.2
8	100	100.4	95.3	93.8	93.9	95.2	89.9	87.8	77.0	64.8
9	–	100	104.9	101.8	100.5	97.8	94.9	95.7	93.9	94.0
10	–	–	–	100	100.3	97.9	94.9	92.7	91.9	89.1
Price index of leading products	100	99.4	97.7	96.3	95.3	94.8	91.6	93.4	92.2	91.7
BLS consumer price index for prescriptions	100	97.6	96.3	95.2	95.1	93.4	91.8	93.0	94.5	94.6

Source: Douglas L. Cocks and John R. Virts, "Pricing Behavior of the Ethical Pharmaceutical Industry," *Journal of Business* 47 (July 1974): 355-358. Reprinted with permission of the University of Chicago Press.

Table 5-9
Price Trends in the Drug Industry, Ten Ethical Drug Product Sets, 1962-1971

Product Set	1962	1963	1964	1965	1966	1967	1968	1969	1970	1971
1. Vitamin and hematinic	100	100.3	98.5	97.4	97.4	97.2	97.1	100.4	101.3	101.3
2. Antiinfective	100	92.8	90.4	87.9	84.9	77.6	74.8	73.7	71.3	63.2
3. Cough and cold	100	107.0	101.6	99.9	99.7	99.5	99.9	104.5	105.7	108.3
4. Analgesic and antiinflammatory	100	100.7	100.0	103.0	99.0	97.5	95.7	96.3	95.6	98.0
5. Antihypertensive and diuretic	100	98.4	97.4	97.2	96.1	95.8	93.1	91.4	92.3	93.4
6. Psychopharmaceutical	100	99.4	97.7	96.3	95.3	94.8	91.6	93.4	92.2	91.7
7. Antiobesity	100	103.1	101.4	100.8	99.2	99.7	98.6	100.2	101.3	105.1
8. Oral contraceptive	100	85.9	79.7	76.3	75.5	70.6	69.1	73.0	75.3	77.0
9. Anticholinergic and antispasmodic	100	101.2	99.8	99.8	99.9	98.8	99.0	99.1	101.0	100.7
10. Diabetic therapy[a]	100	95.7	89.0	87.1	83.8	81.7	82.3	81.6	80.3	81.0
BLS consumer price index for prescriptions	100	97.6	96.3	95.2	95.1	93.4	91.8	93.0	94.5	94.6

Source: Douglas L. Cocks and John R. Virts, "Pricing Behavior of the Ethical Pharmaceutical Industry," *Journal of Business* 47 (July 1974): 355-358. Reprinted with permission of the University of Chicago Press.

[a]In the diabetic set the pricing data for the products of the company with whom the authors are associated was not complete. These numbers were directly obtained from the company.

firms with smaller market shares were aggressive price cutters seeking to increase market share so that the firms with the larger market shares were eventually forced to cut their prices due to losses in market shares.

Schwartzman observes that the prices of some generic products manufactured by relatively small companies are lower than the prices of major companies' products. In such cases the price of antibiotic products would not have been reduced to marginal costs. Price differentials for generic products may result from uncertainty in comparing the quality of the products and the reputation of their producers.

Government Controls on Prices of Successful Drugs

Government requirements that drug prices bear some specified relation to costs may achieve savings in the short run, but they result in high drug prices per unit of quality in the long run. The initial impact of government-imposed price reduction on successful products is to result in lower prices. The decreased prices will result in lower returns from successful products. Both the incentives and the ability to conduct research for innovative drugs are thereby reduced. The effects of reduced incentives to conduct research and development in the effort to produce innovative drugs extends to all firms in the drug industry. This is because price controls on successful products reduce the prospective returns to research and development for all firms that potentially will have successful products.

The longer-run effects are especially pernicious. Lopping off the top of returns from successful products decreases overall returns. But no provision is made for offsetting the losses from unsuccessful research and developments efforts and unsuccessful drug products. This has perverse effects on research. If the rewards from significant successes are reduced to moderate returns but no assistance is provided on significant failures, the natural reaction would be to avoid high risk projects. But most significant innovations represent high-risk activity. Incentives are pushed in the direction of moderate changes related to existing products where the risks are much lower. The possibilities of achieving major new breakthroughs are reduced because such high-risk activities will be avoided. Thus in the longer run price controls on successful products reduce both the incentives and ability to conduct fundamental research that produces significant breakthroughs in drug therapies.

At some stage in price control programs on drugs it will be necessary to take the overall position of individual drug companies into account. Otherwise it is patently inequitable to control the prices of successful products without taking into account the unsuccessful research efforts and unsuccessful drug products. A firm with a few outstanding successes and many failures would be in an overall loss position if prices were controlled on the successful products.

Equity considerations therefore lead to the necessity of taking the overall profitability position of the firm into account. When this occurs, other perverse incentive effects begin to take place.

If the overall profitability of a firm is to be taken into account, the incentives for cost control and efficiency that are normally very strong in unregulated drug companies begin to be anesthetized. If price controls take the overall profitability of the firm into account, rising costs will be compensated by the higher prices allowed. It is difficult for managements to be convincing in applying pressures for cost efficiencies and cost controls in such an environmental framework. As a result costs inevitably move upward.

Over a period of time cost levels will be higher, and as a consequence price levels will move upward as well. However, profits for individual firms and for the industry will be at lower levels. Hence in the long run price reductions to reduce the profitability rates on successful drug innovations will slow the rate of introduction of new innovative drug therapies, cause costs and prices of drugs to move upward, and lower the rates of profitability of the drug companies. The results are adverse for the public, the government, and the drug companies, with no offsetting benefits to any group.

Conclusions

The foregoing data on drug price flexibility and the general downward trend are consistent with the existence of vigorous, dynamic competition in the pharmaceutical manufacturing industry. They are also consistent with monopoly, since monopoly prices could be flexible with shifting demand or cost conditions. The patent privilege provides a monopoly over individual drugs. However, the appearance of similar drugs introduces competition before the expiration of the seventeen-year patent period. Thus the observed patterns of drug prices reflect entry and other competitive processes. The evidence on trends in market shares and in drug prices in the individual therapeutic classes supports a number of generalizations:

1. A leading patented product has an element of uniqueness. This must be so or the patent would not have been achieved in the first place.
2. No product is completely unique in a longer-run context. "Uniqueness" is a matter of degree and what appears to be absolutely unique in the short run is less unique or less competitively superior as time elapses.
3. Product imitations and product substitutions result in high cross elasticities of demand over broad groups of drugs that define a therapeutic product class.
4. Entry of new products and firms is slowed only when the therapeutic

performance of the existing product is high in relation to its price.

5. Historically, no leading product has maintained its market share position for more than a limited number of years. Preeminance is temporary.

From the standpoint of statistical probabilities and economic realism, there will be no exceptions in the long run to these general patterns, summarized from considerable factual evidence. The general pattern is one of temporary preeminance, relatively rapid displacement of leading products, and the rise of similar products and substitutes. All this implies that the demand functions relevant for pricing decisions have relatively high cross elasticities of demand. Hence on the average, in a long-run context, there are not likely to be wide departures between long-run marginal costs and price for most drug products. Furthermore, departures from technical optimal pricing tests are more than off-set by the great advances in innovation, product improvement, and new products resulting in substantial benefits to consumers.

The relation between static welfare losses from negatively sloped demand functions and the gains from innovation is especially relevant for the pharmaceutical industry. After a review of the methodologies involved in calculating welfare losses, Markham constructs a table showing the time required for selected GNP annual growth rates from technological changes to offset various assumed annual welfare losses from monopoly. He points out that "the calculated growth in GNP of 1.2 percent to 1.5 percent per year attributable to innovation overcomes the deadweight welfare loss from monopoly in a surprisingly short period of time—for the Harberger-Schwartzman estimates, approximately one month!" Markham further points out that even if "the monopoly welfare loss is 20 times that estimated by Harberger and Schwartzman, the welfare gains from innovation would still overcome the deadweight loss from monopoly in the short span of 18 months."[12]

In summary, an erroneous new misconception is frequently stated with regard to the nature of competition in the drug industry. It is asserted that there is no price competition. This is a major misconception. Systematic data show that drug manufacturers approach the ultimate consumer via the retail and wholesale market in a variety of ways. Many different types of arrangements are made in sales both to wholesalers and to retail outlets. These special deals represent direct and continuous price competition among the manufacturers.

There is also competition in prices among a wide array of competing drugs. This competition has resulted in a downward trend in the prices of new drugs in the years following their introduction. Thus drug prices compete over their life cycle with the prices of other drugs over their life cycles. This is a continued, real, and active form of price competition. In addition, the data demonstrate that the trends of drug prices, relative to other consumer products, have continuously trended downward.

Notes

1. H. Steele quoted in *Summary and Analysis, Competitive Problems in the Drug Industry,* Select Committee on Small Business, U.S. Senate Subcommittee on Monopoly, Washington, D.C., 1972, p. 22.

2. T. Donald Rucker, "Public Policy Considerations in the Pricing of Prescription Drugs," *California Pharmacist,* September 1974, p. 8. Reprinted with permission.

3. J. Fred Weston, Steven Lustgarten, and Nancy Grottke, "The Administered-Price Thesis Denied: Note," *American Economic Review* 64 (March 1974): 232-234; J. Fred Weston and Steven Lustgarten, "Concentration and Wage-Price Change," in *Industrial Concentration: The New Learning,* ed. Harvey J. Goldschmid, H. Michael Mann, and J. Fred Weston (Boston, Mass.: Little, Brown, 1974), pp. 307-332.

4. Jesse W. Markham, "Economic Incentives in the Drug Industry," in *Drugs in Our Society,* ed. Paul Talalay (Baltimore, Md.: Johns Hopkins Press, 1964), p. 170.

5. W.D. Reekie, "Price Policy, Commercial Success and Therapeutic Advantage of Pharmaceutical Innovation," (Department of Business Studies, University of Edinburgh) April 1976.

6. "The Canberra Hypothesis, the Economics of the Prescription Medicine Market," based on a paper delivered by George Teeling-Smith in January 1975 to the Pharmaceutical Sciences Section of the Australian and New Zealand Association for the Advancement of Science at the Academy of Sciences in Canberra, Office of Health Economics, London, England, September 1975.

7. Ibid., p. 18.

8. Ibid., p. 21.

9. The group I antiinfective drugs were Chloromycetin, Declomycin, Terramycin, Panalba, Achromycin V, and Ilosone. The group II antiinfective drugs were Mysteclin F, V-Cillin K, Erythrocin, Furadantin, Polycillin, Lincocin, and Pentids. The group III drugs were Keflin, Garamycin, Vibramycin, Loridine, Macrodantin, Cleocin, Keflex, and Cleocin Phosphate.

10. Sam Peltzman, *Regulation of Pharmaceutical Innovation: The 1962 Amendments* (Washington, D.C.: The American Enterprise Institute for Public Policy Research, 1974), pp. 47-48.

11. Douglas L. Cocks and John R. Virts, "Pricing Behavior of the Ethical Drug Industry," *Journal of Business* 47 (July 1974): 360.

12. Jesse W. Markham, "Concentration: A Stimulus or Retardant to Innovation?" in *Industrial Concentration,* pp. 253-257.

6

Pricing of Multiple-Source Drugs

David Schwartzman

Overview: *Despite the high concentration of sales in therapeutic classes, manufacturers of multiple-source drugs engage in price competition. This paper analyzes the sources of the competition and describes what has happened in tetracycline.*

A multiple-source drug is a generic-class drug which is supplied by several manufacturers. For example, the generic class of tetracycline includes quite a large number of products sold under either generic or brand names. A company identifies its product as tetracycline, the generic title, adding the company name; or they may use a brand name like Achromycin, which is Lederle's brand name, or Tetracyn, which is Pfizer's brand name. An example of a single-source drug is furosemide. Furosemide is a diuretic and there is only one producer, Hoechst, which sells the product under the brand name Lasix. This discussion will be confined to multiple-source drugs.

Much of the discussion of price competition in this industry has related t drugs generally. No distinction has been made between single-source and multiple-source drugs, but this distinction is important. Multiple-source drugs now account for more than 44 percent of all prescriptions, so they are a large part of the total market.

Most students in the past have argued that there is no price competition in this industry. A discussion that follows the structure-conduct-performance model points out that the conditions in the industry do not encourage price competition, for the following reasons.

First, there is a high degree of concentration of sales among sellers in therapeutic markets. Antibiotics, for example, are a therapeutic market. The concept of market has been used in the ordinary sense as we understand it in economics. The high concentration within each of the therapeutic markets makes it possible for the major sellers to collude.

Second, the elasticity of demand facing each of the sellers is low because physicians who prescribe drugs are indifferent to price. If a firm cuts its price, it cannot expect to increase its sales sufficiently to offset the loss in revenue resulting from the price cut.

This paper is based on chapter 12 of David Schwartzman, *Innovation in the Pharmaceutical Industry* (Baltimore, Md.: Johns Hopkins University Press, 1976).

97

Third, there are barriers to entry that take the form of patents, in the case of single-source drugs, and heavy advertising expenditures for all types of drugs. In addition, the leading brands are familiar to doctors, who continue to prescribe them.

The conclusion is that there is no price competition; therefore pharmaceutical manufacturers earn high profits. My own study suggests that this analysis is incorrect. I only examine multiple-source drugs. In general, a single-source drug becomes a multiple-source drug when a patent expires, although sometimes entry takes place well before that time either because the patent is contested or because the original patentee licenses other manufacturers. In any case, when a drug becomes a multiple-source drug, entry becomes fairly easy. The original brand usually commands a large proportion of the total sales of its generic class even after many competitors have entered. For example, in 1963 Polycillin had 100 percent of total sales of ampicillin compound compared to about 25 percent ten years later.

Entry takes place fairly rapidly. Numerous firms come in because manufacturing drugs is no great problem. The only thing that keeps them out is the patent. In this way the drug industry differs from other industries. In other industries numerous technical problems—manufacture, service, marketing—bar entry. The patent itself may not be a significant element in, for example, computers or communications equipment, but manufacturing may be the nub. Not so in drugs, nor in chemicals generally. It is possible for manufacturers to identify the chemical composition of a drug that is available on the market and then to imitate it.

While the concentration in each therapeutic class may be high, numerous drug manufacturers, both large and small, have the necessary equipment to manufacture duplicate drugs. Usually they can use the same equipment as for other drugs; they do not have to develop new equipment. They will have to develop a process, but this is usually not a difficult problem.

The Food and Drug Administration (FDA) presents a problem, but it is minor. A drug has to be approved by the FDA prior to marketing, but if it is a duplicate of an existing drug, the standards for approval are easily met. Physical quality and clinical tests have to be met, but many firms can quickly fulfill these requirements. So entry is easy. Now the question is how a firm's sales of a duplicate grow.

The appeal of any duplicate is based largely on low price. A company selling a duplicate of an existing drug has no other claim. Obviously the manufacturer cannot claim that a duplicate is superior to the original drug, so they must undercut the price of the original brand, and they do. This is as true for the major manufacturers who enter with duplicates as for the small companies.

This price competition takes place despite oligopoly which suggests that leading firms in an industry will refrain from price competition because they are aware of the disastrous consequences of price competition for profits. The major drug companies have entered into each of the multiple-source markets undercutting prices of original brands. Thus there is a pattern. The ones that come in early make small price cuts, and the ones that come in later make further price cuts; and then the original firm brings its price down.

One of the observations frequently made about the multiple-source markets is that the price disparity between the leading brand, the original brand, and the duplicates continues for some time. The explanation is simple. The original brand has a large share of the market at the outset. Consequently the elasticity of demand facing the producer of that product will be low. Price cuts will not greatly increase total sales of the generic class. If the company does increase sales, it will be largely by increasing its market share, but the share does not have much room to increase. For these reasons the elasticity will be low. The same thing is not true for the duplicates, where the elasticity of demand is very high. Their initial shares are small, and price cuts can increase their sales rapidly.

Two other factors are related to the alleged doctors' indifference to prices.

First, there is considerable generic prescribing once a drug is produced by several well-known manufacturers. The doctors then tend to prescribe ampicillin instead of Polycillin so that in 1973, for example, 50 percent of all ampicillin prescriptions were generic. Pharmacists will use a low-priced drug rather than the original brand to fill a generic prescription. This is not universally true, but the proportion of generic prescriptions filled with low-priced drugs is much higher than the proportion of prescriptions that specify a brand accounted for by the low-priced brands. Substitution occurs. The pharmacist, in effect, acts as a price agent for the consumer.

The second point concerns brand substitution. In 1973, before the repeal of the antisubstitution laws in many of the states, only four states permitted substitution of drugs within a generic class for the one that was specified in the prescription. Twenty-one states now permit substitution. Even so, before it was legal to do so, pharmacists did substitute; and frequently they did so without asking permission from the prescriber. For example, there was brand substitution in 33 percent of all ampicillin prescriptions, and the pharmacists did not obtain permission to make such substitutions in 82 percent of these cases; so they were doing so illegally. When they substituted, they tended to substitute a low-priced brand for the prescribed brand. Again they were acting as a price agent.

In 1952 there were five leading brands of tetracycline: Achromycin, which accounted for 85 percent of the total, Tetracyn, Panmycin, Sumycin, and Tetrex. The patent expired in 1972, but there were many generics on the market by 1962, partly as a result of the challenges to the patent that had been going through the courts. There was some question about the validity of the patent; therefore many generic manufacturers entered, and Pfizer, which held the patent, did not contest their entry.

As a result of the entry of these generics, the share of Lederle (the manufacturer of Achromycin) went from 85 percent to 72 percent between 1962 and 1964. In 1964 Squibb became an active price cutter. Squibb has played an active role in price competition in several markets, perhaps because Squibb, which had not been innovating and had as a result been losing sales, was under great pressure to compete aggressively. The obvious way to compete was to produce duplicates and cut the price. So Squibb cut is price between 1964 and 1968 from $15.60 to $3.98. Its share jumped in 1967 to 7 percent and then in 1968 to 16 percent. It leveled off at about 20 percent and Squibb has not cut its price since.

As a result of Squibb's competition, the other prices came down. Lederle's share of the market fell from 72 percent to 33 percent, and Pfizer's from 11 percent to 4 percent. Lederle, Pfizer, and Upjohn cut their prices in response to Squibb, and in 1968 Pfizer and Upjohn cut their prices to about the same level as Squibb's. Lederle delayed its price cutting, and it was only in 1971 that it reduced its price to $4.65. It took a long time for Lederle's price to approach that of Squibb. The explanation for this may be simply that as long as Lederle had a large share of the market, its elasticity of demand was lower than that of its competitors.

A similar history can be seen in erythromycin, ampicillin, and penicillin VK. These are the other major antibiotics that have become multiple-source drugs.

7

Pricing in the Pharmaceutical Industry in the United Kingdom and the United States

W. Duncan Reekie

Overview: *In my British study (*Pricing New Pharmaceutical Products*) the introductory prices of new chemical entities were analyzed in relation to their incremental clinical significance and to their levels of achieved sales in the first few years of life. The pricing behavior was not inconsistent with what one would anticipate if the firms believed that doctors considered price when writing prescriptions and if firms considered competitive response when setting their own prices. In the United States, where drugs are subject to much less price regulation than in Great Britain, essentially the same pricing behavior was observed. Some new drugs were introduced at lower prices than leading substitutes, and those priced at high levels tended to be important innovations. Other conclusions are that new drug prices tend to fall over time, the price of existing products tends to fall in the face of innovative competition, and price elasticity of demand either increases as products mature or is low if the therapeutic gain is high. From a welfare point of view the drug industry is not perfectly competitive in terms of static microeconomic theory. The monopoly rents are the sources of funds for research and development that provide future innovations. It may be socially optimal for this difference between price and marginal cost to be greatest where demand elasticity is less. The monopoly rents are transitory because prices are eroded over time and converge toward some competitive norm.*

A suspicion has long existed that drug firms in Britain were somehow milking the National Health Service cow. The Sainsbury Committee reported that "the cost [of drugs] to the NHS has been inflated by excessive prices." One explanation given was that on the demand side of the market "neither doctor nor patient has any direct need to concern himself with price." On the supply side the committee "did not gain the impression that there was any significant degree of price competition."[1]

My later American paper, summarized below, developed from a study that attempted to ascertain the validity of some of these explicit and implicit criticisms of the economic behavior of the drug industry in the United Kingdom.

The British Evidence

In the British study[2] almost all new chemical entities (NCEs) launched onto the market between 1962 and 1970 were examined. The NCEs had previously been ranked on a scale of 1 to 5 in descending order of incremental clinical significance at date of introduction. This information was compared with their respective daily dosage costs (relative to close substitutes) and with their levels of achieved sales in their first few years of life.

Approximately one-third of all the innovations were introduced at lower prices than those of leading available substitutes. A high initial price was employed more frequently for major than for minor innovations. But a low price adopted for an innovation (of any rank) was significantly related to a likelihood that competition, in the form of a superseding chemical entity, would soon emerge.

In other words, the pricing behavior was not inconsistent with what one would anticipate if firms *did* believe that doctors took price into consideration when writing prescriptions. It was not inconsistent with what one would expect if firms *did* consider rivals' responses when setting their own price.

I argued that the results were possibly not due to the British government's Voluntary Price Regulation Scheme since the version of the VPRS that existed during the study provided firms with a "freedom period" during which they could pitch their prices at their own chosen levels. I went on to say that this assertion would be worth testing by comparing, for example, what had happened in the United Kingdom with what had happened in a market subject to much less price regulation than the monopsonistic British situation. The logical follow-up study was thus carried out in the United States.

The Empirical Evidence

Four basic questions were posed in the U.S. study.[3]

1. Are NCE prices determined exclusively by forces on the supply side of the market (such as advertising), or does demand have a role?
2. Once determined, do NCE prices converge toward some competitive mean, or can they remain monopolistically high?
3. Do NCEs prompt price cuts in competing products? Or can competitors maintain prices even in the face of innovation?
4. Are doctors price sensitive? What is the price elasticity of demand for NCEs (a) at launch? (b) through the life cycle?

In the United States a longer data series (1958-1975) was used, and the qualitative ratings were those devised by the Food and Drug Administration.

Over 40 percent of the NCEs were introduced at lower prices than leading substitutes. Those priced at high levels relative to competitors tended to be innovations providing "important therapeutic gains." This fits within the behavior
pattern one would expect from simple price theory. Firms can charge a higher
price when consumers are willing to pay that price. Consumers will pay if the
innovation is relatively more productive than alternative products. Minor
variants, conversely, can penetrate a market only if their price is below that of
existing rivals. Given the Sylos postulate, their demand curve is that part of
the market demand curve to the right of ruling price.

More detailed analysis of the data answered the other three questions.
NCE prices tend to fall over time; the price of existing products tends to be
cut in the face of innovation as firms attempt to gain a price advantage where
a quality advantage has been lost; and price elasticity of demand either (a)
increases as products mature (and so are subject to competition from later
drugs) or (b) is lower initially the more important the therapeutic gain represented by the NCE (see table 7-1).

Conclusions

The welfare implications indicated by the study of demand elasticities is that
the industry is not perfectly competitive in the sense of static microtheory.
Monopoly rents are reaped. But these rents are the sources of funds for the
research and development that provide future innovations. Schankerman has
shown that it may be socially optimal for this difference between price and
marginal cost (a difference that funds R&D) to be greatest where demand elasticity is least.[4]

Table 7-1
Demand Elasticities, Analyzed by FDA Rating and
Product Maturity

	FDA Rating	
	Important Therapeutic Gain	*Modest Therapeutic Gain*
Year 1	1.03	1.11
Year 2	1.56	2.68
Year 3	1.30	1.79
Year 4	n.s.	2.83

Notes: n.s. = not statistically significant.

The negative elasticity signs have been discarded.

Figures are rounded to two decimal places.

Our results indicate that the industry is behaving in the way Schankerman suggests is optimal. Moreover the rent reaped is transitory. Prices are eroded over time and converge toward some variant of the competitive norm. This implies a dynamic process of the kind outlined by Cocks.[5]

There are reasons why this process probably does not result in an overall resource misallocation. Many firms may already be operating at price equals marginal cost for their marginal products. In addition, the marginal consumer may buy a product from a firm at a price close to marginal cost. This speculation, bolstered by the fact that the economic rate of return for the industry, as opposed to the accounting rate of return, is reportedly very similar to that for all other manufacturing industries,[6] leads me to wonder whether we are not studying the wrong phenomena. Maybe we should be directing our attention away from price and profit studies. Maybe we should instead be attempting to ascertain what the theoretical margin of profits above the industrial norm should be if we believe it necessary to continue the inducement of innovative activity.

Notes

1. *Report of the Committee of Enquiry into the Relationship of the Pharmaceutical Industry with the National Health Service, 1965-1967* (Sainsbury Report), Cmnd 3410, 1967, paras. 124, 41, 45.

2. W. Duncan Reekie, *Pricing New Pharmaceutical Products* (Croom-Helm, 1977).

3. W. Duncan Reekie, "Price and Quality Competition in the United States Drug Industry," *Journal of Industrial Economics* (1978).

4. Mark A. Schankerman, "Common Costs in Pharmaceutical Research and Development," in *Impact of Public Policy on Drug Innovation and Pricing,* ed. S.A. Mitchell and E.A. Link, (Washington, D.C.: American University, 1976).

5. Douglas L. Cocks, "Product Innovation and the Dynamic Elements of Competition in the Ethical Pharmaceutical Industry," in *Drug Development and Marketing,* ed. Robert B. Helms (Washington, D.C.: American Enterprise Institute, 1975).

6. See, for example, Robert Ayanian, "The Profit Rates and Economic Performance of Drug Firms," and Thomas R. Stauffer, "Profitability Measures in the Pharmaceutical Industry," in Helms, *Drug Development and Marketing.*

8

The Use of Pharmaceutical Profitability Measures for Public Policy Actions

Kenneth W. Clarkson

Overview: *Based on the book* Intangible Capital and Rates of Return, *corrections are made to book profit and net work for intangible capital expenditures (research, development, advertising, and promotion) for computing rates of return. Unlike previous attempts by Jesse Friedman, Robert Ayanian, and others who have used similar techniques, the correcting procedures made here explicitly include nontaxable income from intangible capital and apply the same adjustments to sixty-nine firms in eleven industries with different levels of intangible capital. The results demonstrate that the accounting rate of return is an unreliable indicator of monopoly power of excess profits. In addition, the findings of substantial and differential biases in accounting rates of return among different industries cast serious doubt on previous economic studies in which interindustry differentials based on the accounting rates of return were attributed to risk, entry barriers, concentration, and other related variables. Specifically, the validity of using existing pharmaceutical accounting rates of return for public policy decisions is highly questionable.*

At present there is overwhelming agreement that profitability measures, particularly rates of return on investment, are significantly biased in industries with extensive amounts of intangible capital.[1] Pharmaceutical firms, as is well known, make substantial investments in advertising, promotion, basic research, development, and other forms of intangible capital. Consequently we should not be surprised if corrections to book profit and net worth measures for intangible capital expenditures in pharmaceutical firms yield substantial revisions in the rate of return for these firms. Such corrections, however, may not be sufficient to convince individuals who have noted that the reported profitability of the pharmaceutical industry has stacked up very well over the last twenty-five years in the listings of both the First City National Bank and the Federal Trade Commission. Pharmaceuticals have, during this period, ranked number one in these lists in more years than any other industry.

This paper is based on research presented in Kenneth W. Clarkson, *Intangible Capital and Rates of Return* (Washington, D.C.: American Enterprise Institute, 1977).

The long use of these and related publications has probably been the reason that the theoretical arguments and supporting evidence of significant biases in the rate of return for industries with extensive intangible capital expenditures have been generally ignored by policymakers. For example, Secretary of Health, Education, and Welfare Joseph A. Califano, Jr., in a June 1977 speech before the American Medical Association claimed that "there is precious little competition among pharmaceutical companies." He appeared to base that opinion on the relative earnings of the major pharmaceutical companies, because he went on to declare: "The profits of these drug companies are far above the average for large corporations in America."[2] To change impressions such as Secretary Califano's, it is probably necessary both to identify the appropriate technique for reducing biases in the rate of return and to apply this technique to a representative sample of all industries rather than to a single industry.

The first section of this paper examines the most important variables that affect rate-of-return measures. In the second section the contributions and limitations of previous rate-of-return studies focusing on the pharmaceutical industry are examined. The third part of the paper applies the appropriate corrections to the rates of return and examines the sensitivity of the chosen assumptions for a representative pharmaceutical firm. In the fourth part the correction technique is applied to sixty-nine firms in eleven representative basic industries with differing levels of intangible capital. The paper concludes with some recommendations for future research.

Measuring Profitability

In determining the appropriate method for measuring the relationship between resources committed by and outputs resulting from investment decisions, it is necessary to identify those factors most likely to alter the actual returns from and measurement of investment.[3] These factors include (1) the period of accumulation of intangible capital expenditures before they become assets and production begins, (2) economic life of the assets after production begins, (3) the opportunity cost of the resources used in creating and holding the assets, (4) any changes in absolute or relative price levels, (5) risk (however defined), and (6) the appropriability of rewards from the assets.

Because it may take anywhere from less than a year to three or four years before new plants begin production and much longer before many research projects begin to pay off, the period of accumulation of capital before an asset is created and output begins is extremely important in measuring the comparative profitability of investment alternatives. Of course, once in production, assets have a finite economic life. When the two periods of accumulation of capital and economic life of the asset are combined, they define the economic life cycle of the investment project.

Moreover, since resources used in any project represent alternatives foregone in other possible projects, there is an opportunity cost of using resources
to create an asset in any investment. With the average after-tax rate of return
as a base, the opportunity cost for capital has been estimated to be 10 percent
per year.[4] This is the prescribed rate for U.S. government investment decisions
on deferred costs and benefits.[5] In addition, since changes in relative and
absolute prices will alter the net returns from investment projects, corrections
for price level changes must be made to prevent systematic biases in measurements of expenditures, opportunity costs, and receipts. Equally important,
each investment must be weighted by its corresponding probability of success
or risk.[6] Without such weighting, riskier projects would appear to yield higher
returns than less risky alternatives. Finally all measurements must be corrected
for the appropriability of returns from the investment to the enterprise. When
an enterprise's net receipts or benefits cannot be captured, the returns to the
organization must be corrected accordingly for decision-making purposes.
Under existing income tax regulations, for example, corporate enterprises can
be expected to receive approximately half the net returns (defined under
current accounting procedures) from any investment when the enterprise is
financed by equity capital.

For decision-making purposes, these conditions can be summarized in the
following equation:[7]

$$PV = -\sum_{t=0}^{i-1} \frac{K_t(P_t)}{(1+r)^t} + \sum_{t+i}^{n} \frac{p(R_t - C_t)(P_t)}{(1+r)^t}(A_t) \qquad (8.1)$$

where

PV = present value of the investment

t = index to year

K_t = capital expenditures in year t

P_t = price index for year t

r = opportunity cost of capital

R_t = gross revenues in year t

C_t = manufacturing costs in year t

p = probability of favorable occurrence

A_t = appropriability of returns to enterprise in year t

i = number of years before sales begin

n = end of the economic life for the investment

Thus if the accumulated capital expenditures (corrected for changes in the price level and adjusted for the opportunity cost of capital) is less than expected discounted net revenues (corrected for changes in the price level and for appropriability factors), the present value of the investment will be greater than zero and a wealth-maximizing enterprise would undertake the project.

Modifications of the parameters in equation 8.1, of course, will alter the present value calculations. For example, if the probability of a favorable occurrence increases (p rises), then the present value of that investment will rise. On the other hand, if the appropriability of rewards falls (A_t decreases), then the present value decreases and the investment expenditures will be curtailed or possibly omitted.

Actual measurements of the rate of return require calculation of corrected profits (an income flow) expressed as a ratio to corrected net worth (a stock of wealth). The corrected measure r_c can be expressed as CP/CW where

$$CP = OP + (AE - DA)(1 - TR) + (RE - DR)(1 - TR) + (AR)(r) \qquad (8.2)$$

$$CW = OW + BE + BR + AR \qquad (8.3)$$

CP = corrected profits

OP = original profits

AE = current advertising expenditures

DA = depreciation of current and past advertising expenditures

RE = current research expenditures

DR = depreciation of past research expenditures

AR = accumulated research expenditures

TR = marginal tax rate

r = opportunity cost of capital

CW = corrected net worth

OW = original net worth

BE = balance of undepreciated advertising expenditures

BR = balance of undepreciated research expenditures

Equations 7.2 and 7.3 show that differences between the accounting and economic measurements of the rate of return depend on several variables,

including the magnitude and rate of growth of advertising, promotion, research
and development expenditures, the period of accumulation or depreciation of
these expenditures, the opportunity cost of capital, and price level changes.
Thus we should expect that corrected rates of return will generally differ from
accounting rates of return.

Previous Pharmaceutical Rate-of-Return Studies

While distortions in the conventional rate-of-return measurements have been
known since the end of the nineteenth century, the bias attributable to expensing
advertising, promotion, and research and development outlays has gathered attention only with the past decade.[8] In 1969 both Telser and Weiss independently
identified the basic theoretical problem associated with expensing durable capital
investments. One year later Solomon [1970] provided some examples of the
biases between the book and economic rates of return that occur when intangible
capital is expensed. This was followed by Stauffer [1971] who estimated the
errors involved for specific values of depreciation using simulation techniques. In
addition, there have been a number of studies investigating the relationship
between rates of return and future pharmaceutical investment. For example,
Baily [1972] and Schwartzman [1975] have estimated the change in the rate of
return from research and development expenditures as a consequence of the 1962
regulations governing the testing and introduction of pharmaceutical products.
    More recently there have been attempts to estimate the bias in the accounting
rate of return by Ayanian, Bloch, and Friedman. These studies, however, fail to
incorporate all the factors that create biases in the accounting rate of return or
fail to apply corrections to other industries. Both the study by Bloch [1974] and
the study by Ayanian [1975a], for example, exclude research and development in
their measures of intangible capital expenditures when they investigate the effects
of expensing these expenditures on rate-of-return measurements. Both studies
also fail to incorporate adjustments for inflation. There are, of course, other
differences in these studies. For example, Bloch's study uses a uniformed depreciation period for advertising in all firms, and Ayanian uses different depreciation
periods for intangible capital in each industry for computing rates of return.
Both studies find that the adjusted rates of return for the firms examined are
lower than book rates (with one exception) and that there is a differential impact
among companies.
    Two additional studies, one by Bloch [1976] and one by Friedman and
Associates [1973], limit their investigation of the effects of intangible capital
expenditures to those associated with research and development. In this study
by Bloch depreciation of intangible capital is proportional to the amount of sales
generated in each year. The corrected rates of return in Bloch [1976] are significantly below book or accounting rates of return, but the empirical results are

limited to a sample of pharmaceutical firms. Friedman's study estimated the rates of return from capitalizing research and development expenditures for a sample of six pharmaceutical companies and for the average of all U.S. manufacturing. This study is unique in that research and development expenditures are capitalized with adjustments for price and original costs.[9] Again the results show that firms with extensive amounts of intangible capital are likely to have significant upward biases in accounting rates of return.

Finally, Ayanian [1975] and Stauffer [1975] capitalized both research and development and promotion expenditures to correct for biases in the accounting rate-of-return measures. Unfortunately both studies are limited to pharmaceutical firms and are based on small sample sizes (Stauffer's study investigates only one firm and Ayanian's study examines six firms). Again there are other differences in the adjustments made in each study. For example, Ayanian shows the effects of different depreciation rates for intangible capital expenditures ranging from 9 percent to 13 percent. Stauffer's study uses varying depreciation techniques including declining exponential and straight-line depreciation. Again the corrected rates of return fell in both studies.

While each of these studies uses different methods for correcting rates of return and alternative data sources, their results are clear and strong—that accounting rates of return in firms with intangible capital are biased upward.[10]

My own research, summarized in the next two sections, incorporates corrections for inflation, provides for the accumulation of capital during the basic research and development stages, and employs differing economic life cycles for advertising, for basic research, and for development, which vary among industries.[11] The research also examines alternative opportunity costs of capital and averages the results for periods longer than the typical business cycle.[12] These corrections are applied to sixty-nine firms representing eleven industries with differeing levels of intangible capital.

Applications and Limitations

The use of the appropriate price level adjustments, intangible capital outlay expenditures, and capital accumulation and depreciation periods is relatively straightforward once the data are available. Unfortunately, except for price level adjustments the data are elusive, since conventional accounting procedures do not make it possible to identify all the transactions that should be included as intangible capital outlays, nor do they make it possible to determine true accumulation and depreciation periods.

In the pharmaceutical industry some capital outlays incurred for manufacturing plants (and some other investment activities) are capitalized and depreciated. In most firms capital invested in manufacturing plants represents less than 50 percent of the true economic capital of the firm.[13] This is because advertising and other promotion activities are chosen partly according to their ability to augment revenues over long periods of time.[14] Various studies indicate that the economic life of advertising capital ranges from less than one year in one industry to more than ten years in some industries, depending on such factors as the media used, the scope and clarity of the information, the nature of the product, and the life of the product itself.[15] In the pharmaceutical industry, where new products are patentable and do not become obsolete for ten to twenty years, advertising and other promotional activities would likely be directed toward long-term effects. It is also true that information received through direct personal interaction, which is the dominant form of promotion in pharmaceutical firms, has a more durable effect and correspondingly longer economic life than information received through print or broadcast media. Consequently a lower bound of three years for the economic life of pharmaceutical advertising and promotion activities is reasonable.

More important, pharmaceutical enterprises allocate large capital expenditures for research on and development of new products. These expenditures produce no revenues for some years; then, if successful, they provide revenues over the remainder of the product's life cycle. A small amount of each research dollar is allocated for basic research with no immediate commercial application. The remainder of the funds allocated to general research activities is more specifically directed to development of products which, it is hoped, will become marketable. The preliminary testing, the evaluation, the additional testing to meet FDA regulations, and other related activities are included in this development stage. Once a compound becomes a commercial product, research activity on that compound does not automatically cease. Additional research activities continue during the remainder of the compound's economic life, including the introduction of improved manufacturing procedures, new quality control, and the identification of new uses, new dosages, and the effects and interactions with other drugs. Estimates of the average total economic life cycle of a pharmaceutical product, including research and development time, range from twenty to thirty years.[16] In the initial corrections for a pharmaceutical enterprise's research expenditures, a minimum twenty-six-year economic life cycle for basic research and sixteen-year economic life cycle for development is chosen. Basic research expenditures are assumed to accumulate for eleven years and development expenditures for the last six of the eleven years before the compound is marketed.[17] When data are not available for basic research expenditures, they are assumed to be 16 percent of total research expenditures.[18]

Table 8-1 shows profits (both corrected and uncorrected), advertising outlays, research and development capital, corrected profits, net worth (both corrected and uncorrected), and rates of return (corrected and uncorrected) for 1965 through 1974. Column 2 of this table gives accounting profits adjusted for price changes for each year (1973 is the base year).[19] The adjustment for price level changes permits more accurate comparisons of profits (or other

Table 8-1
Pharmaceutical Manufacturers' Rates of Return on Net Worth and Assets Based on Book Value
(millions of constant 1973 dollars)

Year	Uncorrected Profits	Advertising and Promotion Outlays	Research and Development Capital	Corrected Profits[a]	Net Worth Uncorrected	Net Worth Corrected	Rate of Return Uncorrected	Rate of Return Corrected
1965	53.441	79.498	44.792	96.353	321.060	864.379	16.33%	11.15%
1966	61.673	90.148	48.304	108.365	336.572	941.165	18.32	11.51
1967	66.307	103.100	50.417	120.199	387.466	1,064.078	17.11	11.30
1968	82.917	111.301	55.833	141.783	451.905	1,206.236	18.35	11.75
1969	93.173	119.469	64.265	156.864	513.654	1,350.850	18.14	11.61
1970	97.927	124.024	70.925	165.409	571.098	1,493.943	17.15	11.07
1971	98.936	167.376	78.341	183.914	627.069	1,665.479	15.78	11.04
1972	122.172	170.136	81.215	205.335	699.434	1,844.058	17.47	11.14
1973	129.700	179.400	96.086	209.478	730.200	1,969.534	17.76	10.64
1974	119.596	163.667	109.662	189.533	713.625	2,024.621	16.76	9.36

Source: Kenneth W. Clarkson, *Intangible Capital and Rates of Return* (Washington, D.C.: American Enterprise Institute, 1977), pp. 47 and 49.

[a] Advertising and promotion are depreciated for three years; basic research accumulates for eleven years and development accumulates for six years; basic research is depreciated for fifteen years and development is depreciated for ten years.

variables) over time. Column 3 gives constant dollar advertising and promotion outlays each year. Each year's research and development expenditures from 1955 to 1974 have been price adjusted (using 1973 constant dollars) and apportioned into basic research (16 percent of total R&D expenditures), which is accumulated (at 10 percent per year) for eleven years and depreciated for fifteen years, and development, which is accumulated for six years and depreciated for eleven years. The net result of price adjustment, accumulated and depreciated for each year, is given in column 4. Column 5 takes the original uncorrected profits and adjusts each year's amount according to the relationship specified in equation 8.2. Equation 8.3 is applied to the uncorrected but price-level-adjusted measures of net worth (shown in column 6) to obtain corrected net worth (shown in column 7). Consequently the accounting or uncorrected rate of return (column 8) and corrected rate of return (column 9) can be obtained by dividing column 2 by column 6 and by dividing column 5 by column 7.

Comparisons between the accounting and corrected rates of return show striking differences. For example, the accounting rate of return on net worth in constant 1973 dollars for 1966, 1968, and 1969 exceeds 18 percent. The economic rates of return for the same years, however, are less than 12 percent. The average rate of return for the last ten years shows a similar bias. From 1965 to 1974 the average accounting rate of return on net worth was 17.3 percent. During the same period the estimated economic rate of return on net worth averaged 11.1 percent.[20]

Some indirect evidence of the validity of capitalizing and depreciating advertising, marketing, and direct research is obtained when we examine the variance of the rate of return with and without corrections for intangible capital outlay. When markets are relatively competitive, entry and exit (or expansion and contraction by existing firms) will cause the rate of return to more toward the opportunity cost of capital, adjusted for risk.[21] Risk, information and transaction costs, as well as disequilibrium forces, however, ensure that some variance in rates of return will occur. In addition, if rates of return contain systematic biases for some industries, measured variance will tend to be larger than the variance based on corrected rates of return. Since these corrections are designed to eliminate such biases, we would expect calculated variances to decline after the appropriate corrections have been made. An examination of the variance of rates of return when advertising, marketing, and direct research and corrected confirms this expectation. The variance of the rate of return on net worth for the period covering 1965 to 1974 falls from 0.67 percent to 0.41 percent when capitalization is made.

These results hold even with major modifications of the size of adjustments for price levels, economic life cycles (including depreciation periods), and the opportunity cost of capital. First, if calculations are based on current dollar amounts rather than constant dollar (price-level-adjusted) amounts, there is little change in the outcome. With identical capitalization and depreciation assumptions the average 1965-1974 corrected rate of return on net worth using current dollars is 11.9 percent, or only 0.8 percentage points higher than the average using price-adjusted data.

Second, as might be expected, longer economic lives are generally accompanied by lower average economic rates of return.[22] When advertising and promotion are depreciated for three years, the ten-year (1965-1974) average return on net worth (with price level corrections) is 14.8 percent. This falls to 13.4 percent and 11.7 percent when the depreciation period is lengthened to five and ten years, respectively. Increasing the economic life of research and development expenditures also generally lowers the average economic rate of return.[23] Equally important, with each of these the variances of corrected rates of return in these cases are lower than those calculated with no capitalization of advertising and promotion or research and development expenses.

Third, lengthening the total economic life cycle by increasing the period of either accumulation or depreciation lowers individual yearly and ten-year average economic rates of return. For example, the 1965-1974 average economic rate of return on net worth is 11.7 percent when a sixteen-year life cycle for research and development is chosen and 11.5 percent when a twenty-six-year life cycle is chosen.[24] More important, there is little variation in the ten-year average economic rates of return for relatively large changes in economic life cycles, and all life cycle changes yield corrected rates of return below the uncorrected accounting rates of return. Furthermore the variance of economic rates of return on net worth is always lower than the variance for the uncorrected rate of return.

Fourth, as table 8-2 shows, combining capitalization of advertising and promotion with capitalization of basic research and development produces both a general lowering of yearly and average corrected rates of return as well as a reduction in the variance of the rate of return. For example, increasing the total economic life cycle by five to fifteen years of depreciation for basic research and ten years of depreciation for development expenditures when advertising and promotion are depreciated for three years lowers the estimated ten-year average rate of return on net worth from 11.5 percent to 11.1 percent. Again the variance of economic rates of return is lower than the variance of the accounting rate of return.

Fifth, changes in the opportunity cost of capital do not have any significant impact on the average economic rates of return. When the opportunity cost of capital is raised from 10 percent to 15 percent, the inflation-adjusted ten-year average economic rate of return increases from 11.1 percent to 11.4 percent.[25]

Overall, while we can be sure that other corrections, such as replacing the accounting depreciation schedules with schedules that more closely represent

Table 8-2
Combined Effects of Alternative Capital Expense Corrections on Average Rates of Return, 1965-1974
(in percentages)

Capital Expense Corrections (years accumulated or depreciated)	Corrected Rate of Return on Net Worth
Basic research accumulation (11) Development accumulation (6) Advertising/promotion depreciation (3) Basic research depreciation (10) Development depreciation (5)	11.49
Basic research accumulation (11) Development accumulation (6) Advertising/promotion depreciation (3) Basic research depreciation (15) Development depreciation (10)	11.06
Basic research accumulation (11) Development accumulation (6) Advertising/promotion depreciation (4) Basic research depreciation (10) Development depreciation (5)	11.22
Basic research accumulation (11) Development accumulation (6) Advertising/promotion deprecision (4) Basic research depreciation (15) Development depreciation (15)	10.62
Basic research accumulation (11) Development accumulation (6) Advertising/promotion depreciation (5) Basic research depreciation (15) Development depreciation (15)	10.45

Source: Kenneth W. Clarkson, *Intangible Capital and Rates of Return* (Washington, D.C.: American Enterprise Institute, 1977), p. 55.

true economic depreciation, will increase the accuracy of our calculations, it is highly unlikely that these major general effects will be altered.[26]

Variations in Rates of Return

Differences among rates of return in various industries are the product of many factors. First, the observed rates at any time may not reflect actual steady-state returns because industries are rarely in static equilibrium for long periods. Second, there may be differences in the nonmoney characteristics that would cause money rates of return to differ under competitive market conditions. Third, there are differences in riskiness among different industries, with higher average rates of return required for competitive viability in riskier industries. Industries such as pharmaceuticals are like lotteries—everyone pays to play, but only a lucky handful win high returns. Fourth, differences in the quality of resources may cause variation in observed rates of return if superior resources are unequally distributed and earn unequal rents that are not completely capitalized on the books of the firms owning and using them. Fifth, entry barriers such as those erected by government regulation could cause observed rates of return in some industries to be higher than in others.[27] Finally, differences in rates of return can exist whenever there are systematic errors in measurement differentially affecting firms in some industries. For example, certain forms of intangible capital, such as recruitment, selection, and training of the work force may be omitted. In addition, rate-of-return calculations for industries whose physical assets are more concentrated in age brackets differing from the average for all industries can be expected to contain additional errors.

Given these factors, it would be highly unlikely that observed rates of return among firms within an industry or for all industries would be equal. Nevertheless, if biases from any one of these factors can be reduced, rates of return will move closer together if markets are competitive. If these biases have been reduced and markets are competitive, one would expect a narrowing of calculated rates of return.

A sample of sixty-nine firms representing eleven industries was chosen to test this hypothesis.[28] To reduce the problems associated with disequilibrium forces, data for each firm for 1949 through 1973 were collected from Moody's *Industrial Manual.* Average industry advertising expenditures were taken from the *Statistical Abstract* and the U.S. *Treasury Statistics of Income*, and average company research and development expenditures were obtained from the National Science Foundation (NSF). Table 8-3 gives both of these amounts as a percentage of net sales for each industry. Whenever research and development or advertising expenditures were not available for a firm in Moody's *Industrial Manual,* the industry average in table 8-3 was used.

Data from NSF surveys for several years were adjusted for price and averaged to determine the relative amount of basic research and development in each research dollar (see table 7-3). The period of accumulation for development expenditures in each industry was estimated from several industry sources, with an additional five years added for basic research expenditures.[29]

Industry average accounting rates of return for 1959-1973 were computed for each of eleven industries (shown in table 8-4).[30] As predicted, the corrected average rate of return significantly decreases for industries that were relatively capital intensive in advertising-promotion and research-development expenditures.

Table 8-3
Advertising, Research and Development (R&D) as Percentage of Net Sales,
Basic Research as a Percentage of R&D Expenditures by Industry

Industry	Advertising as Percentage of Net Sales (1949-1971)	R&D as a Percentage of Sales (1961-1971)[a]	Basic Research as a Percentage of R&D Expenditures (1960-1971)[a]
Pharmaceuticals	3.7	5.3	16.0
Chemicals	3.7	3.1	11.5
Foods	2.3	0.4[b]	8.4[c]
Electrical machinery	1.6	3.6	3.6
Rubber products	1.5	1.7	4.1[d]
Office machinery	1.0	3.1	2.0
Motor vehicles	0.8	2.5	2.4[e]
Paper products	0.7	0.9	2.5[f]
Petroleum	0.5	0.9	8.6
Ferrous metals	0.3	0.7	7.3
Aerospace	0.3	3.5	1.3

Source: Kenneth W. Clarkson, *Intangible Capital and Rates of Return* (Washington, D.C.: American Enterprise Institute 1977), pp. 61-62.

[a]Computed using 1973 dollars.

[b]Data not available for 1963.

[c]Data not available for 1962.

[d]Data not available for 1964, 1965, and 1971.

[e]Data not available for 1966-1971.

[f]Data not available for 1960.

The pharmaceutical and electrical industries, which spend relatively more on advertising and promotion and on research and development, experience the largest changes in their 1959-1973 average rates of return.

The pharmaceutical industry experiences the largest decline in its rate of return. Its average corrected rate of return is 5.4 percentage points less than its average accounting return. The next largest drop in the electrical machinery industry is 3.2 percentage points. In the other nine industries the return declines only about 1 percentage point. Overall the estimated average rate of return in all industries falls from 11.2 percent to 9.6 percent. More important, the variance, when corrections have been made, falls substantially from 7.5 to 2.5.

Table 8-4
Average Accounting and Corrected Rates of Return on Net Worth, 1959-1973
(in percentages)

Industry	Accounting Rates of Return	Corrected Rates of Return	Difference
Pharmaceuticals	18.3	12.9	−5.4
Electrical machinery	13.3	10.1	−3.2
Foods	11.8	10.6	−1.2
Petroleum	11.2	10.8	−0.4
Chemicals	10.6	9.1	−1.5
Paper	10.5	10.1	−0.4
Office machinery	10.5	9.9	−0.6
Motor vehicles	10.5	9.2	−1.3
Rubber products	10.1	8.7	−1.4
Aerospace	9.2	7.4	−1.8
Ferrous metals	7.6	7.3	−0.3
Average	11.2	9.6	−1.6
Variance	7.5	2.5	

Source: Kenneth W. Clarkson, *Intangible Capital and Rates of Return,* (Washington, D.C.: American Enterprise Institute, 1977), p. 64.

Despite a 5.4-point drop, pharmaceutical industry profits are the highest under the corrected calculations, as they are under conventional calculations. But the corrected calculations do bring the difference between average returns for the drug industry and for all eleven industries down from 7.1 to 3.3 percentage points. Furthermore the methodology employed to correct accounting rates of return yields extremely robust results. This is true for variations in assumptions examined in my research and for assumptions employed by other studies of intangible capital discussed in the second section. These independent studies further confirm the proposition that accounting rates of return are differentially biased.

Equally important, the corrected rates of return are more useful in explaining variations in stock prices than accounting rates of return. Average yearly stock prices (adjusted for stock splits and dividends) were regressed on both accounting and corrected rates of return for each of the sixty-nine firms.[31] The regressions using corrected rates of return outperformed or matched the regressions using accounting rates of return two to one (based on adjusted R^2). This provides additional evidence that corrected rates of return represent a more accurate picture of each firm's performance than accounting rates of return.

Conclusion and Future Research

The results of this research on profitability clearly support Bain's 1941 argument concerning accounting rates of profit:

> The unadjusted accounting rate of profit, as computed by the usual methods from balance sheets and income statements, is *prima facie* an absolutely unreliable indicator of the presence or absence either of monopoly power or of excess profits. . . . The relationship between price and accounting average cost tells us nothing about the degree of monopoly power, and little about the extent of excess profit.[32]

Unfortunately, until we obtain better information about the levels and economic life of advertising and about the magnitude and life cycle of research activities, precise ex post economic rates of return cannot be determined. However, we should not expect our basic findings of substantial and differential biases in accounting rates of return to be altered with more accurate information. In fact, the consistency of these findings suggests a different approach.

First, the findings of substantial and differential biases in accounting rates of return cast serious doubt on previous economic studies in which interindustry differentials in rates of return were attributed to risk, entry barriers, concentration, and other related variables. Indeed these results suggest that if entry barriers exist, they are not particularly effective and that risk may have been overstated in previous inquiries.[33] Clearly additional investigations using corrected rates of return are in order.

Second and more important, the validity of using existing pharmaceutical probability measures for public policy decision is, at best, highly questionable. The pharmaceutical industry faces an extensive set of existing and proposed regulations from the Federal Trade Commission, the Justice Department, the Food and Drug Administration, the Department of Health, Education, and Welfare, and other federal state and local regulations. In many cases existing regulations are enforced and new ones proposed in the context of "high" profitability measures in the pharmaceutical industry. Rational public policy decision making demands that information on profitability and the factors that determine it be accurate. As a first step we should take the lead from regulatory commissions who have questioned the usefulness of the accounting rate of return:

> There is no difference between research and development costs and any other costs which will benefit future ratepayers. Thus, just as other costs which benefit future rate-payers are capitalized and expensed in the future, so should research and development costs. The fact that accountants often treat research and development expenditures as a current expense is no reason for doing so for regulatory purposes.[34]

Notes

1. The bias involved in expensing advertising, research, and development costs has been recognized by many, including the Federal Trade Commission, Friedman and Friedman, Friedman and Associates, Bloch, Ayanian, Telser, Solomon, Stauffer, Schwartzman, and Clarkson. See the references for papers and articles.

2. *Washington Post,* June 26, 1977.

3. The discussion in this section is drawn from chapters 1 and 2 of Clarkson, *Intangible Capital and Rates of Return.*

4. See J. Stockfisch, "The Interest Rate Applicable to Government Investment Projects," in *Program Budgeting and Benefit-Cost Analysis,* ed. H. Hinrichs and G. Taylor (Pacific Palisades, Calif.: Goodyear Publishing Co., 1969), pp. 187-201.

5. U.S., Office of Management and Budget, *Discount Rates To Be Used in Evaluating Time-Distributed Costs and Benefits,* Circular A-94, March 27, 1972. This is the rate to be used after all inflation adjustments have been made.

6. H. Bierman and S. Smidt, *The Capital Budgeting Decision* (New York: Macmillan, 1966), pp. 322-325.

7. See generally, T. Stauffer, "Profitability Measures in the Pharmaceutical Industry," *Drug Development and Marketing,* ed. R. Helms (Washington, D.C.: American Enterprise Institute, 1975), pp. 97-119.

8. Many of these distortions have been known for some time. See, for example, O. Ladelle, "The Calculation of Depreciation," *The Accountant* 17 (November 1890); and I. Fisher, *The Nature of Capital and Income* (1906; reprint ed., New York: Augustus M. Kelley, 1965).

9. The inflation adjustment is very important if not all firms are growing at the same rate or have different amounts or scheduling of capital investment.

10. Under certain conditions corrected rates of return will be higher than uncorrected rates. For example, comparisons between corrected and uncorrected rates of return for the years when capitalization begins may not be valid unless there were no prior advertising and promotion or research and development capital expenditures. This is because the corrected profits in equation 8.2 will not include depreciation of previous capital expenditures. In addition, if capital expenditures are rising rapidly, other biases may be introduced. However, if the period under analysis is significantly longer than the economic life cycle, and if the earliest years are omitted from comparisons of corrected and uncorrected rates of return, these biases can be decreased.

11. This section is drawn from chapters 3 and 4 of Clarkson, *Intangible Capital and Rates of Return.*

12. This later procedure reduces some of the cyclical factors and averages some of the temporary disequilibrium forces.

13. See table 4 in Clarkson, *Intangible Capital and Rates of Return.*

14. See Y. Brozen, ed., *Advertising and Society* (New York: New York University Press, 1974).

15. See Y. Peles, "Rates of Amortization of Advertising Expenditures," *Journal of Political Economy* 79, no. 5 (September/October 1971): 1032-1058; K. Palda, "The Measurement of Cumulative Advertising Effects," *Journal of Business* 38, no. 5 (April 1965): 162-179; L. Telser, "Advertising and Cigarettes," *Journal of Political Economy* 70, no. 5 (October 1962): 471-499; R. Jastram, "A Treatment of Distributed Lags in the Theory of Advertising Expenditures," *Journal of Marketing* 20, no. 1 (July 1955): 36-46; N. Borden, *The Economic Effects of Advertising* (Homewood, Ill.: Richard D. Irwin, 1952), pp. 105, 135, 137, 140; S. Hollander, "A Rationale for Advertising Expenditures," *Harvard Business Review* 27, no. 1 (January 1949): 79-87; M. Vidale and H. Wolfe, "An Operations Research Study of Sales Response to Advertising," *Operations Research* 5, no. 3 (June 1957): 370-381; D. Tull, "An Examination of the Hypothesis That Advertising Has a Lagged Effect on Sales" (Ph.D. dissertation, University of Chicago, 1956); and M. Nerlove and F. Waugh, "Advertising without Supply Control: Some Implications of a Study of the Advertising of Oranges," *Journal of Farm Economics* 43, no. 5 (October 1961): 813-837.

16. See H. Clymer, "The Changing Costs and Risks of Pharmaceutical Innovation," in *Economics of Drug Innovation,* ed. J. Cooper (Washington, D.C.: American University, 1970); and L. Sarett, "Impact of FDA on Industrial Research and Development," in *Regulating New Drugs,* ed. R. Landau (Chicago: University of Chicago Press, 1973).

17. Recent experience with the 1962 drug amendments indicates the period of accumulation should be longer.

18. See table 7-3.

19. The wholesale price index is used.

20. While the magnitudes differ, similar patterns of individual rates of return are found using either weighted and unweighted assets for the base. This is also true for the average and variance of asset-based rate of return measurements.

21. See L. Telser, "The Supply Response to Shifting Demand in the Ethical Pharmaceutical Industry," and D. Cocks, "Product Innovation and the Dynamic Elements of Competition in the Ethical Pharmaceutical Industry," both in Helms, *Drug Development and Marketing.*

22. If the growth rate of advertising and promotion is very high, the average rate of return could increase with longer economic lives.

23. Clarkson, *Intangible Capital and Rates of Return,* table 8.

24. Ibid., table 9.

25. Ibid., table 11.

26. My estimates make no adjustment for depreciation expenses on physical plant, assuming that it would be trifling. Where it is large relative to reported profits, adjustment from original book dollars to current dollars could have an

important effect. For example, suppose physical plant were acquired in one year at a cost of $20 million. Assuming no other physical plant currently in use a decade later, $10 million in current revenues, $7 million in current operating costs and taxes, and $1 million in depreciation based on book cost and a twenty-year life (straight-line depreciation), the $2 million in profit on the $10 million of depreciated cost would yield a 20 percent accounting rate of return (assuming no working capital were required). If replacement costs for plant were to have doubled, the depreciated value of the plant in current dollars would be $20 million, current depreciation would become $2 million annually, and current profits would be reduced to $1 million. For this reason, retrospective revaluation of past profits to current dollars will still overstate the growth of profits if the depreciation adjustment is more than trifling.

27. See S. Peltzman, "An Evaluation of Consumer Protection Legislation: The 1962 Drug Amendments," *Journal of Political Economy* 81, no. 5 (September/October, 1973): 1049-1091; idem, *Regulation of Pharmaceutical Innovation* (Washington, D.C.: American Enterprise Institute, 1974).

28. Clarkson, *Intangible Capital and Rates of Return*, appendix B.

29. Ibid., table 15.

30. An economic life of three years for advertising was chosen to correct for advertising and promotion biases, and a ten-year period of depreciation was specified for basic research, with a five-year period for development. The pharmaceutical industry was assigned a fifteen-year depreciation period for basic research and a ten-year period for development. This modification was chosen to correct for conditions specific to the pharmaceutical industry. The creation and development of products takes a longer period of time than in other industries, hence entry (de novo or by expansion) involves a longer period of time. When combined with the patentability of ethical drugs, the effective life of products in this industry becomes significantly longer than the average in other industries. See Peltzman, *Regulation of Pharmaceutical Innovation*, and D. Schwartzman, *Expected Return from Pharmaceutical Research* (Washington, D.C.: American Enterprise Institute, 1974).

31. $S = a + \beta R$ where S represents the average stock price and R represents either corrected or accounting rates of return.

32. J. Bain, "The Profit Rate as a Measure of Monopoly Power," *Quarterly Journal of Economics* 55 (February 1941): 291. Copyright 1941 by the President and Fellows of Harvard College. Reprinted with permission.

33. The inclusion of these variables is beyond the scope of this study. For example, testing for the consequences of risk requires inclusion of either all or a significantly large random sample of the firms in the industry. For the pharmaceutical industry this entails knowledge about a large number of firms. Furthermore, data limitations further biased this sample toward the more successful larger firms.

34. Louisiana Public Service Commission, *Opinion,* June 15, 1976, Docket

Number U-12785. The opinion goes on to explain why accountants expense research and development expenditures.

> It appears that the basic reason why accountants reflect research and development as a current expense is that there is uncertainty or at minimum, a high degree of risk associated with the prediction of the future revenue accomplishments associated with research and development costs as compared to other asset expenditures. When faced with a high degree of uncertainty, the accountant invokes the convention of conservation and effects an immediate charge off of research and development costs. This conservative approach is, however, in conflict with the more basic underlying accounting concept which calls for an association of costs with the time periods benefited and/or the revenues produced by such costs.

Selected References

Ayanian, R., "Advertising and Rate of Return," *Journal of Law and Economics,* 18, no. 2 (October): 479-506.

Ayanian, R., "The Profit Rates and Economic Performance of Drug Firms," in *Drug Development and Marketing,* ed. R. Helms (Washington, D.C.: American Enterprise Institute for Public Policy Research, 1975), pp. 81-96.

Baily, M., "Research and Development Costs and Returns: The U.S. Pharmaceutical Industry," *Journal of Political Economy* 80, no. 1 (January/February 1972): pp. 70-85.

Bloch, H., "Advertising Profitability: A Reappraisal," *Journal of Political Economy* 82, no. 2 (March/April 1974): 267-286.

Clarkson, K., *Intangible Capital and Rates of Return* (Washington, D.C.: American Enterprise Institute for Public Policy Research, 1977).

Federal Trade Commission, *Annual Line of Business Report Program: Statement of Purpose* (Washington, D.C.: U.S. Government Printing Office, 1973).

Friedman, J., and Associates, *R&D Intensity in the Pharmaceutical Industry* (Washington, D.C.: Jesse Friedman and Associates, 1973).

Friedman, J., and Friedman, M., "Relative Profitability and Monopoly Power," *Conference Board Record* 9, no. 12 (December 1972): 49-58.

Grabowski, H., *Drug Regulation and Innovation* (Washington, D.C.: American Enterprise Institute for Public Policy Research, 1976).

Helms, R., ed., *Drug Development and Marketing* (Washington, D.C.: American Enterprise Institute for Public Policy Research, 1975).

Peltzman, S., *Regulation of Pharmaceutical Innovation* (Washington, D.C.: American Enterprise Institute for Public Policy Research, 1974).

Schwartzman, D., "Pharmaceutical R&D Expenditures and Rates of Return," in *Drug Development and Marketing,* pp. 63-80.

Schwartzman, D., *The Expected Return from Pharmaceutical Research* (Washington, D.C.: American Enterprise Institute for Public Policy Research, 1974).

Solomon, E., "Alternative Rate of Return Concepts and Their Implications for Utility Regulation, " *Bell Journal of Economics and Management Science* 1, no. 1 (Spring 1970): 65-81.

Stauffer, T., "The Measurement of Corporate Rates of Return: A Generalized Formulation," *Bell Journal of Economics and Management Science 2,* no. 2 (Autumn 1971): 434-69.

Stauffer, T., "Profitability Measures in the Pharmaceutical Industry," in *Drug Development and Marketing,* pp. 97-119.

Telser, L., "Comment" (on "Advertising and the Advantages of Size," by W. Comanor and T. Wilson), *American Economic Review* 59, no. 2 (May 1969): 121-123.

Weiss, L., "Advertising, Profits, and Corporate Taxes," *Review of Economics and Statistics* 51, no. 4 (November 1969): 421-430.

Commentary

Leonard W. Weiss

Overview: *Clarkson's purpose is correct, but some of his procedures and conclusions are questionable. The most important error is that he multiplied advertising and research and development less depreciation on past advertising and research and development by one minus the marginal tax rate. The firms involved did not in fact pay taxes on that imputed income and should not be treated as if they had. Other questions are about the assumed lives for ads (too short) and research and development (too long) and his use of industrywide advertising and (in many cases) industrywide research and development averages. His analysis may imply that drug companies earn smaller rates of return than their corporate reports suggests, but they also imply that they pay less corporate income taxes than other firms whose assets are mainly tangible.*

The sort of corrections that Clarkson makes are something I have advocated for years. I have only a few questions to raise.

First, I presume that in calculating the present value of an investment he means to deflate future capital expenditures, revenues, and manufacturing costs, which means dividing by the wholesale price index, not multiplying by it as he indicates in equation 8.1. This makes no difference to his calculations in the paper because he does not use equation 8.1 and apparently deflates profits, advertising and R&D in the conventional way in table 8-1.

Second, I do not understand why he multiplies advertising expenditures less depreciation on past advertising and research expenditure less depreciation on past research and development by one minus the marginal tax rate. We are interested in how much the companies being studied actually earn, not what they would earn if investments in intangibles were treated as profits and taxed. Similarly depreciation on advertising and R&D are not actually deducted in computing the corporate income tax. This correction seems wrong to me. Its net effect is to reduce corrected profit rates more than they should be.

Third, his three-year life for drug advertising seems short to me. When I reviewed the various studies of the life of ads I concluded that the typical ad has a six-year life. Admittedly ads for durables have much shorter lives— only one year according to Peles—but ethical drugs are not durables. Ayanian put the life of drug ads longer than most nondurables, if anything. The result of understating the lives of drug ads is to overstate corrected profit rates.

Clarkson does not tell us how he accounted for depreciation of ads and R&D. I presume he used straight-line depreciation. The double-declining balance method would come closer to the depreciation patterns shown in econometric models of advertising lives, though this may be due to nothing more than the convenience of the Koyck distributed-lag model in econometric studies of advertising. At any rate, if he did use straight-line, this would tend to offset the short life he assigned to drug advertising.

On a related point, my impression is that detail men (salesmen) are at least as important as advertising in selling ethical drugs. To the extent that he leaves these out, Clarkson overstates corrected rates of return for the drug industry.

I'm on less firm ground on the life of drug innovations, but I had the impression that the effective life a new drug was much less than the seventeen-year life of a patent, though this may have changed because of the Kefauver Act. If Clarkson has indeed overstated the life of drug research, then he understated corrected profits.

My fifth question is, How did Clarkson deflate net worth? He doesn't say. If he merely divided net worth by the wholesale price index, his correction is very crude. Net worth represents a collection of assets of various ages whose value is understated by various amounts because of inflation. The right way to correct its value would be deflate investment in the year it occurred, cumulate deflated investments less depreciation to find total deflated fixed assets at the current date, add deflated current assets, and subtract deflated liabilities to find deflated net worth. I do not know how much difference this would make for drug companies or, for that matter, whether it is possible with the information in corporate reports. It *is* possible for census industries. The incorrect deflation of net worth would tend to relatively understate profit rates for rapidly growing firms such as IBM because most of their plant is new.

My next point is a question, not a criticism. How did Clarkson get company R&D expenditures by firm? If those are what he says he used, I would like to have his data. I can think of lots of uses for it. If he cannot reveal these data because of disclosure promises, I urge him to investigate the effects of firm size and concentration on R&D intensity himself. We need an update of the R&D studies of the 1960s.

At the same time he used industrywide averages for advertising intensity. The industries involved are generally very broad and not representative of many of the firms involved. He can get firm advertising expenditures for the hundred leading advertisers from *Advertising Age*. He should use them where possible.

Finally, I agree that to add investments in intangibles to profits and not subtract depreciation on earlier such investments (perhaps for lack of data) would bias corrected profits upward. Indeed, I wonder how he was able to compute corrected returns on equity for 1959 when he apparently had R&D data only from 1961 (see tables 8-3 and 8-4). I would have thought he needed R&D data back to at least 1949 and earlier than that for drugs in view of the long lives he assigned them.

My main point, however, is that I do not agree that correct profit rates are biased upward when investments in intangibles grow rapidly. I have shown elsewhere[a] that corrected rates of return are more than accounting rates of return when $g/(1 + g)$ is greater than the accounting rate of return, g being the rate of growth in investments in intangibles. The corrected rate of return in this case is right. The rapidly growing firm really does not have much earlier intangible capital to depreciate. I do not see any bias in not subtracting a lot of depreciation to find profits for rapidly growing firms. This will not make much difference for most of the firms in Clarkson's study. For most of them, $g/(1 + g)$ is more than the accounting rate of return. In general, the expensing of intangibles does lead to the overstatement of their rates of return. But I bet that the accounting rate of return for a rapidly growing firm like IBM is close to correct or perhaps even understated.

I agree that public policy has probably been misdirected in many cases because of the apparently large profit rates reported by industries with many intangibles. At the same time, however, the expensing of intangibles has resulted in the understatement of net income (as well as equity) for tax purposes. According to table 8-1, the absolute value of drug profits is understated by an average of 42 percent in 1965-1974. This means drug companies paid far less taxes on their actual profits than other firms. Consistency would seem to call for the capitalization of intangibles for tax purposes as well as for reporting purposes and larger tax collections from firms that invest heavily in intangibles as a result. Perhaps the tax break that such firms get on R&D is a useful tax subsidy that Congress might want to continue, but I doubt that it would support a subsidy to advertising if it knew what it was doing.

---

[a]Leonard W. Weiss, "Advertising Profits and Corporate Taxes," *Review of Economics and Statistics,* 51 (November 1969).

Rates of Return to Investment in the Pharmaceutical Industry: A Survey and Critical Appraisal

Oswald H. Brownlee

Overview: *Accounting rates of return in the pharmaceutical industry exceed "true" or economic rates of return because expenditures for research and development and for advertising are considered current expenditures rather than capital expenditures and because the economic rate of return exceeds the growth rate of the industry. The results of three empirical investigations comparing historical accounting and economic rates of return and two studies estimating future rates of return to research and development are summarized. All the evidence indicates that accounting rates of return have substantially exceeded economic rates of return in the past and that the difference between the two concepts will be even greater in the near future.*

It has been alleged that profits in the pharmaceutical industry have been considerably larger than the average for industry as a whole. This allegation has been made with respect to the United States, Britain, Canada, and New Zealand in the reports of various governmental commissions.[1] Perhaps there are comparable allegations for other countries, but the alleged existence of the phenomenon in four countries and over a fairly long span of time—from about 1950 until the middle and late 1960s when the reports were prepared—has led economists and other investigators to try to describe more precisely the manner in which the profitability of the pharmaceutical industry has differed from that of the average for other industries and, if it truly has been larger, why the differential has persisted for a relatively long period of time.[2]

A persistently larger than average profitability, profitability being defined as the ratio of properly measured earnings to the value of the equity capital, is a rare phenomenon when equity trading takes place, since the current value of the equity is the present value of the stream of future earnings, as that stream is perceived. These earnings and present value are closely correlated.

Current earnings could be consistently higher than the amounts that had been anticipated, that is, investors could repeatedly underestimate the future earnings of an industry for a considerable period of time. Demands for the industry's products might grow at rates considerably in excess of those that generally were expected, costs might be reduced faster than had been anticipated

129

or random events affecting profits might exhibit an unusually long favorable sequence. In any event, in this manner of viewing the capitalization of income streams, differences in profitabilities among industries are "explained" by the preferences of investors for opportunities of various kinds and the ways in which they view the future.

This concept of profitability is not universally considered the most useful one. In particular, it does not seem to describe the relationship between earnings and the capital that was actually employed in obtaining these earnings. Some observers want to view current profitability as a ratio of some concept of current earnings to a capital base whose size is not a tautalogical capitalization of these same earnings but instead is measured by the depreciated value of the assets acquired at various times in the past. Of course, this concept also is not without ambiguities. Should original cost (perhaps corrected for price level changes) or replacement cost (if replacement were possible) be the basis for the undepreciated value of capital, and what depreciation rates should be employed?

An accounting rate-of-return concept of this kind forms the basis for the allegations that the pharmaceutical industry has been considerably more profitable than the manufacturing industry as a whole. Although the industry has been described as one in which the entry of new firms is difficult, using the standards employed by most people who try to describe the extent to which various industries are dominated by large firms, the pharmaceutical industry is relatively unconcentrated. The industry is such that the largest firm has less than 10 percent of the industry's output, a two-digit number is required to describe the smallest number of firms needed to produce three-quarters of the output, and the total number of pharmaceutical producers is more than one thousand.[3] The rank orderings of shares of the market held by various producers for different products has changed frequently and markedly. It is unreasonable to claim that the industry is not competitive.

Another "explanation" for a higher-than-average rate of return is the riskiness of an industry, a premium supposedly being necessary to attract capital into the more risky areas. A relationship between risk and profitability is difficult to establish. It could be that investors with preferences for assuming risk tend to be concentrated in the riskier areas and are satisfied with average rates of return no larger than those obtained elsewhere. Mining, some petroleum exploration, dry-land farming, and many other seemingly risky areas have not appeared to have rendered rates of return as high as the average. Because expenditure on research and development in the pharmaceutical industry is much larger relative to other costs than for industry as a whole, the pharmaceutical industry has usually been classified as a risky one. The risk may have been increased by the changes in procedures required for obtaining drug approval that were initiated in 1962. Some investigators claim that these requirements and the relatively large increases in costs of research and development have reduced the relative profitability of the pharmaceutical industry and that the allegations regarding high rates of return are no longer true.

It could be that neither conditions of entry nor risk are relevant in explaining the "high profitability" of the pharmaceutical industry, for what is alleged may not in fact be true. The entity that has been measured may be quite different from the one that is relevant. If one accepts the internal rate of return as the appropriate measure of profitability, the pharmaceutical industry has not been very different from manufacturing as a whole.

Internal Rate of Return

The concept rate of return is an attempt to characterize by means of a single number some of the features of a stream of income and outlays over time. The internal rate of return is the rate of discount that would make the present value of the contemplated stream equal to zero, that is, is a value of r that satisfies the expression

$$\sum_{i=1}^{t} \frac{Y_i}{(1+r)^i} = 0$$

where Y_i is the outlay or income at time i.[4]

Business investment opportunities are usually such that the incomes in the early years are negative, that is, there are outlays for plant and equipment, research, and so forth which are expected to produce positive incomes in later years. In such situations r must be greater than zero in order for the commitment requiring the outlays and yielding the incomes to be undertaken. However, there are situations—such as those in which tax payments are not to be made until some time after the income constituting the tax base has been received—in which the terms in the early years are positive, and the negative terms appear in the later years when r is a negative number. In such cases the business situation may be equivalent to borrowing at a negative rate of interest.

The internal rate of return is often referred to as an economic rate of return, implying that it is the standard against which other concepts are to be judged. If this were the case and if an accurately estimated internal rate of return could be obtained at little cost, there would be no need to employ other concepts. In practice, the future income attributable to past outlays cannot be precisely predicted. Furthermore, although the internal rate of return (or discounted value of the cash flow) is widely used in decisions with respect to a single project, the corresponding measure for an entire firm is generally not available. Instead various rates of return estimated from accounting data are employed as surrogates.

Book Rates of Return

These measures are generally ratios of income (a flow per unit of time) to assets (a stock existing at a given point in time). Since there are many different ways of defining income and assets from a given set of data, many different measures of rate of return will be obtained in this way. The classification of a given outlay as a current expense rather than as a capital expenditure, the way in which asset depreciation is determined, and the rate of growth of the capital base are among the most important factors that account for differences between the book or accounting rate of return and the internal or economic rate of return.

As has been demonstrated by Solomon [1970], Stauffer [1971], and Ayanian [1974], among others, the relationship between the internal rate of return r_{econ} and the book rate of return r_{acc} can be expressed as

$$r_{acc} = r_{econ} + F\left[(r_{econ} - g)\left(d_{acc} - d_{econ}\right)\right]$$

where F denotes a function, g is the rate of growth of the capital base of the firm, d_{acc} is the accounting rate of depreciation, and d_{econ} is the true economic rate of depreciation. If $F[0] = 0$, that is, if either term in the brackets is zero, then $r_{acc} = r_{econ}$. For other cases the algebraic sign of F is as shown in table 9-1.

Evaluating F is generally not feasible by the usual analytic methods, but its values for some conditions can be approximated by simulation. Solomon [1970] illustrated his conjectures regarding the relationship between book rates and economic rates of return with relatively simple examples, and Stauffer [1971] employed simulation methods to estimate the errors for specific values of certain parameters. True economic depreciation is particularly difficult to determine. However, it should be apparent that for firms investing less than their true earnings (which is usually the case, if dividends are paid) *and* rapidly depreciating

Table 9-1
Algebraic Sign of $F[\ \ ]$ for Ranges of r_{econ}/g and d_{acc}/d_{econ}

	d_{acc}/d_{econ}		
r_{econ}/g	*Less than 1*	*Equal to 1*	*Greater than 1*
Less than 1	+	0	−
Equal to 1	0	0	0
Greater than 1	−	0	+

capital for purposes of defining earnings, the accounting rate of return will be larger than the economic rate of return, that is, F will be greater than zero.

The larger is stated depreciation, for a given cash flow, the smaller is stated earnings, so that if accounting depreciation is less than economic depreciation, accounting earnings are understated. However, for the case in which the growth rate of the capital base is smaller than the true rate of return, the capital base will be understated proportionately more than earnings, so that the ratio of stated earnings to the arbitrarily depreciated capital base is an overestimate of the true rate of return. Of course, accelerated depreciation reduces the income tax bill and increases the present value of a given pattern of cash flow. In fact, if assets are instantaneously depreciated, the effective income tax rate on profits is zero. Using income as stated for tax purposes as the basis for determining true rates of return often gives a distorted picture.

Pharmaceutical Book Rates of Return

Although there are other factors—such as the time profile of cash receipts, the average productive life of assets, the ratio of working capital to total capital and the way in which income is defined for tax purposes—that may affect the relationship between the net profitability ratio and the internal rate of return, the division of outlays according to current or capital expenses seems to be most important in distinguishing the pharmaceutical industry from the "average" industry.

The pharmaceutical industry's expenditures for research and development and for selling activity (advertising and the use of salesmen) comprise a larger percentage of its total expenditure than is characteristic of U.S. manufacturing as a whole. Sellers of cosmetics, soaps, and detergents for home use, cigarettes, and some foods have relatively large advertising expenditures; space and electronics industries' expenditures on research and development are large; and book publishers incur large expenditures for salesmen who perform a role comparable to the drug firms' "detail men." However, few industries have as large combined percentages of total expenditure made up by selling and research and development expenditure as does the ethical drug sector.

In the computation of book rates of return, both selling and research and development expenditures are classified as current expenditures. However, considerable time elapses before selling expenditure exerts its full effect on sales, and research and development requires considerable time before it bears fruit. Furthermore, the return attributable to them continues for some time after the selling or research and development activity has ceased. Thus both selling and research and development expenditures are like what are ordinarily called capital expenditures, in that their effects are retained for some time, that is, they are depreciable. To treat them as current expenditure underestimates both current earnings and the capital base in the same manner as does depreciating any asset too rapidly.

Following a point made by Telser [1969] with respect to advertising expenditure, let

Y = sales receipts minus current expenditure

K = tangible capital

A = "advertising capital"

M = "research and development capital"

a = advertising expenditure

m = research and development expenditure

d_k = rate of depreciation of tangible capital

d_a = rate of depreciation of advertising capital

d_m = rate of depreciation of research and development capital

Denote the true rate of return by

$$r = \frac{Y - Kd_k - Ad_a - Md_m}{K + A + M}$$

and the measured or book rate of return by

$$\bar{r} = \frac{Y - Kd_k - a - m}{K}$$

For algebraic simplicity let $d_a = d_m$. As shown by Telser [1969], Stauffer [1971], and others,

$$r/\bar{r} \geq 1 \quad \text{if growth of } (a + m) \geq \bar{r}$$
$$< \quad \text{if growth of } (a + m) < \bar{r}$$

This is the same result described earlier as $r_{acc} = r_{econ} + F[\quad]$.

The growth rate is generally less than the measured rate of return so that the measured or book rate overestimates the true rate of return when research and development and selling expenditures are considered current outlays. The extent of the overstatement has been estimated in different studies. Stauffer [1975] estimated the effect of capitalizing as a common rate of advertising and research and development expenditure for one firm (Smith, Kline, and French Laboratories) on the return for the period 1953-1969. He assumed that the cycle from basic research activity to the manufacture and marketing of a new drug product required a constant expenditure per unit of time for six years from the initiation of the research program to approval of the drug by the Food and Drug Administration. If the returns from the project were represented by a rectangular distribution over time (the same amount of cash per unit of time for the life of the drug) the rate of return would be 17 3/4 percent; if the cash flow profile over time were represented by a steadily declining trend (a declining exponential), the return was 19 percent. The book rate of return was 31.2 percent. These are rates of return before deduction of federal corporation taxes. Stauffer's estimate of the true rate of return is sensitive to the distribution of research and development expenditure over time. A longer cycle or one in which expenditure is more heavily concentrated at the beginning of the development period reduces the estimated true rate of return; a shorter cycle or one in which expenditure is concentrated at the end of the development period raises the true rate. A cycle of four years instead of six years would have raised the estimates by about two percentage points. If the cycle were eight years instead of six years, the estimated true rate of return would have been about two percentage points less than Stauffer's figures.

Robert Ayanian [1975] also capitalized research and development and advertising expenditure at the same rate. He estimated that the depreciation rate for advertising and research and development capital was not likely to be less than 9 percent nor more than 13 percent per year, the estimates being based on data relating to six major pharmaceutical firms. He had previously estimated the retention rate (one minus the depreciation rate) for drug firm advertising for different firms and years and found it to be about 91.3 percent, so he felt justified in aggregating research and development and advertising expenditure. He estimated that the true rate of return for the six firms for 1973 was from 14.06 percent to 13.69 percent for a depreciation rate for advertising and research and advertising ranging from 13 percent to 9 percent. The corresponding average book rate of return for these six firms was 17.7 percent. Apparently Ayanian's estimates are rates of return after federal corporate tax liability. His estimates do not consider detailing a capital expenditure.

Jesse J. Friedman and Associates [1973] have estimated rates of return to six major pharmaceutical companies and to total U.S. manufacturing, capitalizing research and development expenditures, for the six years 1967-1972. It is stated that 90 percent of research and development expenditure is capitalized and amortized over a period of twenty years, "of which 5 years is estimated average elapsed period before commercial introduction and 15 years is estimated average productive term of R&D investment" (p. 26, footnote 1). This study also makes a further adjustment in the rate of return for increases in the cost of research and development. According to Friedman, for the pharmaceutical companies the book rate of return is 21.2 percent, the rate of return capitalizing research and development expenditure at current prices is 16.8 percent, and the rate of return capitalizing research and development expenditure at a constant general level of prices is 13.7 percent. The corresponding numbers for total U.S. manufacturing are 10.8, 10.5, and 9.3 percent, respectively.

The results of the three studies are summarized in table 9-2. The largest percentage adjustments are obtained by Stauffer. Although Ayanian capitalized both research and development and advertising expenditure, whereas Friedman capitalized only research and development, the percentage adjustments for the two studies are nearly the same. Since advertising is not particularly important,

Table 9-2
Estimated Book Rates and True Rates of Return in the Pharmaceutical Industry

Investigator, Group Analyzed, Time Period, and Nature of Adjustment	Book Rate of Return (%)	Estimated True Rate of Return (%)	Estimated True Rate as Percentage of Book Rate
I. Stauffer Smith, Kline, and French 1953-1969 R&D and advertising capitalized	31.2		
A. Rectangular distribution of receipts		17.75	57
B. Declining distribution of receipts		19.00	61
II. Ayanian Six major drug firms 1973 R&D and advertising capitalized	17.7		
A. Depreciated at 9 percent per year		13.69	77
B. Depreciated at 13 percent per year		14.06	79
III. Jesse J. Friedman			
A. Six major drug companies 1967-1972	21.2		
1. R&D capitalized at current costs		16.80	79
2. R&D capitalized at constant price level with assumed 5 percent rate of inflation		13.70	64
B. Total U.S. manufacturing 1967-1972	10.80		
1. R&D capitalized at current costs		10.50	97
2. R&D capitalized at constant price level with assumed 5 percent rate of inflation		9.30	86

most selling activity being in the form of detailing, this result is not surprising. Both studies analyze six firms, but only four firms are common to both studies, and Ayanian's estimate is for 1973 whereas Friedman's is for 1967-1972. Ayanian employed data from years prior to 1973 in estimating the rate at which to depreciate research and development and advertising expenditure, however. Only Friedman applied the same adjustments to other industries as were made for the pharmaceutical industry, and except for the effect of inflation the correction for total U.S. manufacturing was small. Since the inflation adjustment was applied only to research and development expenditure, the magnitude of this correction for total U.S. manufacturing seems somewhat large. Had both advertising and research and development expenditures been capitalized, the adjustment for total U.S. manufacturing would have been larger, and the ratio of rates of return for the pharmaceutical companies to rates of return for total U.S. manufacturing probably would have been larger than one would obtain from Friedman's numbers but smaller than those obtained from uncorrected book rates of return.

Although these studies do not encompass the entire drug industry nor adequately compare the pharmaceutical firms with the rest of the economy, they indicate that measurements of rates of return, properly capitalizing research and development and selling expenditure, would show the pharmaceutical industry's rates of return to be less above the average than has been reported. Although there is no economic case for government interference in a competitive industry even though its profits are large relative to industry as a whole, a political case for intervention would be weakened by proper rate of return comparisons.

Effects of Inflation on Estimates of Profitability

Among the studies previously cited, only Friedman [1973] made some attempt to correct for inflation.[5] In order that profits be accurately measured, costs and returns must be stated in the same units of account. In valuing assets at their original cost, a part of current costs is measured in dollars whose values differ from those dollars measuring the amounts of receipts. The result, when the price level is rising, is that costs are understated, that is, the absolute amount of depreciation in current monetary terms is greater than the figure used in estimating income. However, the asset base is also understated, since the undepreciated portion of the asset base is worth more in current dollars than in dollars of the dates at which these assets were purchased.

The effect of not adjusting net earnings for the effect of inflation is to overestimate them, thus making the income tax liability larger than would be the case if depreciation were measured on the basis of replacement cost. The effect of not adjusting the asset base is an understatement of net worth in current dollars. Since the accounting rate of return is a ratio of net income to net worth and the numerator is too large and the denominator too small when allowance is not made for inflation, the unadjusted rate of return is unambiguously too large.

This means that comparisons of profit rates for a firm or an industry or an economy over time will give a distorted picture, if allowance is not made for inflation. However, the errors in comparisons among firms or industries at a given point in time cannot be assessed so easily. Profits are generally overstated for every firm. Growing firms have a larger proportion of their assets priced at levels near the current ones than do declining firms. Consequently both the overstatement of earnings (understatement of depreciation) and the understatement of net worth will be less for growing firms than for decaying ones. The pharmaceutical industry has been growing more rapidly than the economy as a whole. However, the costs of research and development, one of its principal assets, have risen more rapidly than the price level as a whole. These two factors work in opposite directions; the more-than-average growth makes the pharmaceutical industry's accounting profits appear relatively smaller compared with the average of industry than would its economic profits, and the more rapid increase in the cost of one of its principal assets and one that is not included in the asset base makes book returns appear relatively larger compared with industry as a whole than would economic returns. A more detailed investigation than has been made here would be necessary to ascertain correctly how inflation has affected the relative profitability of the pharmaceutical industry.[6]

Expressing the various incomes and outlays in units of constant value probably cannot be accomplished without ambiguity, since the prices of the items on which outlays are made and the prices for things that are sources of income do not change exactly in the same manner during periods of general inflation (or deflation, if it should occur). However, using any of a number of different price indexes that have been nominated as deflators would be an improvement over making no correction for the change in the value of money.

Future Rates of Return in the Pharmaceutical Industry

The change in Food and Drug Administration requirements for drug approval initiated in 1962 appear to have coincided with a marked decrease in the number of new drugs placed on the market per unit of time. The additional evidence required by the Food and Drug Administration, in an attempt to increase the probability that a drug will not have harmful side effects and at the same time will be effective in the treatment of ailments, requires additional resources, including a lengthening of the time between the initiation of a research and development project and the actual marketing of the product.

This change is not fully reflected in all the estimates cited previously. Stauffer's rate of return is an average for the period 1953-1969. Friedman and Associates assumed a twenty-year amortization period, so their estimated rates of return reflect the effects of decisions made both prior and subsequent to 1962. However, their data show no marked trend in book rates of return for the six years 1967 to 1972 but do show a downward trend in the rate of return to assets including capitalized research and development expenditure. Stauffer estimated that adding two years to the development period would reduce the true rate of return by about two percentage points but leave the book rate of return unaffected.

Martin Neil Baily [1972] and David Schwartzman [1975] have prepared estimates on rates of return to research and development expenditure. Baily notes the fall in the number of new drugs introduced after 1962 and the increase in research and development expenditure and roughly estimates that the change occasioned by the 1962 regulation change will cut the rate of return by a least 50 percent. He estimated the rate before tax to be about 25 percent in 1961. Schwartzman estimated the expected rate of return on research and development expenditure made in 1973 and obtains a lower limit of 3.3 percent (after tax) for a ratio of profits to sales of 15.4 percent and a fifteen-year commercial life for a drug. His upper limit is 7.5 percent for a ratio of profits to sales of 20 percent and a twenty-year commercial life for the drug. These numbers compare with 11.4 percent and 18.4 percent for ratios of profits to sales of 15.4 percent and 20 percent, respectively, for 1960.

One would expect investment in the pharmaceutical industry to take place at a slower pace in accordance with the reduced expected rate of return. However, the ratio of research and development capital to other capital will have increased due to the 1962 requirements. Book rates of return may fall very little or might even rise at the same time that true rates of return fall. It is imperative that regulatory agencies and critics of the industry's alleged high profitability look at the appropriate numbers, or a substantial loss in general welfare will ensue.

Notes

1. For the United States the *Final Report of the Task Force on Prescription Drugs* (U.S. Department of Health, Education, and Welfare, Office of the Secretary, February 7, 1969) presents a brief summary of the contention that the drug industry makes high profits. The pharmaceutical industry in Great Britain is described in the *Report of the Committee of Enquiry into the Relationship of the Pharmaceutical Industry with the NHS* (Cmnd. 3410, 1967). The Canadian experience is described in the report of the Harley Commission, and the Public Expenditure Commission reported on New Zealand.

2. The ratio of annual net income after taxes to net worth for six major drug companies in the United States, as estimated from FTC-SEC Quarterly Financial Reports for Manufacturing Corporations and from company data, was relatively constant from 1964 through 1972. M.H. Cooper claims that the ratio of net income to net worth for the aggregate of pharmaceutical companies in Great Britain declined from the early 1950s through 1963, although the variance among companies was large. He reports a similar trend for pharmaceutical companies in other western European countries, although he cites few data. See M.H. Cooper, *Prices and Profits in the Pharmaceutical Industry* (London: Pergamon Press, 1966), especially ch. 2.

3. From U.S. Census of Manufacturers, FTC, and industry data.

4. The rate *r* is expressed as a solution to a polynomial equation that is generally economically meaningful if the polynomial consists of a set of nonpositive terms (some are negative) succeeded by a set of nonnegative terms (some are positive) or vice versa. See J. Hirschleifer, *Investment, Interest, and Capital* (Englewood Cliffs, N.J.: Prentice-Hall, 1970), pp. 77-79.

5. For a survey of literature on the effects of inflation on the relationship between true earnings and reported earnings see Eric Schiff, *Inflation and the Earning Power of Depreciable Assets* (Washington, D.C.: American Enterprise Institute, 1974).

6. If capital gains are also counted as income, inflation's effects are different to generalize. Inflation causes a gain due to the reduction in the real value of a firm's debts that are fixed in money terms and a loss from the reduction in the value of assets nominated in money.

Bibliography

Ayanian, Robert, "Advertising and Rate of Return" (Ph.D. dissertation, University of California at Los Angeles, May 1974).

———, "The Profit Rates and Economic Performance of Drug Firms," in *Drug Development and Marketing,* ed. Robert Helms, Washington, D.C.: American Enterprise Institute for Public Policy Research, 1975.

Baily, Martin Neil, "Research and Development Costs and Returns: The U.S. Pharmaceutical Industry," *Journal of Political Economy* 80 (January/February 1972): 70-85.

Cooper, M.H., *Prices and Profits in the Pharmaceutical Industry,* London: Pergamon, 1966.

Friedman, Jesse J., and Associates, *R&D Intensity in the Pharmaceutical Industry,* Washington D.C., September 1973.

Hirschleifer, J., *Investment, Interest, and Capital,* Englewood Cliffs, N.J.: Prentice-Hall, 1970.

Schiff, Eric, *Inflation and the Earning Power of Depreciable Assets,* Washington, D.C.: American Enterprise Institute for Public Policy Research, Domestic Affairs Study 25, November 1974.

Schwartzman, David, "Pharmaceutical R&D Expenditures and Rates of Return," in *Drug Development and Marketing,* ed. Robert Helms, Washington, D.C.: American Enterprise Institute for Public Policy Research, 1975.

Solomon, Ezra, "Alternative Rate of Return Concepts and Their Implications for Utility Regulation," *Bell Journal of Economics and Management Science* 1, no. 1 (Spring 1970): 65-81.

Stauffer, Thomas R., "The Measurement of Corporate Rates of Return: A Generalized Formulation," *Bell Journal of Economics and Management Science* 2, no. 2 (Autumn 1971): 434-469.

_____, "Profitability Measures in the Pharmaceutical Industry," in *Drug Development and Marketing,* ed. Robert Helms, Washington, D.C.: American Enterprise Institute for Public Policy Research, 1975.

Telser, Lester, "Comment" (on a paper by William S. Comanor and Thomas A. Wilson), *American Economic Review* 59, no. 2 (May 1969): 121-123.

**Part III
The Impact of Government
Regulations on
New Drug Development**

10 The Impact of Regulation on New Drug Development

William M. Wardell

Overview*: The major social costs of government regulations are: (1) limitation of drug innovation and development; and (2) interference in the practice of medicine. New approaches in drug research and development are needed in order to achieve a proper balance between the pursuit of medical advances and the avoidance of undue hazards. Congress should give the Food & Drug Administration a mandate to pursue positive policies designed to improve the flow of beneficial new drugs rather than merely a negative mandate of avoiding harmful ones.*

Regulations on the development and use of drugs and the way such regulations are enforced have a substantial influence on medical care. Therefore it would be logical to subject drug regulations to the same close scrutiny and to the same criteria for safety and efficacy that the regulations themselves require for drugs. To date, the regulations have not been so scrutinized, and their full impact has not been measured; but there are indications that they are not always beneficial.

The federal government's first major attempt to regulate the food and drug industries was the Pure Food and Drugs Act of 1906. This law gave the government control over the labeling, but not the testing or advertising, of any substance used to affect disease. At the time prescription drugs were of secondary importance; the correction of abuses in food and patent medicines was far more urgent.

By the 1930s the deficiencies of this law were fully appreciated. The result was the Food, Drug, and Cosmetic Act of 1938 (passed in response to the Elixir Sulfanilamide tragedy)[1] which increased the government's control over the advertising and labeling of food, drugs, and cosmetics. It also stipulated that before being permitted in interstate commerce, a new drug had to be judged "safe" by the FDA. These regulations were intended to prevent the marketing of untested, potentially harmful drugs not generally recognized as safe by experts.

The legislation that has undoubtedly had the greatest impact on the development of new drugs is the 1962 set of Kefauver-Harris amendments to the

---

This article was originally published under the title, "New Drug Development: The Impact of Regulation," in *Medical Student* 3 (November 1976), copyright 1976 by Miller & Fink Corp., Darien, Conn. Reprinted with permission.

1938 law. The amendments were passed at the time that the teratogenic effects of thalidomide were becoming apparent in Europe. Under these amendments both the requirements for preclinical toxicity testing and the process of clinical testing of a new drug were subject to greater control by the FDA. In addition, manufacturers were now required to demonstrate not only the safety of a new drug, but also its therapeutic efficacy.

When one examines the achievements of the FDA in light of history and of the aims of these various laws, there is cause for satisfaction. Major achievements in the regulation of drugs include

Elimination of "patent medicines"

Elimination of untested new drugs from the market

Elimination of unduly hazardous drugs

Elimination of totally ineffective drugs

Control over the accuracy and scope of drug claims and promotion

Application of rigorous scientific standards to drug evaluation and promotion

These are impressive achievements for which the FDA and the congressional actions that established it have earned a deservedly high place in world esteem. Nevertheless these achievements have been accompanied by appreciable medical, scientific, and financial costs, especially in recent years. The costs include limitation of drug innovation and development and interference in the practice of medicine.

Limitation of Drug Innovation and Development

Limitation of drug innovation and development is reflected in delays in the availability of effective new therapies (the drug lag and its effects) and in the limitation of industrial research.[2] Only now are studies beginning to focus on the impact that increased regulations and their attendant costs have had on the basic discovery process within the American pharmaceutical industry, and there are already several indications that the discovery rate has declined—or at least failed to increase as expected—over the past fifteen years. In addition, there has been a massive shift of research and development abroad by American companies in the past five years. Nearly half of all drugs developed by American companies are now first studied clinically in other countries.

It is the American patient who will suffer directly if major therapeutic advances no longer originate in the United States, since new drugs developed

abroad (and even American drugs first introduced abroad) generally take several
additional years to gain FDA approval for use here. For example, the first widely
used bronchoselective (and hence safer) beta-adrenergic bronchodilator, meta-
proterenol, was available in Europe for twelve years before becoming available
in the United States. Cromolyn sodium was available six years earlier in Europe
than in the United States. The beta-blocking agent propranolol was available
in Britain in 1965 but was not available at all in the United States until 1968,
and then it was approved only for relatively minor uses.[3] It took another five
years for the same drug to be approved for its first major use, angina, and still
another three years (until 1976) before it was approved for its other major use,
hypertension. This, and the lack of availability of certain other beta blockers
in the United States, resulted in a marked backwardness in American sophistication in the treatment of hypertension over much of the past ten years.

Other beta blockers, such as practolol and alprenolol, have been shown
abroad to produce a 40 percent reduction in the incidence of myocardial re-
infarction and cardiac death in postcoronary patients.[4] Although this effect
could result in saving several thousand lives annually in the United States, these
beta blockers are no longer available in this country even for investigational
purposes. *As a result of these interminable delays, American textbooks of
pharmacology and medicine are in some fields so hopelessly out of date that
when used abroad they are often irrelevant.*[5]

Interference in the Practice of Medicine

While the primary focus of new regulations is on drugs, the ultimate effect is to
regulate the practice of medicine. This stems first from the regulations that
control the access of new drugs to the market. The practice of medicine is also
affected by the regulations' control, through the package insert, over the way
in which drugs are used by physicians. One example is propranolol. Another
example is carbamazepine which, although available here, was not approved
for epilepsy for many years. An American physician who prescribes a drug for
a use that is not "approved" in the labeling risks certain indirect legal sanctions
related mainly to increased liability if a malpractice action arises. While this
point is contested vigorously by the American Medical Association, lack of an
indication on a drug's labeling does the use of a drug for the unlabeled indication. In some situations such deterrence may be generally desirable, but in
many instances it is not. What is particularly disturbing is the way in which the
drug labeling—in some instances years out of date—is coming to supplant or
overrule the entire body of expert medical opinion together with the world's
literature on a topic.

This encroachment of regulation on the practice of medicine was not
apparent in the early days when so much work was needed to improve the

drugs themselves. Now, however, the FDA and the medical profession clash frequently over issues such as "approved" and "unapproved" uses for drugs. The potential for such clashes will increase in the future as the existing regulations penetrate the practice of medicine.

The FDA's most successful achievements have come from regulating issues that are easily defined—for example, in areas of production, quality control, and distribution. There are, however, parts of the development process of new drugs where the issues are hard to define and where regulation has been less effective and less readily accepted. One such area is the intermediate stage of a drug's development where it advances from a purely experimental to a potentially therapeutic compound, and then from experimental therapy to marketed drug. Here attempts at regulation have met with justifiable resistance from clinical investigators because at this stage judgment and maximum flexibility are required. For example, many of the major discoveries in therapeutics have resulted from serendipitous observations of the effects of drugs that had already been introduced to human use for an entirely different purpose. Examples include the major tranquilizers, both types of antidepressants (monoamine oxidase inhibitors and tricyclics), carbamazepine for trigeminal neuralgia, the antihypertensive actions of beta blockers, the antiparkinsonian action of amantadine, and many others. It is precisely this delicate, unstructured process that is the most adversely affected by regulation. Any action that reduces the flow of new drugs to areas in which clinical observation is possible could bring much of this activity to a halt, since the total number of new drugs available for serendipitous findings would be reduced.

New approaches in drug research and development are needed. The following are some actions that should be considered by the FDA and other concerned groups in the field.

Define the public interest in the process of drug research and development in order to achieve a proper balance between the pursuit of medical advances and the avoidance of undue hazards.

Regulate positively to stimulate drug innovation and development. Congress should give the FDA a mandate to pursue policies designed to improve the flow of beneficial new drugs to the patient. What is really needed is a mandate to maximize therapeutic benefit and to protect the patient from disease. The existing philosophy, to protect the public from drug-induced harm, is very different. A more positive legislative approach is needed, and was addressed in part by the Drug Regulation Reform Bill (1978), although not all would agree that the bill's total effect would be positive.

Appoint an ombudsman to investigate and arbitrate on regulatory disputes between the FDA and industry.

The medical profession should support the FDA in its recent improvements that benefit patients.

It is unlikely that the medical, scientific, and economic costs of regulating new drugs were foreseen, much less intended, by Congress when it wrote the laws. In my opinion, implementation of the suggested improvements could reduce some of these costs without undermining the important gains that have resulted from food and drug regulations. The law itself does not need to be changed (except for the need for a positive statement on maximizing benefit); rather, it needs to be applied more sensibly by the regulators.

Notes

1. In 1937 over one hundred people died after ingesting Elixir Sulfanilamide. An investigation revealed that diethylene glycol, a toxic substance, was present in the elixir and was the cause of the deaths. See P.N. Leech, "Elixir of Sulfanilamide-Massengill," *JAMA* 109, no. 19 (1937): 1531; C.I. Ulmer and R.P. Fischelis, "The Sulfanilamide Tragedy and Its Lesson," *J. Med. Soc. N.J.* 35, no. 1 (1938): 35-38; A.P. McGinty, "Complications Following the Use of Sulfanilamide," *J. Med. Assn. Georgia* 26 (1937): 569-570.

2. See the following articles by W.M. Wardell, "Introduction of New Therapeutic Drugs in the United States and Great Britain: An International Comparison," *Clin. Pharmacol. Ther.* 14 (1973): 773-790; "British Usage and American Awareness of Some New Therapeutic Drugs," *Clin. Pharmacol. Ther.* 14 (1973): 1022-1034; "Therapeutic Implications of the Drug Lag," *Clin. Pharmacol. Ther.* 15 (1974): 73-96; "Developments in the Introduction of New Drugs in the United States and Britain, 1971-1974," in Helms, R.B. (ed.), *Drug Development and Marketing* ed. R.B. Helms (Washington, D.C.: American Enterprise Institute, 1975), pp. 165-181; "Drug Development, Regulation, and the Practice of Medicine," *JAMA* 229 no. 11 (1974): 1457-1461.

3. Wardell, "Introduction of New Therapeutic Drugs."

4. C. Wilhelmsson, J.A. Vedin, L. Wilhelmsson, G. Tibblin, and L. Werko, "Reduction of Sudden Deaths after Myocardial Infarction by Treatment with Alprenolol," *Lancet* 2 (1974): 1157-1160; C. Ahlmark, H. Saetre, and M. Korsgren, "Reduction of Sudden Deaths after Myocardial Infarction," *Lancet* 2 (1974): 1563; "Improvement in Prognosis of Myocardial Infarction by Long-Term Beta-Adrenoreceptor Blockade Using Practolol," (Multicentre International Study), *Brit. Med. J.* 3 (1975): 735-740.

5. Wardell, "Drug Development."

11

The Pharmaceutical Development Process: Estimates of Development Costs and Times and the Effects of Proposed Regulatory Changes

Ronald W. Hansen

Overview: *Prior to the research reported on in this article, there was very little published information about the cost and time requirements for developing a new chemical entity. Most cost estimates were based on a division of annual R&D expenditures by the annual flow of new products, a procedure that is inappropriate for an investment activity extending over many years. In the study described in this article cost estimates were based on confidential data on actual expenditure on a representative sample of development projects. When expenditures are capitalized to the date of marketing approval at an 8 percent interest rate, the estimated cost per marketed new chemical entity is $54 million.*

The data obtained in the study can also be used to estimate some of the effects of proposed changes in pharmaceutical regulations. As an illustration, the effect of a Health Research Group proposal on the cost of new drug development is estimated.

Although the "Drug Regulation Reform Act of 1978" failed to secure congressional approval, it reopened public debate of the effects of pharmaceutical regulation. This debate brought out many important issues but it also demonstrated the difficulty of predicting the effects of proposed regulatory changes on pharmaceutical innovation and the health of the population.

Most existing studies of the impact of regulation on pharmaceutical innovation have focused on the effects of the 1962 amendments to the Food, Drug, and Cosmetics Act. A summary and critique of many of these studies appear

This material is based on research supported by the Center for Research in Government Policy and Business of the Graduate School of Management, University of Rochester and from the National Science Foundation under Grant No. 75 19066. Any opinion, findings, and conclusions or recommendations expressed in this publication are those of the author and do not necessarily reflect the views of the Center or the National Science Foundation.

151

in a paper by this author and in Henry Grabowski's *Drug Regulation and Inno-vation.*[1] Most studies of the effects of the 1962 amendments employed time series models in which the observations were typically annual industry R&D expenditures, annual introductions of new chemical entities, annual sales data, and measures proxying the stock of existing drugs. The fact that many of the provisions of the 1962 amendments were not fully implemented until late in the 1960s and the gradual implementation coincided with other important changes makes it difficult to estimate the independent effect of regulatory changes. While these studies provided some insight on the probable impact of provisions in the 1978 bill, the usefulness of these studies in assessing the pro-posed reforms was limited by the fact that the nature of these changes was substantially different from the changes made by the 1962 amendments.

Since the estimating techniques of these studies relied on aggregate measures rather than exploring the impact on specific aspects of the development process, it is difficult to adapt their results to novel regulatory changes.

One of the major difficulties in assessing new regulatory proposals is the lack of published information on the characteristics of the pharmaceutical development process, particularly the economic and managerial decisionmaking characteristics. The study reported in this paper attempts to fill in a portion of this void.

This study represents the first attempt that I know of to estimate the cost of new drug development based on data supplied by several companies on the level and timing of their expenditures on specific development projects. As a result it avoids many of the pitfalls inherent in approaches based on simple divisions of R&D budgets by current-year new product introductions. The paper treats the development expenditures as an investment and capitalizes the outlays to the point of marketing approval. The total investment cost consists not only of actual outlays but also foregone earnings or interest on funds invested for many years prior to marketing approval. It also recognizes that there will be many unsuccessful projects for each one that results in a marketed product; and in the calculation of the cost per marketed new chemical entity, the expenditures on unsuccessful projects are allocated to the successful projects.

To construct profiles of drug development expenditures, it was necessary to examine the length of time devoted to testing NCEs at various stages of the development process. The paper thus provides an estimate of the time pattern of attrition of new drug products from the testing process and estimates of the length of time required for various phases of the development process.

The bulk of the data used in this study was provided by fourteen U.S. pharmaceutical firms. Since these firms were supplying data that they regarded as confidential, they were guaranteed anonymity. Among the fourteen firms were some of the largest in the industry, as well as several firms with relatively small R&D budgets. The conditions under which the data were obtained pre-vents the publication or dissemination of the raw data.

At the time this project was initiated, the Health Research Group (HRG) petitioned the Food and Drug Administration (FDA) for a change in the manner in which drug development tests could be conducted. The impact of this proposed restructuring on the cost of new drug research is estimated in this paper as an illustration of a policy analysis application of the data generated in this project.

The first section of the paper describes the general nature of the development process and may be skipped by readers who are already familiar with the process. The second section presents new empirical data on the time required to complete development stages and the attrition rates of compounds during the testing process. The third section considers the cost of development, and the final section discusses the use of these estimates in the assessment of proposed regulatory changes.

The Nature of Pharmaceutical R&D

Although many different activities take place in the process of pharmaceutical research and development, it will be useful for our purposes to focus on the activities that occur after a new chemical entity has been selected for extensive testing. The other activities include synthesizing new chemicals, early pharmacological studies on these chemicals, and attempts to improve the understanding of the physiopathological processes. These activities are sometimes referred to as basic research, although in the context of industrial R&D the meaning of this term is different from its meaning in university R&D. Since some of the activities do not fit classic definitions of "basic research," we shall refer to this stage as the discovery phase.

The discovery research produces new chemical entities (NCEs) that show enough potential activity to be identified as candidates for extensive testing. It is at this point that an NCE enters the development stage. During this development phase most regulations regarding the safety and efficacy of the drugs come into direct application. Of course, the effects of regulations and market forces on the development stage have implications for the level and nature of discovery activities.

The first tests performed during the development stage are short-term animal toxicity tests. These tests provide the investigators with information about the activities of the new chemical in animals which helps predict its safety in man and its likely therapeutic activity. Only a small percentage of the NCEs testing in animals are judged to be suitable candidates for further development.

If the results of the initial animal toxicity studies are encouraging, the firm submits to the FDA a "Notice of Claimed Investigational Exemption for a New Drug" (IND). The requirement to file an IND was initiated as part of the 1962 amendments. So long as the animal pathology-toxicity tests have been properly conducted and have no significant adverse findings, the granting of the IND exemption is virtually automatic. Prior to 1970 the firm could begin testing in human subjects as soon as they had filed the IND, but now they must wait thirty days.

The human (or clinical) testing period is considered under the regulations to occur in three phases. Phase I testing usually involves giving doses of the NCE to healthy human volunteers. The principal objectives of these tests are to check for evidence of toxicity in humans and to determine basic properties of the pharmaceuticals, for example, absorption of the NCE. Compounds that have considerable activity in animals often have little or no desirable activity in the human body.

If a compound still appears promising after phase I studies, it is studied in patients. In addition to providing more information on possible toxicity, the purpose of phase II studies is to determine whether the drug candidate has any therapeutic value in the treatment of disease. If it displays sufficent therapeutic value without significant adverse side effects, it is further studied on a wider scale; this is phase III. The wide-scale tests help to uncover less common side effects and come closer to replicating the type of drug utilization that would occur if the drug were available on the market.

The firm must also subject the compounds to long-term animal studies to check for effects that may take a prolonged exposure or a long time to appear, such as carcinoginicity and effects on reproduction. These tests usually include studies on second generations of the test animals and usually last two to three years depending on the types of animals used and the number of generations to be studied. Long-term animal testing is usually conducted concurrently with phases II and III.

If, after all of these tests, a compound is judged by the firm to be suitable for marketing, the firm will file a New Drug Application (NDA) with the FDA. The NDA includes the raw data on all of these tests on the compound. The FDA reviews the NDA to determine whether the drug can be marketed or whether additional tests are required. For successful candidates the review process averages about two years before approval is granted.

Not all new chemical entities follow this process. New chemical entities that show promise of treating serious diseases for which no existing therapy is effective may be tested immediately in patients. In such cases the possible adverse side effects may be outweighed by the hoped-for improvement in treating the disease. Such a decision may be based on the results of foreign experiences with the NCE or on in vitro studies. In other circumstances the testing sequence may follow this general pattern, but no sharp division exists between the study phases. Despite these occasional deviations, this division of the drug development process into phases provides convenient benchmarks for discussing and analyzing the NCE development process.

Estimate of NCE Development Times

Only about 12 percent of the drugs that enter the human testing process reach the market. The others are dropped from consideration because they have unacceptable toxicity, they fail to produce the desired therapeutic effects, or the potential market for which the drug may prove acceptable is too small to warrant the expenditures required to complete its development for marketing. Very little information has been published about the speed with which NCEs drop out of testing, the reasons for suspension of testing, or the profile of development expenditures on unsuccessful and successful NCEs. In this section we discuss the procedures used to obtain this additional information and then present the estimated time estimates for NCE development. The costs of NCE development are considered in the next section.

More detailed information on the NCE development process was obtained by collecting information from firms on a random sample of NCEs that had entered human testing. The 1975 NCE survey conducted by William Wardell generated a list of all NCEs that were first tested in humans by the responding firms.[2] The information obtained from this survey made it possible to classify virtually all NCEs first tested in man after 1963 according to expected pharmacologic category (which gives an indication of expected therapeutic use), date of first clinical trial and current regulatory status: approved for marketing, NDA submitted but still pending, IND closed, or IND open but no NDA submitted. It was also possible to calculate the length of time between the filing of an IND and either the closing of the IND or the submission or approval of an NDA.

This information on the NCEs was utilized in designing a more detailed survey and in selecting the sample of NCEs to be covered. Since a firm's willingness to supply the requested data would be affected by the amount of work required to complete the questionnaire, as well as by the confidential nature of the data requested, no firm was asked to supply detailed information on more than eight NCEs. Smaller firms were questioned on less than eight in order to avoid asking them to supply information on all or a large percentage of their total NCEs tested in humans. These constraints, imposed to increase the likelihood of response, dictated that the sample for the detailed follow-up be approximately one hundred NCEs. This number constituted about 15 percent of the NCEs taken into humans by the twenty-five U.S. firms who had replied to the 1975 NCE survey by the date of this detailed second survey. Since a 100 percent return rate was not anticipated for the second survey, the sample was structured to obtain the maximum amount of information about the testing process.

The NCEs with INDs open less than two years constituted 37 percent of all NCEs tested by the twenty-five firms, but they progressed only through the early testing stages. By contrast the NCEs that had completed all three phases of clinical testing and had either been approved for marketing or had an NDA submission pending constituted only 6 percent of the total. Thus a survey selection procedure designed to produce a completely random sample of the NCEs would generate a relatively large amount of information on the early testing stages but little on the later stages. It was also expected that the variances in costs and testing times would be greater in the later phases of clinical testing than in the somewhat more standard first phase. For these reasons it was decided that the follow-up sample should contain a greater than proportional share of NCEs that had progressed to advanced testing stages and a reduced share of NCEs with INDs open less than two years. The selection procedure was therefore first to categorize the NCEs according to whether they were marketed, had an NDA submission, had an open IND, had an IND closed within two years of filing, had an IND closed after two years from the filing date, or were tested abroad first. Within these categories the NCEs were randomly selected. However, proportionately more drugs were selected from the categories with longer expected testing periods. Since the NCEs for which information was obtained in the follow-up questionnaire could be identified as belonging to one of these categories, it was possible to weight the responses in order to obtain a representation of the total population. For example, in the calculation of the average phase I testing times, average phase I time for NCEs with INDs open less than two years was given a weight of 37 percent even though these NCEs constituted less than 10 percent of the replies received.

In the questionnaire (a copy appears in the appendix to this chapter) firms were asked to supply the date at which an NCE began each phase of clinical testing and the date at which the testing phase was completed or testing was suspended. Starting and completion dates were also requested for the preclinical animal pathology and toxicity tests and the long-term animal studies. Firms were also asked to estimate their expenditures, both in-house and external, on each sampled NCE by testing stage. For nonmarketed NCEs that had been removed from active testing firms were asked to identify the reason for removal. Firms were asked to indicate whether an NCE had been tested abroad prior to U.S. clinical trials or marketed abroad prior to U.S. marketing. The final section of the questionnaire asked for annual data on total NCE R&D expenditures as well as a breakdown of the total by type of expenditure (basic, preclinical animal toxicity, or clinical) and by location of expenditure (United States, Great Britain, or other foreign).

The questionnaire was sent to twenty-five U.S. pharmaceutical firms. Fourteen of these firms completed all or parts of the questionnaire. The responding firms included some of the largest pharmaceutical firms, as well as some firms with modest R&D budgets. The NCEs for which information was received represented approximately 10 percent of the total number of NCEs that the twenty-five firms first tested in man from 1963 to 1975. Over 20 percent of their NCEs that had reached the point of NDA submission or approval were included in the responses.

One of the first tasks of the analysis was to estimate the rate of attrition of NCEs in the testing process. The 1975 NCE survey indicated that over one-third of the NCEs that entered human testing after 1963 had had their INDs closed after two years. Since clinical trials cannot be performed in the United States without an IND, the IND closure points set a maximum estimate of the length of time an NCE is actually being tested. However, it was not possible to estimate more precisely testing times from that survey, since some firms keep an IND open long after active testing has stopped. In fact, since the passage of the Freedom of Information Act many firms are reluctant to close an IND, because as long as the IND is open much of the data on an NCE that they have submitted to the FDA has trade secret status, thus preventing the FDA from publicly disclosing the data. However, once the IND is closed the trade secret status is lifted. The increase in the number of NCEs with open INDs makes it impossible to estimate testing times from data on IND closings.

The detailed survey asked specifically for the date of first clinical trial and the date at which testing was completed or suspended. The results indicate that the actual testing times are on average only half as long as the period during which the IND is open. By the end of fifteen months of clinical testing, testing has ended on over 50 percent of the NCEs that entered human trials. By three years the fraction that has been removed from clinical trials is approximately 75 percent. Figure 11-1 graphs the attrition rate for NCEs. The initial attrition is due primarily to the decision not to develop the NCE for marketing, whereas

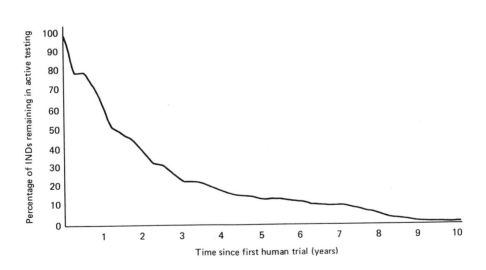

Figure 11-1. Expected Duration of Active NCE Testing Following First Human Trial

the later removal from active testing is due in part to the successful completion of the tests required prior to marketing.

In the construction of these time profiles all NCEs that had open INDs but had not reached the NDA submission stage were omitted. This would normally have the effect of overstating the attrition rate, because the NCEs that entered testing close to the survey date and had short testing times were likely to have a closed IND whereas those with longer testing times would still have an open IND and thus not be in the sample. However, the reluctance of firms to close INDs after the passage of the Freedom of Information Act has resulted in the inclusion in the open IND category of many NCEs that have already been removed from testing. Moreover recent NCEs that have completed testing and have advanced to the stage of NDA submission would be included in the sample of open INDs. The omission of these NCEs imparts an opposite bias to the attrition rate. As a check we constructed estimates that omitted all NCEs that entered testing after 1970 and found little difference in the testing profiles.

An exponential decay function was used to estimate the attrition of NCEs from clinical testing. If N_0 NCEs enter testing at time 0, then t years later $N_t = N_0 e^{-\delta t}$ would remain, where δ is the attrition rate. The attrition rate δ was estimated using two different formulations for the error term:

$$N_t/N_0 = \exp[-\delta t + \epsilon] \tag{11.1}$$

$$N_t/N_0 = \exp[-\delta t] + \mu \tag{11.2}$$

where ϵ and μ are normally distributed error terms with mean 0. The estimated attrition rate was 41.5 percent and 43.9 percent for the two forms:

$$\left(\frac{N_t}{N_0}\right) = \exp[-0.415t], \quad R^2 = 0.947 \atop (-24.32) \tag{11.1'}$$

$$\frac{N_t}{N_0} = \exp[-0.439]\, t, \quad R^2 = 0.978 \tag{11.2'}$$

Equation 11.1' was estimated using ordinary least squares. Equation 11.2' was estimated using a nonlinear iterative procedure. The t statistic for the coefficient in the ordinary least squares regression is in parentheses.

The percentage of all NCEs tested in humans that eventually become marketed products is of special interest. However, it is difficult to estimate this percentage from the available data. Since the data included only NCEs that began human testing during 1963 or later, the maximum time between the beginning of clinical testing and market approval prior to the 1975 survey date is twelve years, and NCEs that began later will have a correspondingly shorter period during which to obtain approval. NCEs approved for marketing have averaged approximately six years from IND submission to NDA approval. This relatively long period required for approval makes it hazardous to estimate success rates of NCEs that have been in testing for relatively short time periods. Although only 6 percent of NCEs in the sample had been approved by the date of response to the questionnaire, the percentage for this sample will increase after further time has elapsed if any of the NCEs currently being tested are approved for marketing.

As a cohort of NCEs ages, all NCEs should eventually either be approved for marketing or be removed from active testing. At this point it would be a relatively simple matter to calculate an overall success rate. Unfortunately, we do not have such a long horizon for the NCEs in our data sample. However, it is possible to use the information available to calculate the probability of success as a function of the time elapsed since the IND approval point. Such an analysis of success probabilities was performed by Christopher Cox on this sample of NCEs.[3] He calculated the probability of an NCE's reaching the NDA submission stage as a function of time elapsed since IND approval and also calculated the probability of an NDA approval as a function of time since NDA submission. He found that ten years after IND filing, the probability that an NDA had been submitted was 12.5 percent. He estimated that six years after NDA submission 88 percent of NDAs would be approved. (Using the data collected in the 1975 NCE study the approval rate for all NDAs that were submitted at least five years prior to the survey date was calculated to be 88 percent.) Taken together these two estimates imply that at least 11 percent (0.125 X 0.88) of NCEs will eventually reach the market. A similar analysis for IND closures which would have placed a ceiling on the approval percentage was not performed. However, the small number of open INDs in the cohort of NCEs for which at least ten years have elapsed since IND filing indicates that the eventual NDA submission percentage cannot rise much above the current 12.5 percent rate. Since not all NDAs will be approved, 12.5 percent may be even optimistic for the eventual success rate; however, for purposes of estimating testing costs per successful NCE the 12.5 percent estimate was used. If a lower figure had been used the calculated costs per marketed NCE would be higher.

A similar problem with the elapsed testing time was encountered in estimating the probability that an NCE would successfully complete a specific clinical development phase. Fortunately the problem was less serious for this estimation, since the time spent in a particular testing phase is relatively short. In calculating this probability all NCEs in active testing in the clinical phase under consideration on the reporting date were omitted. Although this may appear to create an upward bias in the estimate of the failure rate since NCEs that would successfully complete the testing phase might be expected to have longer testing times and thus be more likely to be omitted, in fact there was little difference in the within-phase testing times for successful and unsuccessful NCEs.

Although the clinical testing of some NCEs does not follow the standard phase I, II, and III distinction, the survey results indicated that approximately 50 percent of the NCEs entering phase I clinical trials do not advance to phase II. Only 19 percent continue to phase III, and 13 percent reach the point of an NDA submission.

The large attrition of NCEs from testing during phase I points to the importance of early clinical trials in screening out NCEs. Many NCEs were removed from testing during early trials because of excessive toxicity in humans or because they exhibited a lack of clinical usefulness despite early promise in animal screens. Since long-term animal tests are typically conducted concurrently with phases II and III, one cannot assume that NCEs removed from testing during those clinical phases are dropped because of human test results. For NCEs that had been removed from testing firms were asked to identify the reason for the suspension, that is, to indicate whether animal or human test results were the principal cause. Although about 20 percent of the NCEs removed from testing during phases II and III were dropped prior to the start of long-term animal testing, for NCEs on which both clinical and animal studies were taking place, the reasons for suspension were evenly divided between human and animal test results.

For the NCEs that enter clinical testing the average testing times were estimated to be 9.1 months for phase I, and 23.2 months for phase II. The reported testing times for phase III testing averaged 33.6 months. However, it was found that many firms were reporting terminal dates for phase III testing after the NDA submission dates. Some firms choose to continue testing after an NDA submission, and occasionally the FDA requires them to conduct additional tests during the NDA review process. No information was obtained on how extensive this testing is vis-a-vis pre-NDA submission testing. If the testing period for these NCEs is estimated by using the NDA submission date as the terminal point for phase III testing, the average pre-NDA phase III testing time was 22.6 months. The long-term animal toxicity tests which are usually conducted concurrently with phase II and III clinical tests averaged 36.8 months in duration.

Estimates of NCE Development Costs

Published estimates of the average cost of developing a marketable new chemical entity have generally been based on a division of annual R&D budgets by the number of NCEs approved for marketing. Such estimates do not account for the fact that the bulk of the expenditures necessary to bring an NCE to the market have been made over a period of several years prior to its entry into the market. Thus the level of R&D expenditures in one year has little effect on the number of NCEs marketed in that year, and the calculated ratios are affected by any increasing or decreasing trends in R&D efforts. Moreover, since the expenditures are made over several years, one should treat the development process as an investment expenditure and the total cost should include interest or earnings foregone on funds invested. To capitalize the past expenditures, one needs to obtain information on the time pattern of expenditures necessary to market an NCE; such information was not available prior to this study. The section that follows discusses estimates of development costs based on the actual expenditures on the sample of NCEs.

In the questionnaire sent to U.S.-owned pharmaceutical firms the respondents were asked to report on the expenditures made for the development of a sample of NCEs tested by their firm. All drugs in the sample were first tested in humans by the responding firm and thus the sample excluded products licensed from other firms. Expenses for modifications or postmarketing testing of existing compounds were not included as part of the R&D expenditures for NCEs. Although the sample of NCEs included in the survey overrepresented those categories of NCEs with more extensive testing, the information obtained on an NCE was grouped according to the sampling category of the NCE, and the data from each category were weighted according to the categories' share in the total distribution.

Since there has been considerable inflation during the time period covered, 1963-1975, it was necessary to convert all costs into constant dollar terms. The major price indices for this period use 1967 as the base period, and thus that year was selected for the estimates. There is no published price index designed specifically for the inputs to pharmaceutical development, so the wholesale price index compiled by the Department of Labor was used. Development costs were reported by phase of development, which in most cases extended over two or three years. The midpoint of each development phase was used as the reference point for adjusting the reported dollars to 1967 dollars. To convert these estimates to 1976 dollars, the 1967 values should be multiplied by 1.829 since the wholesale price index for 1976 was 182.9 compared to its 1967 base value of 100.

The average cost per testing stage was computed without distinguishing between NCEs that advanced to the next phase and those that were dropped from testing during the phase. A distinction between the two groups was made in initial calculations on the premise that drugs that did not complete the phase successfully (did not enter the next phase) would exhibit a lower average cost. However, the difference turned out to be small, and the dropouts actually had slightly higher average costs. One possible explanation for this observation is that some of the failures were held longer in the early phases in order to investigate the complications, whereas had no complications arisen they would have advanced to the next phase earlier.

Table 11-1 summarizes the average cost per testing stage. The reported testing costs for phases II and III exhibited a high variance due to the very high testing costs encountered by a few NCEs. The median phase III testing cost was $548,000 in 1967 dollars versus the average cost of $1,546,000.

Table 11-1
Average Testing Cost for NCEs Developed by U.S. Firms by Phase of Testing
(in thousands of dollars)

Testing Phase	Average Cost in 1967 Dollars	Average Cost in 1976 Dollars
Preclinical animal	97	177
Phase I clinical	166	304
Phase II clinical	881	1611
Phase III clinical	1546	2828
Long-term animal	420	768

Obviously one cannot simply add these figures in table 11-1 to obtain the expected cost per marketed NCE, since for every marketed NCE there are approximately seven failures. Most of the failures do not enter all the testing phases, so an expected value estimate must take into account the probability of reaching the testing phase. Finally one must consider the timing of these expenditures in order to generate the present value of expenditures at the point of marketing.

Pharmaceutical development costs can be estimated from the expenditures made on a representative cohort of NCEs that enter human testing. Approximately 50 percent can be expected to be dropped from testing during phase I testing, and other members of the cohort will be removed from testing at later stages. Eventually some of the NCEs will have completed all required testing and will be approved for marketing. The expenditures on tests for this cohort can be used to compute the average post-IND testing cost per NCE entering clinical testing or the average post-IND testing cost per marketed NCE. To calculate the present value or capitalized value of these expenditures the pattern of expenditures on this cohort over time must be estimated and then these expenditures should be discounted or capitalized to a given point in time. For this analysis the expenditures are capitalized to the date of marketing approval, since this is the point at which a firm begins to receive a return on its expenditures for developing NCEs.

This analysis is expressed in terms of probabilities of an NCE's entering testing phases and of expected values for expenditures. This is equivalent to a cohort analysis except that all values are expressed on a per NCE basis.

At the time an NCE is first tested in humans it faces only a 50 percent probability of advancing to phase II studies and a 19 percent probability of entering phase III studies. The probability that long-term animal tests will be conducted is 29 percent. We can calculate the expected value of post-IND testing expenditures per NCE entering human testing by multiplying the probability of reaching each testing stage by the average cost of testing for that phase. This calculation results in an estimated post-IND testing expenditure per NCE of $1.02 million in 1967 dollars, as shown in table 11-2 or $1.87 million in 1976 dollars.

Prior to the filing of an IND, firms must conduct short-term animal pathology tests which may be as short as three months. The average reported duration was 13.7 months at an average cost of $97 thousand in 1967 dollars or $177 thousand in 1976 dollars.

If the probability that an NCE entering clinical testing will be approved for marketing is 12.5 percent, then the average expenditures for post-IND testing per marketed NCE is $8 million in 1967 dollars or $14.9 million in 1976 dollars. These values have not been adjusted to reflect the fact that these expenditures are spread over several years. To calculate the present value or capitalized value the time pattern of these expenditures must be estimated.

The average duration of testing was 9.1 months for phase I, 23.2 months for phase II, 22.6 months for phase III up to the NDA submission point (33.6 months if the reported phase III time is used), and 36.8 months for the long-term animal studies. Assuming that expenditures are evenly distributed over the testing period, we can calculate the average monthly expenditure per phase as shown in table 11-3. Two values for phase III costs are calculated; the first assumes all costs occur prior to the NDA submission point, and the second assumes the costs are evenly distributed over the whole reported time. Multiplying these expenditures by the probability that an NCE entering clinical trials will reach that phase generates the expected value of the monthly expenditures for an NCE entering clinical trials.

Table 11-2
Expected Post-IND Testing Expenditures per NCE Entering Clinical Trials by Testing Phase
(in thousands of 1967 dollars)

Testing Phase	Probability of Reaching Test Phase	Average Cost for Testing during Phase	Expected Expenditure per Phase (2) × (3)
(1)	(2)	(3)	(4)
Phase I	100	166	166
Phase II	50	881	440
Phase III	19	1,546	294
Long-term animal	29	420	122
Total			1,022

Table 11-3
Average Monthly Expenditure on Testing by Phase of Testing
(in thousands of 1967 dollars)

Testing Phase	Average Cost for Testing during Phase	Duration of Phase in Months	Average Testing Cost per Month During Phase (2)÷(3)	Probability of NCE's Reaching Phase	Expected Monthly Expenditure per NCE by Phase (4) × (5)
(1)	(2)	(3)	(4)	(5)	(6)
Phase I	166	9.1	18.2	100	18.2
Phase II	881	23.2	38.0	50	18.5
Phase III[a]	1,546	22.6	68.4	19	13.0
Phase III[b]	1,546	33.6	46.0	19	8.7
Long-term animal	420	36.8	11.4	29	3.3

[a]Based on phase III times prior to the NDA submission point. Testing costs are assumed to occur prior to NDA submission.

[b]Based on reported phase III development times. Costs are assumed to be evenly distributed over reported times.

If we assume that there is no time delay between the clinical phases of testing and that long-term animal tests commence six months after the start of phase II tests, then we can construct the expenditure profile for an NCE that completes all testing phases, as shown in figure 11-2. Adjusting this profile for the probability of reaching each phase generates the expected profile per NCE as shown in figure 11-3.

To capitalize these expenditure flows to the date of marketing approval, we need to determine the time elapsed between the end of phase III studies and the NDA approval date. Based on the 1975 NCE survey by Wardell, the time between NDA submission and approval averaged two years. We use a date two years after the estimated completion of pre-NDA submission phase III studies as the point of marketing approval.

To calculate a present value or capitalized value of expenditures, one must select an appropriate interest rate. We are dealing in constant value dollars (1967 dollars), so the rate of interest selected should be a real rate of interest rather than a nominal rate that reflects anticipated inflation. Since the investment in pharmaceutical R&D is risky, the interest rate selected should incorporate a risk premium. Due to the erratic behavior of the economy during the period under consideration, it would be hazardous to attempt to estimate the market rate of interest appropriate for an investment of this character. We

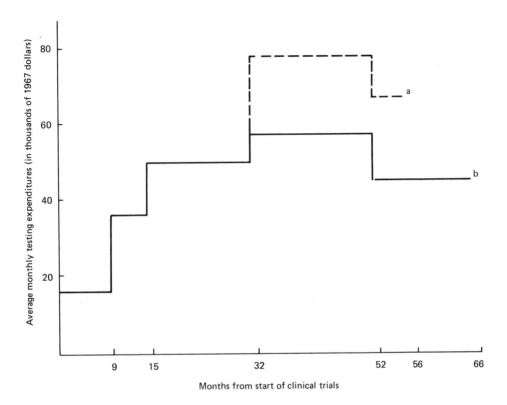

^aBased on phase III times prior to the NDA submission point. Testing costs are assumed to occur prior to NDA submission.

^bBased on reported phase III development times. Costs are assumed to be evenly distributed over reported times.

Figure 11-2. Time Profile of Average Post-IND Testing Expenditures for an NCE Completing All Testing Phases (in 1967 dollars)

therefore present estimates of the capitalized testing expenditures using interest rates of 5, 8, 10, and 15 percent, with the 8 percent rate being the one we consider most appropriate.

Table 11-4 presents the estimated capitalized cost of preclinical and post-IND testing for interest rates of 0, 5, 8, 10, and 15 percent. Phase III costs are allocated evenly over the reported testing period. Allocating them only over the pre-NDA submission period would raise the capitalized value slightly.

Some costs cannot be directly attributed to a particular NCE tested in humans. Short-term animal toxicity tests are performed on many NCEs that

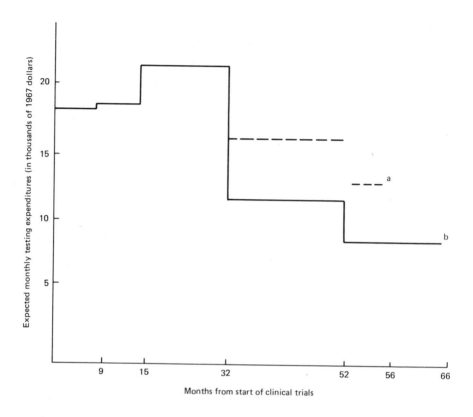

[a]Based on phase III times prior to the NDA submission point. Testing costs are assumed to occur prior to NDA submission.

[b]Based on reported phase III development times. Costs are assumed to be evenly distributed over reported times.

Figure 11-3. Time Profile of Expected Post-IND Testing Expenditures per NCE Entering Clinical Testing (in thousands of 1967 dollars)

firms decide not to test in humans. But by far the largest expenditures not included are those for discovery or predevelopment research. Schwartzman estimated that these expenditures are 50 percent of total R&D expenditures.[4]

In part III of the questionnaire firms were asked to report total NCE R&D expenditures in the U.S. and basic research expenditures in the U.S. by year from 1962 to 1975. Firms were asked to include in basic research expenditures "all outlays on activities prior to the point at which NCEs enter the preclinical animal pathology and toxicity tests". The basic research expenditures reported by the firms represented 51 percent of the total NCE R&D expenditures. Based

Table 11-4
Expected Cost by Development Phase per NCE Entering Clinical Trials
Capitalized to Point of Marketing Approval Using Alternative Discount Rates
(in thousands of 1967 dollars)

Testing Phase	Capitalized Expenditures for Alternative Interes Rates				
	0%	*5%*	*8%*	*10%*	*15%*
Preclinical animal toxicity	97	138	170	195	227
Phase I clinical	166	226	273	309	420
Phase II clinical	440	561	649	715	911
Phase III clinical	294	330	353	370	415
Long-term animal	122	148	165	178	215
Total Post-IND	1,022	1,265	1,440	1,572	1,960
Total, including preclinical	1,109	1,403	1,610	1,767	2,187

on this result each NCE was attributed a discovery research expenditure equal to the uncapitalized identifiable testing expenditures, $1.1 million in 1967 dollars. These expenditures occur before the development phase but there is no way to precisely allocate them to a particular NCE or to estimate the time pattern of the expenditures. Schankerman has suggested allocating these expenditures evenly over a three year period prior to clinical testing, however, some projects are known to have required much longer to produce NCEs for human trials, and some never result in clinically tested NCEs.[5]

In preparing table 11-5 we have considered three periods for allocating the discovery expenditures. For later work we will generally use the most conservative of these—allocating discovery costs evenly over the three years prior to the start of clinical tests. Although the dollar outlays are estimated to be the same in the discovery and development stages, when the costs are capitalized to the point of marketing approval using a positive interest rate, the capitalized value of discovery expenditures exceeds the capitalized value of development expenditures.

All these estimates have been presented in terms of expected cost per NCE entering clinical trials. Only one NCE out of eight entering clinical trials will be approved for marketing. The costs per marketed NCE are thus eight times the values calculated before. The discovery and development cost estimates per marketed NCE expressed in 1967 and 1976 dollars are presented in table 11-6.

Our estimated cost per NCE is higher than many existing estimates. One of the major sources of this difference is that we have treated the R&D expenditures as investment expenditures and have capitalized them to the date of marketing approval. This capitalization adds considerably to the magnitude of the costs that occur early in the R&D process, such as the allocated discovery costs. The

Table 11-5

Estimated Discovery Cost per NCE Entering Clinical Tests Capitalized to Point of Marketing Approval Using Alternative Interest Rates and Allocation Periods *(in millions of 1967 dollars)*

Years over which Discovery Costs Are Allocated	Capitalized Value of $1.1 Million Discovery Costs for Alternative Inteest Rates				
	0%	5%	8%	10%	15%
Three years prior to clinical tests	1.1	1.64	2.08	2.45	3.65
Five years prior to clinical tests	1.1	1.73	2.26	2.71	4.24
Seven years prior to clinical tests	1.1	1.81	2.45	2.99	4.93

magnitude of the estimated costs also depends on the interest rate selected. Although I believe an 8 percent real rate of interest is appropriate for this investment, estimates for alternative rates are presented.

Another source of difference between our estimated cost and most others arises from the method of estimation. We have selected a sample of NCEs that U.S. firms first entered into clinical testing and have obtained the expenditures

Table 11-6

Discovery Costs and Testing Expenditures per Marketed NCE Capitalized to Point of Marketing Approval Using Alternative Discount Rates

	Millions of 1967 Dollars				Millions of 1976 Dollars			
	5%	8%	10%	15%	5%	8%	10%	15%
Post-IND test only	10.1	11.5	13.8	15.7	18.5	21.0	25.2	28.7
Post-IND tests plus preclinical animal toxicity	11.2	12.9	14.1	17.5	20.5	23.6	25.8	32.0
Allocated discovery cost using three-year allocation period	13.1	16.6	19.6	29.2	24.0	30.4	35.8	53.4
Total	24.3	29.5	33.7	46.7	44.5	54.0	61.6	85.4

on this sample by stage of development. Other estimates have been based on a division of annual R&D budgets by the annual number of new drugs marketed. Even if the researcher is careful to eliminate new dosage formulations of existing products, the cohort of NCEs introduced includes many that are initially produced or tested by foreign subsidiaries (whose R&D budgets may or may not be included in the aggregate R&D expenditure base) or ones that have been licensed from foreign firms. Since licensing fees are typically not included in R&D budgets are the foreign firms' R&D will not appear as U.S. R&D expenditures, the existence of these NCEs will bias downward the estimated R&D cost per NCE. This study estimated the cost of developing a marketed NCE in the United States, which is different from an estimate of R&D expenditures in the United States, per NCE marketed in the United States.

The small size of the sample can be criticized. The cost data was obtained for only 8 percent and development time data for 10 percent of the NCEs introduced by the twenty-five United States firms surveyed. However, the sample was structured in order to obtain more data on the NCEs with long development times, since it was expected to find a greater variability of costs among these NCEs. A sample of approximately 20 percent of NCEs with NDA submission was achieved. The sample was reweighted to remove the bias imparted by over-sampling NCEs with long development times. It is still possible that the sample of NCEs picked had abnormally high development cost.

The cost estimates derived in this study were based on a sample of NCEs which entered human testing between 1963 and 1975. Although the estimates are presented in terms of 1967 dollars and 1976 dollars, the difference between these two numbers represents only an inflation adjustment. The real cost of drug research and development has also grown over this period. However no attempt was made to estimate the time trend due to the size of the sample. To the extent that real costs are growing, the estimates derived from this study of NCEs entering human testing from 1963 to 1975 will be underestimates of the current real cost of NCE development.

Assessment of Proposed Regulatory Changes

In addition to the 1962 amendments to the Food, Drug, and Cosmetic Act of 1938 a series of other regulatory changes have affected pharmaceutical research. It is likely that changes will continue to occur, particularly in light of the wide variety of proposals now being advanced, such as those contained in the proposed "Drug Regulation Reform Act of 1978."

It would be a difficult task to assess the impact of all the recent proposals. Not only are there a large number of proposals, but many of them express only objectives and are not specific in their operational content. Even ones that are well specified may represent such a large change from past practices that it would be difficult to predict the effects of the proposed change.

An assessment of many of the proposed changes would require detailed data about the process of pharmaceutical innovation. Prior to the research conducted by William Wardell, Louis Lasagna, and myself for the National Science Foundation there was very little published information on the fate of NCEs in the development process or on the cost of pharmaceutical R&D by the stage of development. Even though data similar to that collected during this research are essential to the evaluation of some of the proposed regulatory changes, it is recognized that the assessment of many of the current proposals requires additional types of data depending on the nature of the specific proposal. Moreover, if one is attempting to evaluate a proposal prior to its enactment, one may be forced to make strong assumptions regarding some aspects of the impact of the proposal. As an illustration of methodology as well as the importance of analyses of changes, the remainder of this section is devoted to an evaluation of one recent proposal.

The Health Research Group has proposed that all normal animal tests be conducted before a drug is allowed to enter clinical testing. It is contended that the current preclinical trials do not provide adequate protection for the individuals who participate in the testing of a new drug. Under the current test sequence all NCEs have been screened in short-term animal toxicity tests prior to the start of human testing. However, some NCEs that enter clinical testing are later discovered to have adverse effects on some animals used in the long-term animal tests. Although opinions vary, there is no comprehensive data on the extent of harm that these NCEs may have caused to individuals participating in clinical tests. Likewise little has been done to assess the effects of the proposed change on pharmaceutical R&D. It was beyond the scope of the present study to address the extent to which test subjects are harmed by NCEs that have adverse effects on animals. The impact of the HRG's proposal on the economics of pharmaceutical research in the United States was investigated.

Although a major change in testing requirements may result in international changes in the location of R&D, the initial analysis was designed to measure the impact on testing conducted entirely in the United States. Thus the initial analysis was limited to an investigation of the effects of the proposed change in testing sequence on the time and cost involved in pharmaceutical development in the United States. Changes in expected U.S. development times or costs will have implications for the level and international location of pharmaceutical R&D.

Since the regulatory change to be investigated has not been implemented and cannot be considered a simple extension of similar past regulatory changes, it is not possible to empirically measure the effects by observing the pharmaceutical R&D process during two different periods. However, by making what seem to be realistic assumptions concerning a few key parameters in the altered testing environment and by using empirical data from the existing development process, estimates of the effects of the proposed changes can be constructed.

Following the discussion of the assumptions the procedure to estimate the effects of these proposed regulatory changes is described.

The proposal at issue would require that all normal animal tests be performed prior to the start of clinical trials. This means that the long-term animal tests would be performed prior to phase I clinical tests instead of being conducted concurrently with phases II and III, as is the case for most current NCEs. Since our initial interest is in the effect of this change on the costs and time requirements for the development of NCEs in the United States, we shall assume that all testing is done in the United States and that the NCEs to be tested are the same under both the current and the proposed regulatory environments. Hence we will be comparing the cost and time requirements for testing the same cohort of NCEs in the United States before and after the proposed regulatory change.

One of the major effects of the proposed change in the testing sequence would be to increase the amount of animal testing performed on a cohort of investigational NCEs and to reduce the amount of clinical testing. Currently less than a third of NCEs investigated in humans are subjected to long-term animal tests. Under the altered testing sequence all would enter long-term animal testing but some NCEs that would enter clinical trials under the current test sequence would be dropped prior to clinical testing as a result of the animal test findings. The crucial question for our analysis is the determination of the testing points at which unsuccessful NCEs will be dropped from testing.

Since many NCEs are currently dropped from testing prior to the start of long-term animal studies, it was necessary to make assumptions about the fate of these NCEs if they were initially subjected to long-term animal studies. Under the present testing sequences NCEs that have been given long-term animal tests may either advance to the stage of NDA submission, be removed from testing principally due to animal test results, or be removed from testing principally due to information from the clinical tests performed after the start of the animal tests. Data was collected to determine the percentage of NCEs that fall into each of the these categories for NCEs that reach the stage of long-term animal studies. However, some NCEs dropped principally as a result of human test results while the long-term tests were in progress may have had evidence uncovered later in the animal tests that would have resulted in their suspension; thus the measured failure rate for animal reasons is subject to some downward bias.

There is no way of empirically determining the long-term testing results on the NCEs that do not reach this stage. The NCEs in question have all been subjected to the pre-IND short-term animal tests and have been dropped from testing as a result of clinical test findings. One reasonable assumption is that if these NCEs were initially subjected to long-term animal studies the percentage dropped prior to clinical studies would be equal to the current ratio of NCEs dropped as a result of long-term animal test findings to the total of NCEs dropped after the beginning of long-term animal testing. An alternative assumption would be that the long-term animal results for these NCEs would be the same as that of all NCEs that have been subject to long-term animal testing; that is, the NCEs that reach the NDA submission point should be added to the base. This would reduce the percentage of NCEs that would be assumed to drop from testing during long-term animal studies in the altered sequence. However, since the estimated rate of failure due to animal studies is biased downward due to the concurrency of the animal and clinical tests, the first assumption probably results in a more plausible estimate.

Implicit in the discussion of suspension of NCEs from testing based on particular test results is the assumption that the decision to suspend or continue the testing of an NCE following some adverse animal test results will not be affected by the absence of clinical data under the altered test sequence. Currently the firms' project managers can judge the seriousness of adverse animal results in light of the partial clinical test results. Without this clinical information project managers may change their decisions; however, it is not obvious that they will be more or less prone to continue the testing when they face adverse animal results in the abasence of human test results.

It is also assumed that the same set of NCEs will ultimately reach the NDA submission stage under the altered test sequence as under the current sequence. Again one could generate arguments that more or fewer NCEs would emerge, depending on one's perception of the errors that firms make in eliminating potentially successful NCEs based on limited adverse data.

This list of assumptions is rather lengthy because we are trying to make predictions about a regulatory environment that has not been implemented. Basically the current testing environment in the United States is being compared to one with an altered testing sequence that results in more long-term animal tests and fewer clinical tests, but eventual outcome in terms of the number of NCEs that reach the NDA submission stage is held unchanged. Once this basic analysis is done, one could alter some of the assumptions or consider the likely effects of this change on the R&D decision of firms.

The first step in the analysis of the effects of the proposed regulatory change is to estimate the probability that an NCE will reach particular testing phases under the proposed sequencing. An NCE that has been selected for further investigation after completing short-term animal pathology tests must first complete long-term animal tests. Thus all NCEs of concern will enter this stage. Of the NCEs entering long-term animal trials concurrently with clinical trials under the present testing sequencing, 55 percent will not reach the NDA submission point and 50 percent of these nonsubmissions were due principally to long-term animal test results. If under the altered sequence a similar 50 percent of the NCEs that eventually fail to reach the NDA submission stage (87 percent of the total NCEs advancing past short-term animal studies) do so as a result of long-term animal tests, then 43.5 percent of the NCEs entering long-term animal trials will not enter clinical trials.

The clinical test results will further eliminate NCEs from consideration for marketing. It was assumed that the percentage of the NCEs entering the long-term animal studies that will eventually reach the NDA submission point will be the same as the NDA submission percentage for NCEs currently entering clinical trials. Thus 13 percent of the original entrants will reach the NDA submission stage, and the other 43.5 percent will be dropped from testing during the clinical phases. Currently 50 percent of drugs entering clinical trials are dropped during phase I testing. This represents 57 percent of the NCEs that enter phase I but do not reach the stage of NDA submission. If a similar percentage applies to the eventually unsuccessful NCEs that enter Phase I clinical trials under proposed test ordering, then 25 percent of the original cohort will be dropped following phase I, leaving 31.5 percent to enter phase II.

Under current testing sequencing 31 percent of the post-IND NCEs are removed from testing during phase II testing. Some are removed as the result of the concurrent long-term animal tests and would not be in phase II studies under the proposed system. Similarly some of the NCEs currently dropped in phase II prior to the start of long-term animal tests would be eliminated prior to phase II testing. Since the failures due to long-term animal results have already been removed, only 15.5 percent of the original cohort will fail during phase II, leaving 16 percent of the original cohort for phase III testing. The probabilities of reaching each stage of the testing process under the existing and proposed regulatory environments are summarized in table 11-7.

For the purpose of estimating the expected testing cost under the altered sequence we shall assume that the sequencing change will not affect the cost per phase for those NCEs that enter the testing phase. This allows us to estimate the expected testing costs per NCE entering long-term animal testing by

Table 11-7
Probability of an NCE Entering Testing Phases under Current Testing Sequence versus Proposed Sequence with All Animal Tests prior to Clinical Tests

Tests	Current Probability	Probability with Revised Sequence
Phase I	100	56.5
Phase II	50	31.5
Phase III	19	16
Long-term animal	29	100

multiplying the probability of entering a testing stage by the current average cost for that stage. This is done in table 11-8. The total outlay per NCE entering long-term testing is very similar to the outlay per NCE entering clinical trials under the current testing sequence. However, the time pattern of expenditures will be different. To calculate the effect of the proposal on the capitalized value of testing costs, the timing of the expenditures must be estimated.

For the NCEs that enter clinical trials no significant change in the duration of each phase following the sequencing change is expected. There may be a slight increase in the average duration of phase II or phase III, since NCEs for which testing was stopped during the middle of one of these clinical phases as a result of adverse animal data will not enter these phases in the new sequence. The existing duration times for the clinical phases is used to construct the development time profile.

The average duration of long-term animal tests is currently three years. If these tests are required prior to clinical testing there would appear to be a three-year delay in the start of clinical trials. However, some reduction in this delay is possible. It may be possible to overlap the long-term animal tests with the short-term animal toxicity studies. Firms need not begin all their long-term animal tests at the same time, and the firms may currently find it to their advantage to delay some of the tests. Currently the long-term animal tests are usually completed before the end of the phase III clinical trials, so firms face little likelihood of delaying their NDA submission date when they postpone some long-term test. However, under the proposed sequencing, delays in long-term animal testing will delay the start of clinical tests. In the absence of changes in the long-term animal tests the delay probably will be less than three years. A two-year delay in clinical testing is used for the estimated time profiles. This is

Table 11-8
Expected Expenditures per NCE Entering Long-Term Animal Studies by Testing Phase under Proposed Test Sequence
(in thousands of 1967 dollars)

Testing Phase	Probability of Reaching Test Phase	Average Cost for Testing during Phase	Expected Expenditure per Phase (2) × (3)
(1)	(2)	(3)	(4)
Long-term animal	100	420	420
Phase I	56.5	166	94
Phase II	31.5	881	278
Phase III	16	1546	246
Total			1038

probably a very conservative estimate of the delay, since long-term studies required recently have been of longer duration. Any future changes in long-term test requirements will have further effect on this delay time.

Combining these duration times, the probability of an NCE's reaching a testing stage, and the average cost per testing stage results in the expected time profile of expenditures per NCE entering long-term tests shown in figure 11-4. For comparison the expected expenditure profile for the current test sequence is also shown.

The value of these expenditures capitalized to the expected marketing point has been calculated using interest rates of 5, 8, 10, and 15 percent.

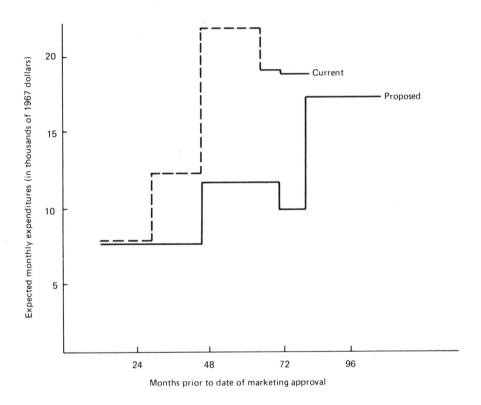

Figure 11-4. Expected Monthly Expenditures per NCE Entering Long-Term Animal Test under Proposed Sequence and per NCE Entering Clinical Trials Under Current Sequence, Measured from Date of Market Approval (in thousands of 1967 dollars)

Although there was virtually no difference in the expected expenditures per NCE tested, the lengthening of the development process and the higher cost of the initial testing phase under the reordered sequence combine to make the capitalized value of the expenditures higher under the proposed sequence. For low interest rates this difference is only about 10 percent. However, if the higher interest rates are selected, the difference is on the order of 20 percent, as shown in table 11-9.

The two-year delay in the date of marketing approval will also increase the capitalized value of the discovery costs allocated to each NCE by a factor equal to two years' additional interest charge on this investment. For our estimates, that utilize an 8 percent rate of interest this would imply an approximate one-sixth increase in the capitalized discovery cost per NCE tested. The estimated capitalized testing and discovery costs per NCE tested for the current and proposed sequence are presented in table 11-10.

The delay in the time of marketing approval and the increase in capitalized value of R&D costs per marketed NCE would have several implications for pharmaceutical innovation, should this proposal be implemented. The increased investment required to develop a drug for marketing will in itself discourage the development of new therapies. Even if research were to continue at the same level in the United States, there would be a two-year delay in the introduction of new therapies which will have consequences for the health of the public.

The pharmaceutical firms would also be affected by the delay in the date of marketing approval, which reduces the effective patent life for new drugs. NCEs that have been marketed in the past five years have received marketing

Table 11-9

Expected Cost by Development Phase per NCE Entering Long-Term Animal Tests Capitalized to Point of Marketing Approval Using Alternative Discount Rates

(in thousands of 1967 dollars)

| Testing Phase | Capitalized Expenditures for Alternative Interest Rates | | | |
	5%	*8%*	*10%*	*15%*
Preclinical animal toxicity	153	201	241	380
Long-term animal	614	770	896	1309
Phase I	128	154	175	238
Phase II	354	410	452	575
Phase III	284	310	329	380
Total excluding preclinical	1390	1644	1852	2502
Total including preclinical	1533	1845	2093	2882

Table 11-10
**Discovery Costs and Testing Expenditures per Marketed NCE Capitalized to Point
of Marketing Approval Using Alternative Discount Rates Under Current and
Proposed Test Sequence**

	Millions of 1967 Dollars				*Millions of 1976 Dollars*			
	5%	*8%*	*10%*	*15%*	*5%*	*8%*	*10%*	*15%*
Current sequencing								
Post-IND tests plus preclinical animal toxicity	11.2	12.9	14.1	17.5	20.5	23.6	25.8	32.0
Allocated discovery cost using three-year allocation period	13.1	16.6	19.6	29.2	24.0	30.4	35.8	53.4
Total	24.3	29.5	33.7	46.7	44.5	54.0	61.6	85.4
All animal test prior to clinical								
Post-IND tests plus preclinical long- and short-term animal tests	12.3	14.8	16.7	23.1	22.5	27.1	30.5	42.2
Allocated discovery cost using three-year allocation period	14.5	19.5	23.9	39.4	26.5	35.7	43.7	72.1
Total	26.8	34.3	40.6	62.5	49.0	62.8	74.2	114.3

approval approximately twelve years prior to the expiration of their patent.[6]
If NCEs were to face a two-year delay in marketing approval, the effective
patent life would fall to around ten years. This reduction in the period during
which firms have exclusive marketing rights will affect the receipts they obtain
from a successful R&D project. While the innovative firm currently enjoys a
marketing advantage past the patent expiration date due to its ability to establish
its branded name for the product, this source of return is being eroded by the
recent repeal of antisubstitution laws in many states. This means the effective
patent life is becoming more important to firms, and alterations in the length of
the effective patent period will have a greater effect on the return to R&D investments.

The combination of somewhat higher expected costs per marketed NCE and the decline in expected receipts that would occur under this proposal will mean a reduction in the overall profitability of R&D if the same numbers of NCEs are tested. Firms will be less willing to conduct research in areas where the potential market is small, and we would expect a decline in the level of pharmaceutical R&D.

Although these estimates were made under the assumption that the same NCEs would be tested following the implementation of the proposal, it is unlikely that this would occur. Firms could avoid some of the increase in cost by conducting clinical trials abroad and then do research in the United States only on the NCEs that were not screened out in the initial trials. While this strategy could probably reduce the expected testing expenditures per NCE, it is likely to result in a further delay in the marketing approval point since the long-term animal tests would not begin until after the early foreign clinical trials.

The reordering would reduce the number of individuals involved in clinical trials but by a relatively small percentage. Most of the clinical trials that would be eliminated are phase I trials involving small numbers of patients for relatively short durations. Under the assumptions of this study there would be approximately a 15 percent reduction int he number of drugs reaching the large-scale phase III trials (16 percent of the total versus 19 percent currently). Of course, to the extent that the proposed testing sequence eliminated drug development, there would be a further reduction in human testing. Currently I know of no evidence on the extent of possible harm to test subjects. Obviously this information would have to be weighted in an overall assessment of the petition.

Another factor not considered is the effect of the reduction of drugs tested in humans on the number of serendipitous therapeutic discoveries made in the process of clinical trials. Some pharmacologists noted this as one of the sources of potential loss from a reordered sequence.

While the analysis in this section cannot conclusively answer the question whether the changes proposed in the HRG petition are desirable, it does point to an adverse impact on the incentive to innovate.

Summary

Prior to the research reported in this chapter there was very little published information about the cost and time requirements for developing an NCE. Most of the existing estimates of the cost of developing a marketed new chemical entity were based on a division of the annual R&D expenditures by the annual flow of new products. This method of calculating average costs would be appropriate if the development process were short enough that one could reasonably assume that the annual flow of new products resulted from expenditures that year. However, the average clinical development times for new pharmaceuticals is on the order of six or seven years and the preclinical research prior to development extends several years earlier. Thus any estimates of the dollar outlays per NCE will be biased by any increasing or decreasing trends in R&D expenditures. Moreover, since the expenditures are made over a period of years prior to the marketing of a new drug, one should capitalize the expenditures. Finally, some new products are licensed from foreign firms, and only a portion of the R&D expenditures on these products will appear as R&D expenditures in the United States.

To overcome some of these difficulties it was decided to calculate the expected development times and costs from information on the development times and costs of a representative sample of new chemical entities that had been tested in humans. The sampling procedure was designed to produce an estimate of the post-IND expenditures on an average cohort of NCEs.

Several firms supplied information by phase of development on a sample of their NCEs that we selected. The responses to the same questionnaire were used to calculate the time spent in each phase and the probability that an NCE would reach the later phases.

Estimates were also made of the length of time NCEs remain in active testing. The attrition rate of NCEs from testing was found to be very high. The distribution of NCEs that remained in active testing was closely approximated by an exponential function with a delay rate of 42 percent per year. After approximately fifteen months, testing had been suspended on half the drugs entering clinical trials. This early rapid decline in the number of NCEs continuing in testing indicates the importance of the early human trials as a screening procedure.

Information was obtained on the reasons for suspending the testing on NCEs. For the NCEs that were dropped early, the decision was virtually always based on information obtained in human trials. However, as the products advanced in testing and long-term animal studies were undertaken, the information that led to the decision to suspend a drug from further testing was rather evenly divided between results of human trials and animal studies.

This information made possible the construction of an expected expenditure profile for each NCE entering human trials. The average expenditures on each NCE entering human trials was estimated to be approximately $1 million in 1967 dollars, or $1.8 million in 1976 dollars. Since approximately only one NCE in every eight that enter clinical trials will eventually reach the market, this figure should be multiplied by eight to obtain the expected dollar outlay per marketed NCE.

Since these expenditures are spread over several years, the outlays were capitalized to the time of marketing approval. To do this the actual pattern of expenditures was estimated. The expenditure per month for the development of an NCE increases as the testing progresses from the early human trials to the larger-scale clinical tests, but the number of products that remain in active testing declines. The attrition of NCEs from active testing roughly offsets the growth of monthly expenditure per remaining product during phase I and phase II, with the result that the expected program expenditure for clinical trials on a cohort of NCEs remains fairly constant over this range. By the time phase III is reached, the attrition rate dominates, with the result that expected expenditures decline. This pattern of expenditures was capitalized to the expected approval point, based on an 8 percent rate of interest. This resulted in an estimated post-IND development cost of $14 million in 1967 dollars, or $24 million in 1976 dollars, per NCE approved for marketing.

This estimate is for post-IND expenditures and does not include the expenditures for pre-IND activities. The annual expenditures by firms for discovery research are roughly the same as the expenditures during the development phase. If these early costs are allocated to the marketed NCEs and capitalized to the marketing approval point, they add $17 million in 1967 dollars, or $30 million in 1976 dollars, to the R&D costs per marketed NCE. The total cost is thus $30 million in 1967 dollars, or $54 million in 1976 dollars. The estimates presented are higher than existing estimates based on the division of R&D budgets by the number of successful products. This difference is due chiefly to the exclusion of licensed products and the capitalization of expenditure flows.

The data that we collected on the cost and time requirements for NCE development can be used to predict the effects of some proposed changes in the regulations governing pharmaceutical development. One proposed change that we investigated using these data was a proposal advanced by the Health Research Group to change the sequence of tests. In particular they suggested that all normal animal tests be completed prior to the start of testing in human subjects. We used our information on the reasons for suspension of testing under the current testing sequence to estimate the point at which unsuccessful NCEs would drop out of testing in the proposed altered test sequence. We then estimated the expected expenditure pattern and the time required to develop an NCE. The reordered testing resulted in an increase in the capitalized value of the expected expenditures, and such a sequence would result in a two-year delay at the minimum in the introduction of new products. This would have an effect on the time at which patients could receive the new therapies and on the length of time in which a company would be able to market its product under patent protection. Currently this effective patent life is approximately twelve years; thus the reduction in effective patent life would have a significant impact on the return to R&D received by the firm.

Notes

1. Ronald W. Hansen, "Regulation and Pharmaceutical Innovation: A Review of the Literature on Monetary Measures of Costs and Benefits,"

University of Rochester, Center for Research in Government Policy and Business, working paper GPB-77-9, June 1977; Henry Grabowski, *Drug Regulation and Innovation: Empirical Evidence and Policy Options* (Washington, D.C.: American Enterprise Institute, 1976).

2. William M. Wardell, Mohammed Hassar, Sadanand N. Anavekar, and Louis Lasagna, "The Rate of Development of New Drugs: Entry into Human Testing, and Regulatory Disposition in the U.S., of New Chemical Entities Produced by the Pharmaceutical Industry from 1963 to 1975," in "Technological Innovation and Government Regulation of Pharmaceuticals in the United States and Great Britain," Louis Lasagna, William M. Wardell, and Ronald W. Hansen, a report submitted to the National Science Foundation, August 1978.

3. Christopher Cox, "A Statistical Analysis of the Success Rates and Residence Times for the IND, NDA, and Combined Phases," in "Technological Innovation and Government Regulation of Pharmaceuticals in the United States and Great Britain."

4. David Schwartzman, *Innovation in the Pharmaceutical Industry* (Baltimore: Johns Hopkins University Press, 1976), p. 70.

5. Mark Schankerman, "Common Cost in Pharmaceutical Research and Development: Implications for Direct Price Regulation," in ed. S. Mitchel and E. Link, *Impact of Public Policy on Drug Innovation and Pricing,* (Washington, D.C.: American University, 1976).

6. This is based on data collected by the Center for the Study of Drug Development, University of Rochester.

Appendix 11A: NCE Development Questionnaire, February 1976

**Instructions and Explanatory Notes
for Completing Questionnaire**

This questionnaire is a follow-up to the one sent earlier by Dr. William Wardell. The purpose of this questionnaire is to obtain economic information about the development process for new chemical entities. As with the earlier questionnaire, all responses will be kept strictly confidential and will not be used in any manner in which your firm can be identified.

This survey asks for greater detail about the drug development process. However, to keep the survey manageable, we are requesting information on a preselected subsample of the NCEs that you have tested. The code numbers for these NCEs have been listed in column 1 of the questionnaire and are the same code you used for the earlier questionnaire. (For the few firms receiving a revised code from Dr. Wardell, these numbers refer to the revised code.) If you did not retain a copy of your earlier responses, we will be happy to provide you with one. We did not automatically mail one out in order to reduce the chance that the confidentiality would be breached.

The questionnaire has been divided into three parts. The first part relates to the time spent to develop both successful and unsuccessful NCEs. Part II concerns the costs of development by NCE testing stages, and part III relates to annual research and development expenditures. An explanation of specific items in each part follows. Thank you for your cooperation.

Ronald W. Hansen

Part I: Testing Time Profile

Drug # (1)	Animal Pathology-Toxicity Test		Phase I Clinical Tests		Phase II Clinical Tests		Phase III Clinical Tests		Long-Term Animal Toxicity and Carcinogenicity Test		Date Testing Suspended for Nonmarketed NCEs
	Date Begun Mo./Yr. (2)	Date Completed Mo./Yr. (3)	Date Begun Mo./Yr. (4)	Date Completed Mo./Yr. (5)	Date Begun Mo./Yr. (6)	Date Completed Mo./Yr. (7)	Date Begun Mo./Yr. (8)	Date Completed Mo./Yr. (9)	Date Begun Mo./Yr. (10)	Date Completed Mo./Yr. (11)	Month/Year (12)

Notes: Column 1, Drug Number: The numbers in the column represent a subsample of the NCEs reported in the earlier questionnaire. This subsample has been selected so as to reduce the data collection requirements and still provide a representative picture of the total industry. If, in addition, these data, or some of them are easily accessible for your other NCEs, we would welcome their inclusion.

Columns 1-12: Self-explanatory.

Questions 13-16. Please use a separate sheet for each NCE.

Part I, page 2

Drug #_____

Question 13: If testing was suspended for this NCE (a) what were the major factors responsible for the suspension (for example, toxicity, difficulty in showing efficacy)? If toxicity was a contributing factor, please identify the nature of the main toxicity.

(b) Which type of test was primarily responsible for this decision (for example, human versus animal; large-scale clinical)?

Question 14: Were additional tests required after the submission of the original NDA for this NCE? If so, were they designed to defend the original NDA or to establish new indications for the NCE? Please indicate whether the tests were animal or clinical and the time period covered by these tests.

Question 15: If the NCE was first taken into humans abroad, how much foreign testing was performed prior to the U.S. IND filing? If possible express in terms of the U.S. testing phases.

Question 16: When was NCE first marketed abroad? (month/year)

Part II: Testing Expenditure Profile by Stage of Development

Drug # (1)	PreClinical Animal Path-ology-Toxicity Test Cost for this NCE (2)	Phase I Human Testing Costs (3)	Phase II Human Testing Costs (4)	Phase III Human Testing Costs (5)	Animal Test Costs Incurred after Start of Human Tests (6)	Foreign Test Costs Prior to U.S. Testing (7)	Other Please Explain (8)

Notes: Column 1: Same as column 1, part I.

Column 2: If preclinical animal pathology-toxicity costs are not retained for the NCE requested, please supply an average preclinical test cost for the relevant years.

Columns 2–7: We expect that some firms will be unable to cost out the testing stages or unwilling to release such information. In theses cases, we would appreciate whatever descriptive data you can supply about the nature, extent, and duraction of the tests.

For post-IND animal tests, please indicate the object of the studies, the numbers and types of animal used and the duration of the tests. For clinical tests, please indicate the object of the study, the number of subjects, whether healthy or patients, whether performed on an in- or out-patient basis, and the duration of the tests.

For firms able to supply cost data, the methodology used in treating overhead charges or in-house versus out-of-house expenses is likely to differ. We would appreciate a brief description of methods used or items included in arriving at the cost figures. Please indicate whether the figures supplied include overhead or other nondirect cost charges.

Part III: NCE R&D Expenditures, Annual Aggregate Expenditures

Year (1)	Total NCE R&D Expenditures in U.S. (2)	Basic Research Expenditure in U.S. (3)	NCE Preclinical Animal Path/Tox Testing Expenditures in U.S. (4)	NCE Clinical Testing Expenditures in U.S. (5)	Total NCE R&D Expenditures in Great Britain (6)	Basic Research Expenditure in Great Britain (7)	NCE Preclinical Animal Path/Tox Testing Expenditures in Great Britain (8)	NCE Clinical Testing Expenditure in Great Britain (9)	Total NCE R&D Expenditures outside U.S. and Great Britain (10)	Basic Research Expenditure outside U.S. and Great Britain (11)	NCE Preclinical Animal Path/Tox Testing Expenditures outside U.S. and Great Britain (12)	NCE Clinical Testing Expenditures outside U.S. and Great Britain (13)
1962												
1963												
1964												
1965												
1966												
1967												
1968												
1969												
1970												
1971												
1972												
1973												
1974												
1975												

Notes: Report only the R&D expenditures for the discovery and development of new chemical entities. Basic research expenditures should include all outlays on activities prior to the point at which NCEs enter the preclinical animal pathology and toxicity tests.

Please note if British expenditures are reported in terms of pounds or dollars.

If your reporting year does not coincide with the calendar year, please note the period covered, for example, June 1, 1962-May 31, 1963.

If the methodology used in arriving at cost figures differs from that used in part II, please indicate the nature of the differences.

Commentary
Gail E. Updegraff

Overview: *Some questions are raised about the data and methodology used by Ronald Hansen. Included in these questions are criticisms of the comparability and representativeness of the data and some suggestions to improve these data aspects in future studies. The policy application that Hansen makes of his work is lacking in relevance to the major issues of debate on proposed changes in drug regulation, legislation, and policy. The applicability of Hansen's work to the emergence of a drug issue of considerable impact is discussed.*

Hansen's work is of interest and importance for two reasons. Although he estimates something that has been examined in several previous studies, namely development costs and times for new chemical entities (NCEs), he does so with a set of data that was seldom analyzed for widespread distribution. Second, and perhaps of greater import, is that Hansen did not stop with his estimates of development costs and times; he engaged in policy analysis by applying them to a proposed regulatory change. However, the estimates were applied to a proposed policy alternative that is not likely to receive much consideration from either the Food and Drug Administration or Congress. Unfortunately this is merely another example of a problem that has persisted for decades, if not centuries: a lack of communication between government and academia.

Before returning to the policy application of Hansen's estimates of development time and costs, a few questions and constructive criticisms of his work seem in order. How comparable are the research and expenditure data submitted by the fourteen U.S. pharmaceutical firms? We do not know how the data were compiled by the firms, nor can we have the data reviewed by an entity such as the Food and Drug Administration; thus it would seem logical to ask some basic accounting questions on the questionnaire when it is not possible to muck around in the raw data. Nevertheless Hansen's estimates seem reasonable compared to previous work in this area. In fact, I wondered whether he wasn't a bit disappointed when he discovered that the estimates were comparable.

What, if any, bias resulted from a 56 percent response rate? That is, do such things as economies of scale and management styles play an important role for development costs and times? I am not sure whether any adjustments to the data are necessary or feasible, but an aggregate profile of such things as the size of the firms and their productivity in terms of NCEs compared to these same characteristics for the nonreporting firms might have been enlightening.

Now for the more interesting side of Hansen's paper: the application of his findings to a public policy alternative. I feel that Hansen should have picked a more "relevant" policy alternative to analyze, and I feel the report of the Review

189

Panel on New Drug Regulation, commonly referred to as the Dorsen Report, offers a more relevant alternative: namely its recommendation that FDA release safety and efficacy data submitted by drug firms when seeking permission to market a drug. The panel believes its recommendation would result in increased public scrutiny of FDA decisions on new drugs and that it would reduce duplicative testing (I find the second reason for the recommendation increasingly hard to understand).

An obvious question is why this policy option is more relevant than the one analyzed by Hansen. To answer this question, one has to examine how policy evolves, or seems to evolve, in Washington, D.C., a city, that often appears to thrive in illogical thought. (Please keep in mind that this paper was written in Rockville, Maryland, the headquarters of the Food and Drug Administration).

The answer to the question starts with the fact that usually some entity first makes or strengthens a case at a congressional hearing. This entity may be part of Congress, the executive branch, industry, or a consumer organization. Next, the executive branch or Congress can decide to press the issue by calling for an ad hoc study or review, as was the case when the Department of Health, Education, and Welfare created the Review Panel on New Drug Regulation. If the results of this study or review indicate the need for action, then the executive branch or Congress takes note and begins work on estimating the consequences of the report recommendations and the resources and legislation necessary to implement them. And so it was that the release of safety and efficacy data became an important issue for the federal government.

The FDA is presently, with the aid of a contractor, examining the impact that safety and efficacy data release could have on drug innovation and pricing; we are particularly concerned with the impact on innovation. The study will examine, for drugs only, three basic options for releasing safety and efficacy data: (1) a user time lag (that is, the data could be used by another pharmaceutical firm only after a specified time period); (2) a user fee (the user would have to compensate the firm that developed the data); and (3) full and immediate disclosure with no restrictions on the use of the data. There are, of course, many variations for each of these options.

A model that estimates the change in the discovery of NCEs over time, for each of the three basic options, has been developed. Clearly any such model requires the input of qualitative as well as quantitative data. And, like any other study, this one has its weaknesses. For example, are NCEs really an appropriate measure of productivity? And then, of course, there is the continuing debate over the relationship between research and development expenditures and the discovery of NCEs. This debate had to be taken into account in the study, since the relationship is one of the linkages in the model.

To elaborate on the study approach, the model estimates the change in research and development expenditures that result for individual pharmaceutical firms when data on their marketed NCEs are released. This model is based on

changes in the prices and revenues of a selected sample of NCEs introduced
into the marketplace since the 1962 amendments to the Food, Drug, and
Cosmetic Act became effective. These price and revenue changes came about
because substitute drugs were gaining earlier access to the market than was
possible when safety and efficacy data were not released. In addition to the
statistical analyses and study reviews that are part of this study approach,
interviews of several pharmaceutical firms that have a large research and development effort have been conducted, as have interviews of medical officers
and their supervisors in the Food and Drug Administration's Bureau of Drugs.

It seems logical that data on the cost of discovering and developing
specific NCEs would be useful in analyzing the Dorsen Report's recommendation on safety and efficacy data release. The cost of discovering and developing
specific NCEs could be compared with the revenue figures for these NCEs
after they have lost whatever protection they derive from the FDA's treatment
of safety and efficacy data as a trade secret. This comparison could be expected
to help determine whether it would have been profitable to develop the NCEs
if it was known that the safety and efficacy data would be available to competitors in some manner.

It appears that work such as Hansen's can be quite helpful to the FDA and
others in assessing the impact of policy alternatives. Certainly one application is
evident. My hope is that we can bridge the gap that often separates good economic analysis such as Hansen's and the application of this analysis to policy
options that are relevant to the executive branch and Congress.

**Part IV
The Economic Impact of
Government Regulations**

12 Economic Regulation of Prescription Drugs

John R. Virts

Overview: *Much of the economics literature on the regulation of the pharmaceutical industry has concentrated on safety regulation as it relates to the Food and Drug Administration, especially the 1962 drug amendments. A new focus is provided by looking at other types of regulation that are affecting the industry. These regulations, which can be thought of as demand-side related as contrasted with the supply-side regulation by the FDA, include formularies, maximum allowable cost programs, repeal of antisubstitution laws, and monopsony purchase programs.*

The provision of drugs under Medi-Cal is a vendor payment system where the government does not directly supply products but finances their supply. Under this type of system the director of the drug program is faced with various stimuli and constraints that in essence place him in a no-win situation. On the one hand the "social" mandate is for his program to serve the target population; in doing this both the number of recipients and their utilization (the number of units received per recipient) increases, in turn increasing the total costs of the program. On the other hand, state legislators and administrators are applying pressures to reduce program costs. Faced with this situation, the program director searches for ways to achieve cost reductions without directly affecting utilization. Thus he focuses on drug prices as a means of reducing costs. His rationalizing this effort is reinforced from external stimuli indicating that drug prices are "wrong." As data reveal, drug prices are not really the problem. However, as costs continue to escalate, unless the director's focus changes, he will seek to further constrain drug prices. In California this resulted in the imposition of a price control program with reimbursement made only for products whose prices were equal to or below an allowed maximum. Since this measure, predictably, failed to contain costs, the regulatory drift became even greater when a proposal was made for a monopsonistic central procurement program.

A complete cost-benefit analysis of regulation is necessary. Such analysis must go beyond short-run considerations such as program cost and must include long-run costs and benefits for all government and all society.

There is economic regulation of some aspects of the market for prescription drugs. It occurs more on the state and local than the national level—although forces for regulation have definitely been national. The forms of regulatory action have names like formularies, maximum allowable costs, repeal of antisubstitution laws, volume purchase plans.

Society today is stumbling into economic regulation of prescription drugs. One role for economic analyses is to judge whether more or less economic regulation is better for society than the status quo. I fear that economists and economic analyses are failing to fulfill that role. As the corporate staff economist of one of the major firms supplying prescription drugs, I am indicting myself as much as anyone else: I do not know how to get the job done. Maybe I'm expecting the impossible. Maybe my reading of the public policy implications of economic analyses is wrong. We want that policy to be formed on the basis of good analysis, but how to do this and by whom it should be done are questions whose answers are far from clear.

Public policy issues concerning drugs, whether they are economic or safety or social in nature, must be examined in the context of total health care. Prescription drugs, after all, are tools—means of achieving a desired result. A crucial characteristic of analysis for public policy purposes is that drugs are not only alternatives for each other in health care regimens but are also alternatives for other sorts of health care.

Table 12-1 shows some data on health care over the last decade. Let me draw some inferences from these data:

1. If increasing health care costs are the problem, the prices of drugs are clearly not a significant cause. Prescription drug usage per capita has increased, but the decline in prices relative to the average of other prices has more than offset this increase.

Table 12-1
Increases in Health Care Spending, FY1965-FY1976

Sources of Increases	Amount of Increase
Population growth	$ 8.2 billion (8.2%)
General price inflation[a]	47.5 billion (47.3%)
Medical care price inflation[a]	7.0 billion (7.0%)
Utilization per capita	37.6 billion (37.5%)
Total increase	$100.3 billion (100%)

Notes: Prescription drugs: 8 percent health care costs (declining), 22 percent increase in prices (1967 = 100), total CPI: 82 percent; contribution to inflation: significantly less than average.

Health care: 8.6% of GNP (rising).

[a]General price inflation and medical care price inflation, 102 percent (1967 = 100).

2. If increasing health care costs are the problem, even the inflation of average health care goods and service *prices*, beyond the level reasonably expected as a pass-through of general inflation, has contributed less over the past decade than population growth. (A recent Congressional Budget Office analysis concludes: "It is clear that the CPI overstates medical price changes" (Congressional Budget Office *Expenditures for Health Care: Federal Programs and Their Effects*, August 1977, p. 5, footnote).

3. The largest single contributor to increasing health care costs has been general inflation.

4. The largest single contributor to increasing health care costs associated with health care has been that the per capita consumption of health care goods and services in real terms nearly doubled from 1965 to 1976.

Table 12-2 shows the FY1976 flow of expenditures to health care providers as recorded by standard Social Security Administration data. An aspect of health care spending essential to establishing the context for public policy formation is how the consumer financed his consumption of health care. In 1929 patients paid directly for about 89 percent of the care they received. By 1965 this had fallen to 53 percent. In 1975 it was 34 percent. Despite the CPI-measured relative increase of health care goods and services prices of some 10 percent (over total CPI)—labeled by the CBO as an overstatement—the trend toward increased payment of costs by insurors and government resulted in a

Table 12-2
U.S. Health Care Spending, FY1976
(in millions of dollars)

Category of Spending	Amount
Personal health care	
Hospital care	$ 55,400 (59.6%)
Physician's services	26,350 (28.4%)
Drugs and drug sundries	11,168 (12.0%)
Subtotal	92,918 (100.0%)
Other[a]	27,513
Total personal health care spending	120,431
Other health care expenditures[b]	18,881
Total U.S. health care spending	$139,312

[a]Dentists, eyeglasses, nursing homes, other professionals, and so forth.

[b]Public health, research and medical facilities construction, expenses for prepayment and administration.

substantial reduction of the real "price" perceived by the consumer as relating to his consumption of goods and services. From 1965 to 1975 these numbers would indicate a reduction of 30 percent in the real, relative price of consuming health care among the consumers' choices.

This reduction of apparent price to the consumer of health care by insurance or various forms of government subsidization is a highly important aspect of the economics of this sector. It has not had equal impact on all health care goods and services, as the data in table 12-3 show.

There are, of course, many problems of definition and interpretation of numbers like these. Examples: not all prescription drugs are included in the drugs and drug sundries line because such products are also administered in hospitals and doctors' offices and the costs are included as expenditures with those providers; in addition, products other than prescription drugs are included in the drug and drug sundries category. However, these numbers are good enough for the purpose at hand—especially since they are all we have.

The most likely analytical justifications for economic regulation of goods or services consumed in an environment and structure like that for the provision of health care are (1) some basic structural defect somewhere that should be exposed by the proper use of the I-O framework as modified to fit the case and (2) such heavy subsidization of the consumer or provider that no economic choice decisions could be decisive enough to achieve reasonable allocation of resources except by regulation.

Much has been written and spoken about health care in general relative to the consumer subsidization, zero-price, insurance phenomena not leading to proper allocation of resources relative to the efficiency achieved by pure economic choice. It is not our task to analyze the rest of the health care situation where numbers like these should probably raise questions, at least questions about how much of the growth in per capita utilization has been economically

Table 12-3
Personal Health Care Expenditures, FY1976
(in millions of dollars)

Expenditure	Total	Direct Payment	Private Insuror, Philanthropy, or Industry	Government
Hospital care	$ 55,400	$ 4,909	$20,095	$30,396
Physicians' services	26,350	10,198	9,520	6,632
Drugs and drug sundries	11,168	9,423	722	1,023
Other	27,513	14,568	2,580	10,365
Total	$120,431	$39,098	$32,917	$48,416

efficient. Relative to prescription drugs, however, these numbers contain sufficient evidence to support the contention that the total of private and government subsidization of individual transactions has not yet reached the point where these forces need be feared as the cause of the need for economic regulation. National health insurance of certain forms could generate such problems, as could some forms of extended subsidization of the prescription drug costs of segments of the population. I hope that society will consider the need to overcome the effects of subsidization with regulation among the costs of things like National Health Insurance.

Economic regulation of drug costs, prices, and consumption exists and is increasing, even though neither type of economic-analytical justification seems to call forth the need for, or predict cost-effectiveness of, economic regulation. That is, neither the subsidization of consumers nor the I-O criteria approach generates conclusive signals for regulation, yet economic regulation continues to increase.

A combination of experience, intuition, and analysis convinces me that such regulation has not yet intruded on enough of the total U.S. market to deny future society a viable, innovative, competitive set of firms to provide improving drug therapy with some semblance of close-to-optimum economic efficiency. However, the regulation continues to increase, and which straw will break the camel's back is hard to predict.

Table 12-4 lists the generic types of regulatory devices that are in place or are being proposed in various states. (The basic designs of Medicare and Medicaid have been largely responsible for state and even local economic regulatory

Table 12-4
Outline of Regulatory Initiatives and Generating Forces

Initiatives	Forces
I. Economic regulation	
Formularies	Program limitation
(Lists of "allowable drugs")	Cost-effectiveness
	Budgets
Maximum allowable cost (MAS or MAIC)	"Inexpensive duplicates"
Multiple-source drugs (generics)	
Volume purchase plans (VPP)	Achieve volume discounts
State purchases total supply	
"Contract" distribution	
II. Deregulation	
Repeal "antisubstitution" laws	MD sensitivity to cost-benefit
Permit pharmacist to select alternative	
generic drug	

initiatives. Medicare, the federal health insurance for the elderly, leans heavily on financial intermediaries like Blue Cross to monitor utilization and costs. In turn, reliance is put on "prudent buyer" kinds of criteria or even "usual and customary charge." Medicare is heavily hospital oriented, and hospitals are heavily nonprofit institutions and importantly state and local government institutions. Medicaid is a federal program to share states' costs of providing health care, partly of the states' choosing, to both certain categories of other welfare recipients and, optionally, to the states' definition of "medically indigent"—under federal guidelines. Medicaid has a large impact on states' budgets.)

A formulary is, in essence, simply a listing of the drugs that can be dispensed to program recipients. Many individual hospitals—public, nonprofit, and proprietary—have had such lists for a number of years. The costs incurred in hospital practice have been minimal because of the ease of both "prescribing around" the formulary, the relatively small population of prescribers and patients affected, and the relative ease of influencing and changing decisions. In some hospitals the benefits have probably been significant, especially in terms of inventory management and purchasing efficiency.

In the setting of a statewide Medicaid program, the formulary becomes a form of regulation. In effect, exclusion from the formulary establishes a list of drugs that cannot be dispensed. These excluded drugs are in the state's distribution system for all non-Medicaid patients. Physicians presumably are prescribing them or there would be no reason for the exclusion. Some are excluded by the elimination of the payment for the treatment of some conditions, as in the exclusion of antiobesity agents or oral contraceptives. In others the exclusion is on the basis of some group's perception, or analysis, of positive cost-effectiveness of included drugs along with the lower cost-effectiveness of the excluded. Although not labeled "regulators" the state departments that construct formularies, in effect, become regulators through such cost-effectiveness judgments and the presumably scientific judgment about patient welfare embedded in the cost-effectiveness analysis. In still other cases sets of drugs are excluded from formularies on the strictly short-term budget consideration that the program cannot afford these particular drugs and the embedded hope that whatever alternative doctors and patients elect will be affordable.

The maximum allowable cost (MAC) or maximum allowable ingredient cost (MAIC) type of regulation is even more easily recognized as economic regulation than formularies. So-called single-source drugs are usually the newer chemicals or product forms still subject to patent. As a rule there is a single fairly observable price for such a single manufacturer's product, and the formulary concept allows the regulators to determine whether the product will or will not be paid for if ordered by a physician and dispensed to a patient. Most drugs—but not necessarily most of the sales of prescription drugs—are not subject to patent restrictions, and multiple manufacturing sources are available to pharmacies, who must be paid by the state. Manufacturers' versions frequently carry brand names that the physician uses to communicate his order to the pharmacist. The prices asked by different manufacturers can be very different, especially list prices.

In states using the MAC or MAIC concept (and soon in all states, since MAC is being put in place as a federal regulation) the pharmacists' compensation by the state consists of two parts: the cost of the ingredient dispensed and a "fee" set by the state to presumably cover business and professional costs of operating and dispensing. The MAC or MAIC concept—operating in the area where many possible prices may be paid by a pharmacist for either a particular brand or for alternative brands or for nonbranded goods—simply limits the ingredient charge reimbursed by the state for dispensing an amount of a particular drug. The effect of such simple-sounding regulation is identical to that of a formulary; certain manufacturers' products are excluded from use on strictly the regulatory judgment that prices above some regulated level represent non-cost-effective merchandise. Presumably, of course, for non-Medicaid drug business, either markets are moving toward such a judgment or private consumers are being ripped off, depending on one's biases or analysis.

So far volume purchase plans have been only proposed and not put in place. Under such a plan the state becomes in effect the single purchaser for the drugs supplied to Medicaid recipients, and wholesalers and retailers are paid handling charges or fees for services rendered to the state. To the economist words like monopsony and public utility regulation are possibly more relevant to economic understanding than volume purchase or central procurement. At the very root of this program of regulation is again the idea of "formulary": include the drugs that are right and cost the right amount. Behind this thinking at any stage— formulary, MAC, or VPP—lies the implicit assumption that markets are not properly determining prices and that doctors are not properly prescribing in view of the need for relative cost-effectiveness to be a part of any economic, resource allocation decision. Without either this implicit assumption or an equivalent analytical conclusion, these forms of regulation are instantly recognizable as not only unnecessary but counterproductive.

The final political thrust that falls somewhere among the forces toward economic regulation of prescription drugs is repeal of the states' so-called anti-substitution laws. I am not sure whether this subject belongs in a discussion of regulation or not. If it does, I think deregulation is a better word to describe it, at least to economists.

Just after World War II the flow of patented discoveries of therapeutically useful new chemical entities began to become great. The number of therapeutically useful agents became large, with agents and therapy also growing more complex. These forces generated a need to fix exactly which of the professionals, doctors or pharmacists, would decide which agent the patient would receive. "Copies" of patented new agents were also present in the marketplace.

Patent holders and pharmacists saw great advantage in having a state law prohibiting substitution to bolster patent law and professionalism. The FDA's inspection and other regulatory capabilities were far less pervasive and sophisticated than today.

I believe every state passed a law prohibiting a pharmacist from making any form of substitution for the specific drug, manufacturer, and trademark prescribed by the physician. These laws joined the existing emphasis on prescription-only drugs and the licensed-physician as the only prescriber to further restrict the free flow of therapeutic drugs in a marketplace. The antisubstitution laws, however, in no way inhibited the physician's freedom to prescribe nor the patient's or pharmacist's freedom to communicate to the physician any knowledge or desire concerning the physician's prescribing.

A proper regulatory analysis of antisubstitution law is a complex problem requiring the full gamut of economic analysis. Imagine a young mother calling the family pediatrician in the late evening about a young child with a high fever. The doctor's questions and the mother's answers limit the causes to those susceptible to treatment by a drug that we'll call therapeutic class X. This class of drugs contains three entries; two are single source, probably patented with no manufacturer licenses, and their effective actual transactions prices to the area's pharmacists are like those in table 12-5. If the physician in calling in the prescription specifies either the Beta or Gamma product, with or without the brand name, the concept of antisubstitution in no way applies in any state. The pharmacist could inform the physician that he had no stock of the prescribed product, and the physician might prescribe one of the other drugs. But in no state could pharmacist substitution be legal or ethical. If the physician prescribed Alphacycline, the generic name, the pharmacist would dispense his selection of brand in any state regardless of the status of antisubstitution law. Only if the physician prescribed brand A, would the legal-economic question of substitution arise. The following cases can be distinguished.

1. Antisubstitution law: pharmacist must dispense Brand A.
2. In all states, if the physician says (or writes) do *not* substitute, or words to that effect, the pharmacist must dispense brand A.

Table 12-5
Prices per Hundred Pediatric Doses

Alphacycline		Betacycline		Gammacycline	
Brand A	$11.00	Brand E	$7.00	Brand F	$21.00
Brand B	7.00				
Brand C	6.50				
Brand D	6.00				

3. In some states, if the patient requests a lower-priced drug, the pharmacist may substitute the brand mutually agreed on with the patient.
4. In some states the pharmacist may substitute the brand of this choice, unless the physician or patient has forbidden substitution.
5. In one state the pharmacist is required to substitute a lower-priced brand if he has it in stock and unless the physician or patient has forbidden substitution.

The repeal of antisubstitution question seems to be principally the question: who has and can best use the relevant therapeutic and economic information? The potential economic consequences of deregulation or regulation in the form of government's requiring least-price dispensing are relatively straightforward. If antisubstitution markets behave efficiently, the question becomes one of behavior under an alternative. Empirical evidence to date indicates very little impact on consumer prices under any alternative observed in practice. This, of course, raises the problem of consumer-voter expectations where antisubstitution law has been debated with a great deal of rhetoric and publicity.

These regulatory forms, combined with the FDA's regulation of what chemicals can be marketed as drugs and for what uses they can be promoted—regulation akin to airline route regulation—form the bulk of the economic regulation of prescription drugs. The remainder of this presentation will deal with a sort of combination analysis some political, some social, some psychological, with some economic analysis always lurking in the background and jumping up front on occasion.

If there is a difference between the practice of academic economists in policy areas and business economists in policy areas, it is partly related to the need of the business economist to develop broader explanations and understandings. He needs to deal with the why of the real world as he gropes toward policy-level understanding. He is also living in a world of advocates and frequently must supply the needs of advocacy even though he is never asked to exceed the bounds of his professional judgment.

The academic economist should try to read the remainder of this presentation with the firm understanding that it is written by a business economist. I hope the presentation is free of both advocacy and rhetoric; but clearly it must be colored by an environment in which analysis is useful only if it generates more effective action than action without analysis.

In bureaucratic jargon Medicaid is a vendor payment program. It is designed to redistribute income by transfers-in-kind to recipients who qualify. Government has decided to give away, but what we desire to give away must come from the same sources as the identical goods and services consumed by the paying public. In this way we attempt to assure quality and program cost-effectiveness. Government, then, need not supply but only finance under a vendor payment plan like Medicaid. The conflicts inherent in such schemes may be leading toward the economic regulation of prescription drugs. (Is it possible for such vendor payment programs to survive in the long run?)

It is useful to speculate on the situation faced by a vendor payment program director whose environment includes the stimuli outlined in table 12-6. We might choose specifically the California Medi-Cal drug program director for our speculations. I suggest this for only two reasons: first, most of the data from this program are readily accessible thanks to the cooperation of the Medi-Cal administrative staff; and second, because Medi-Cal has led the way in initiating regulation.

In today's world everything seems to add to the perception that prices, all prices, are wrong. This is particularly true of the prices we pay, and program directors must pay for what others consume: *he* pays. And no matter what he does, his program costs too much. Tax revenues cannot possibly do everything that needs to be done; we must cut, we will cut. But a program director cannot decide who does not receive, nor even the kinds of things received. Nevertheless he receives orders like, Cut that budget 10 percent. Most especially must he stop program cost increases.

Suppose he calls in an analyst. He might get a preliminary report like that summarized in table 12-7. These data are from the total U.S. programs, but any state program analysis would be similar but with smaller magnitudes of expenditure and increases. Let's use California's Medi-Cal drug program data and follow through a summary of an analysis. Table 12-8 presents some history and results. In the period 1971-1976 in this California program there was a formulary in place which effectively excluded many drugs from use. In addition, a maximum allowable ingredient cost (MAIC) was established for reimbursement of pharmacists for dispensing many multiple-source products. The state promoted cost-consciousness with both recipients and providers, particularly with regard to the size of prescriptions. Under Medi-Cal's pharmacist reimbursement scheme with a negotiated fee paid for each prescription filled, the fee-cost

Table 12-6
Stimuli Acting on Vendor Payment Program Director

Price Differentials	Budget constraints
Media Reports, Analyses	Legislative contraints
Congressional hearings	
"Economists"	
Conventional wisdom	
Big companies	
Multinationals	Program costs "out of
Prices wrong	control": always

Table 12-7
Sample Preliminary Report of Medicaid Increases, 1970-1976

	Total Increases	*Drugs*
Expenditures	$4.8b to $14.2b (196%)	$403m to $944m (134%)
Eligibles (recipients)	11.5m to 15.4m (34%)	Same
Dollars per eligible	$417 to $922 (121%)	$35 to $61 (74%)
Prices (BLS-CPI)	+46%	+11%
Real dollars per eligible	+31%	+54%

Note: Sources of increases: utilization per capita, 52 percent; number of eligibles, 35 percent; prices, 13 percent (with no correction for general inflation (+43 percent).

per unit of medication declines with larger prescriptions. Physicians were urged to write larger prescriptions thus requiring fewer refills.

A principle point exposed by the data in table 12-8 is that programs can lead to changes in patient-provider actions by both incentive-disincentive direction and by marketing. As intended, prescription sizes grew markedly in Medi-Cal from 1971 to 1976, and the pharmacist fee per unit of medication consequently declined while the fee per prescription rose. Medi-Cal instituted a new form of regulation—MAIC or MAC—while continuing formulary restrictions. Program prices paid for drugs, however, increased marginally more than the national average increase. Table 12-9 continues the analysis.

In the period 1973-1976 Medi-Cal achieved a significant saving by a shift

Table 12-8
Analysis of Medi-Cal Drug Program, FY1971-FY1976

	1976 (1971 = 100)
Medi-Cal Data	
Prescription price (unweighted)	143.6
"Pills" per prescription (unweighted)	147.4
Ingredient cost per pill[a]	112.7[b]
Fee cost per pill	91.7[b]
National BLS, CPI for prescription drugs	110.9

Notes: Prescription price = ingredient cost + fee; average prescription price = number of pills per prescription × [ingredient price per pill + fee per pill].

[a]Manufacturer's price

[b]Prescription price per pill, 102.2

Table 12-9
Analysis Medi-Cal Drug Program, FY1973-FY1976

Total program cost increase	64.0%	
Increase in number of pills dispensed	57.1%	
Increase in cost per pill	4.5%	
1976 index of prescription price per pill	114.0	(1973 = 100)
Savings due to increased cost consciousness or consumption pattern	8.4%	
Index of general inflation (CPI)	129.6	(1973 = 100)

Note: Program cost increase (before savings) = increase in prescription price per pill × increase in prescription size × increase in number of prescriptions per recipient × increase in California's population × increase in Medi-Cal participation rate.

in the mix of drugs consumed by recipients. Whether this resulted from a change in the mix of conditions treated or continuing promotion of cost consciousness or a combination of these factors is not known. In any event the 1976 program costs were 8.4 percent lower than they would otherwise have been without the change in product mix.

As the data of table 12-10 show, Medi-Cal drug program price increases of 14 percent during a period when general inflation caused the total CPI to increase by 30 percent accounted for only 22.6 percent of the program cost increase from 1973 to 1976. Yet drug price regulation was a primary direction for control exercised by Medi-Cal throughout the period. This control was of the MAC-MAIC type buttressed by formulary restrictions. Changes in regulatory

Table 12-10
Analysis of Medi-Cal Drug Program, FY1973-FY1976: Contributions to Increase (before Savings)

Price	22.6%
Pills per prescription	32.5
Number of prescriptions	35.3
Population	6.0
Participation	3.6
Total	100.0%

Note: 1.640 ÷ 0.926 = 1.140 (price) × 1.208 (pills per prescription) × 1.228 (number of prescriptions per recipient) × 1.036 (population) × 1.022 (participation).

force were principally in the MAC-MAIC direction impinging, of course, mainly on the so-called multiple-source drugs. However, the average price of a Medi-Cal unit of medication rose 14.0 percent during the period while the national average increase was 11.6 percent. Furthermore, the products' prices subject to MAIC rose 24.7 percent, significantly more than the prices paid by Medi-Cal for the drugs whose prices were *unaffected* by the MAC-MAIC regulation!

Table 12-11 summarizes the vendor payment program director's position after his analyst has presented his report. Frustration must rule the day! A plot of the drug program history for Tennessee—before and after the imposition of MAC—reveals a picture virtually identical to that in figure 12-1, but with an interesting possible addition. For at least the first few years after the leveling period of a year or so, the rate of program cost growth has seemed to increase faster than the earlier rate.

By way of conclusion I would like to discuss the concept of VPP which to date has been the most advanced position of regulatory drift. It has not been instituted in any state, but it has been discussed in several and actively proposed in California with characteristics as outlined on table 12-12. Active planning in California has ceased after lengthy debate.

The decision to implement regulation should always be made after analysis of the cost-effectiveness of regulation relative to at least the next-best perceived alternative. Failure to pass this test should lead to rejection of proposed regulation. The status quo should be a useful alternative for analysis.

Table 12-11
Vendor Payment Drug Program
Director's Position

Conflict
    Stimuli: Prices wrong
    Analysis: Price increases not the problem
Mission: Control cost increases
Programs from stimuli (weak political forces)
    Formularies
        Eliminate high-priced drugs
        Eliminate types of drug
        Limit to acceptable price
    MAC type
    VPP
Programs from analysis (strong political forces)
    Monitor eligibility
    Monitor utilization

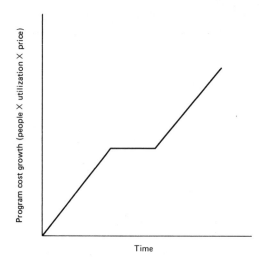

Figure 12-1. Any Program that Controls Increases in Costs by Eliminating Certain Drugs Because of Their Price Must Continually Eliminate More and More Drugs.

Table 12-13 outlines some of the considerations for cost-effectiveness analysis of a regulatory program like VPP. A minimum requirement for such analysis is that consideration must be given not only to departmental costs overseen by a program director and his staff, but also to all government costs and to costs to society influenced by the program and its administration. VPP in California was interesting because it was first tested only against department

Table 12-12
California VPP Program Outline

1. State negotiates for bids for drugs from manufacturer.
2. Wholesaler orders from manufacturer; state is billed.
3. State pays fee to wholesalers to service drugstore orders of "special label" drugs.
4. State pays pharmacist a fee for dispensing to Medi-Cal recipient; fee is increased to cover physical inventory and administrative costs.
5. State maintains audit trail that accounts for units dispensed on prescription, wholesaler inventories, and retailer inventories against state payments to manufacturers for shipments to wholesalers.

Table 12-13
Regulatory Cost-Effectiveness Considerations (Example: California VPP)

Analysis from departmental viewpoint (program director)

New departmental budget against forecasted budget under old system

Will product limiting plus price reduction gains outweigh costs of administration? (Balance discounts and fees, inventory management and costs, data processing costs.)

Additional analysis from total government viewpoint

Costs incurred in other departments

    Quality assurance

    Legal costs, liability

Additional analysis from societal viewpoint

Impact on distribution of goods through drugstores

What are effects of exercise of monopsony power after limiting product selection (economic, therapeutic)?

(If such regulation is limited to Medicaid or a state or two, little damage is likely even if compctition is workable or better.)

---

considerations. Only after more complete analysis of costs external to the proposing department was it shown not to be cost-effective.

Determining the socioeconomic impact of programs such as Medicare and Medicaid is a complex task. If the administration of such programs does result in economic regulation, then the total spectrum of costs of such regulation must be included not only in studies of the relative cost-effectiveness of different patterns of administration, but also in studies of the cost-effectiveness of the programs themselves. Program and regulatory cost-effectiveness studies are challenging areas. The need for such studies seems clear, even though neither the technology for study nor the mechanism for achieving political impact is especially clear. Since the future structure and output of the entire health care economic sector hangs in the balance, the need cannot be ignored. This paper has attempted to present a preliminary justification for the need for such analysis and some of the elements that will need to be included as related to the economics of the pharmaceutical industry.

Commentary

Oswald H. Brownlee

John Virts has described for us the various elements of the increase in health care expenditure from 1965 through 1976 and has indicated that very little of this increase can be attributed to the relative price of health care. The relative average price for prescription drugs has actually declined; that is, prescription drug prices received by drug manufacturers have risen less than the general level of prices of all goods and services. Also expenditures for prescription drugs constitute a relatively small portion (less than 10 percent) of total personal health care expenditures.

Why, then, have prescription drug prices been a favorite target for government regulation? One reason might be that third-party payments for drugs make up only about 16 percent of total expenditures for drugs and sundries in the fiscal year 1976, whereas such payments constituted nearly 90 percent of outlays for hospital care and more than 60 percent of expenditures for physicians' services. If someone else seems to be paying the bill, one doesn't worry so much about its size. The population receiving Medicare and Medicaid are less important as taxpayers than they are as recipients of publicly financed medical care, and they have been strong supporters of measures that they believe would reduce the prices that they would pay for drugs.

Another reason might be the generally low repute of the drug manufacturers in the eyes of the public. One could easily infer that the industry is employing the same public relations firms as those used by the petroleum industry and the government of Chile. The public image of the industry, first created by the Kefauver Committee hearings in the early 1960s, is one of a group of robbers making high profits from selling harmful or ineffective products. Almost every criticism of government regulation of the industry is labeled by the industry's critics as emanating from the industry itself.

Still another reason may be the manner in which regulation is formulated and administered. Virts has emphasized that one could view the bureaucracy as one in which each department attempts to minimize its own costs or to maximize the attribution of benefits to itself and therefore tries to shift its costs elsewhere—ot other departments or to the nongovernmental sector—and to convince the public that it is conferring benefits that may have originated elsewhere. He has cited the California drug regulatory process as conforming to this view. I wish to cite two other examples. The Internal Revenue Service spends about $2 billion annually to collect federal taxes, but taxpayers incur costs of at least $50 billion in keeping records, completing forms, making payments and all of the other activities associated with complying with the tax system. Collection and compliance are substitutes, and the taxpayers need do less if the IRS does more. Minneapolis minimizes its costs of snow removal by heavy salting of the streets. Taxpayers' autos collapse in piles of rust after five winters of driving on these salted streets. The city's snow removal costs are kept low at the expense of rapid depreciation of citizens' cars.

I agree that regulation would be improved if there were accurate cost-benefit analyses of various regulations. However, there is probably not sufficient agreement with respect to the nature of the costs or the benefits to secure the kind of improvement one might expect. For many reformers the outcome is graded according to the degree of equality achieved in the distribution of income, often without respect to the amount of income to be distributed. I find it difficult to rationalize National Health Insurance on grounds that do not weigh very heavily the expected increased equality in the distribution of health care. Whether greater equality will actually be achieved has not been adequately analyzed. If greater equality is the outcome, it might come from reducing the care given to some persons. If it is achieved by raising the levels provided to some without reducing those provided to others, one can legitimately question whether such an outcome represents best use of our resources.

Some of our mishaps are the result of politicians' failure to recognize the important side effects of regulatory legislation. The 1962 amendments to the Food, Drug, and Cosmetic Act increased the costs of developing and marketing new drugs in a manner that I do not believe was anticipated by Congress. It expected that the use of ineffective drugs would be diminished but did not consider that the process that eliminated some ineffective drugs might also eliminate some effective ones as well. Medicaid and Medicare were expected to improve the health care of some parts of the population, but it was not generally realized that such could not be done without reducing the care for others unless the total supply were substantially expanded. Cost controls will only make things worse. In addition to restricting supply, the distribution of available services may be wasteful in requiring the recipients of health care to spend more time in line or in cutting red tape. Time can only be wasted; it cannot be transferred.

Virts made a statement to the effect that we are stumbling into price controls in health care. I would like to conclude my comments by describing my experience with the repeal of state antisubstitution laws. First, let me describe briefly why such laws were enacted and why they are being repealed.

If you were to go to a bar and order a glass of Budweiser, you would not expect the bartender to serve you a glass of Bub's beer instead, and there are no laws specifically prohibiting such action. I suppose that you could bring suit against the bartender, if such an event occurred. Laws specifically prohibiting the substitution of one brand of drug for another were enacted by all of the states in the early 1950s *at the request of pharmacists* because the substitution of one brand of drug for another is more difficult to detect than the substitution of one brand of beer for another and can be much more harmful to the patient.

The new laws generally repeal the antisubstitution provisions enacted

twenty-five years ago; some also require the pharmacist to substitute a generic
drug for a brand name one, under certain conditions. The new situation is
analogous to your going to a bar, ordering a Budweiser, and having the bartender give you a Bub's beer and an additional nickel in change, informing you
that the beer he has served you has been found by Ralph Nader and the Federal
Beer Agency to be chemically and nutritionally equivalent to Budweiser and to
cost less.

Much of the testimony at the various legislative hearings dealt with the
chemical and bioequivalences of various drugs. Pharmacologists are no more
inclined to agree about how their evidence should be interpreted than economists are inclined to agree about what causes inflation. However, the consensus
seemed to be that patients' health would not be improved and might be harmed
by the new laws. Also since pharmacists generally insisted that their fees for
filling prescriptions with generic drugs should be no lower than those for filling
prescriptions with brand name drugs, the reduction in the cost of the drug bill
resulting from the new laws will be trivial.

The legislative committees seemed to understand that the new laws would
not improve health and would not significantly lower paitents' drug costs.
Why did they send such bills to the floors of their chambers? The legislative
action was usually rationalized by statements such as "The pharmacists and the
old people want this law. It won't do much harm, so let's pass it."

Perhaps the laws won't do much harm in the short run. But their sponsors
gave the "public" the impression that marked reductions in drug costs would
result from such legislation, and this will not be the outcome. The "public,"
disappointed by these laws and believing that they have been taken again by the
industry, will demand stronger and more harmful controls. The long-run cost
can be large.

I don't wish to generalize from this experience. I relate it to support
Virts's contention that we are stumbling into price controls. This may jeopar-
dize the freedom of funding for drug innovation.

13 The Economic Consequences of Regulating without Regard to Economic Consequences

Oswald H. Brownlee

Overview: *The director of the Bureau of Drugs, FDA, has stated that the agency does not pay any attention to economic consequences and that the law does not ask it to do so. However, the agency's actions do have important economic effects that cannot be ignored in evaluating drug regulation. This paper summarizes some of the economic effects of the 1962 amendments and discusses some of the economic impacts of limitations on drug advertising and promotion, the proposed weakening of patent rights, the regulations that diminish the value of a brand name after the patent expires, and proposals to reveal the "trade secrets" of drug firms. All will reduce the extent of drug research and development by private firms.*

Some current and proposed regulations affecting the pharmaceutical industry are designed to have certain economic consequences. Price controls such as maximum allowable costs, central procurement of drugs, and the payment of drug bills by third parties are designed to affect the costs of drugs to those who receive them or pay for them. Other regulations were designed with no or little regard for their economic consequences.

J. Richard Crout, director of the Bureau of Drugs, Food and Drug Administration, stated:

> A third thing I would emphasize strongly is that the Food and Drug Administration regulates health policy, not economic matters. That is terribly important to understand. We do not pay any attention to the economic consequences of our decisions and the law does not ask us to. That does not mean that FDA people are necessarily lacking in breadth as people or that we are blind to costs, but the point I emphasize strongly is that our decisions deal solely with the safety and effectiveness of chemicals intended for use as drugs. Because its primary mission is the regulation of health matters, the FDA is a different kind of regulatory agency from many of the others in the government.[1]

Although this statement seems to refer to the manner in which the FDA administers the laws, the attitude that regulations have economic consequences

215

that can be ignored or that it is not government's function to consider such
consequences characterizes much of the regulatory process. I wish to talk about
some of the economic consequences of some of the regulations designed without
reference to their economic effects.

The Effects of the 1962 Amendments on the
Introduction of New Drugs

The 1962 amendments to the Food, Drug, and Cosmetic Act gave the Food and
Drug Administration the power to prevent a drug from being made available to
the public until the FDA was satisfied that its curative powers were those
claimed by its seller. Since 1938 the FDA has had the power to require that a
marketer of a new drug prove that the drug is safe for human consumption.

Since 1962, the proof of both safety and efficacy rests with the industry.
The cost of obtaining a new drug approval has increased markedly since 1962
because of (1) the expanded information requirements imposed on the applicant for a new drug approval and (2) the increase in the time that elapses
between the initiation of the development of a new drug and its approval by the
FDA.

Because a manufacturer was not certain until its evidence had been submitted and evaluated by the FDA whether the method for obtaining and evaluating
evidence was admissible, much of the industry has chosen to try to induce the
FDA to state how it would prefer the data be obtained and to follow this
procedure, even though it might be inefficient, rather than having to hit a
moving target.

Estimates of the magnitude of the increased cost of research and development vary. Harold Clymer estimated that the cost in 1971 was about ten times
the pre-1962 cost. Allowing for a doubling of the cost of research resources, the
real cost would be about five times as large. David Schwartzman estimates that
costs must now be incurred for ten years instead of five years before revenues
begin to flow in from the marketed drug. Also he estimates the annual outlay
(1974) to be about ten times as large as it used to be in 1960. His undiscounted
and undeflated estimate for 1974 is thus about twenty times that of 1960.
Either estimate, however, indicates a big jump in real costs.[2]

The additional costs would be expected to reduce the flow of new drugs.
This reduction has been dispassionately described by Wardell and Lasagna.[3]
It is estimated that the rate of introduction of new drugs was cut by about 60
percent. New drug sales were reduced by about the same amount, and there has
been a delay of at least two years in the marketing of drugs that have been
introduced.

The changes since 1962 are not attributed by all analysts to the 1962
regulations. Many pharmaceutical companies welcomed the 1962 amendments

in the belief that these changes would silence the charges made during the hearings held by the Kefauver Subcommittee that the drug companies were producing harmful and ineffective drugs for which they were charging high prices and making exorbitant profits. (Similarly new regulations such as MAC are also held by some analysts to be potentially beneficial to the industry because of the greater public trust they would engender.) In fact, some pharmaceutical technical staffs have used tests more demanding than those required by the FDA, thus adding to the cost of drug research and development. Also it has been claimed that some of the delays in obtaining FDA judgments about whether a new drug could be marketed were due to the inadequate staffing, low morale, and poor organization of the agency. Some observers have implied that the 1962 regulations are thus not inherently so costly and that proper administration and cooperation between the industry and the FDA would make the additional cost of the 1962 regulations small. During 1973 and 1974 there was an increase in the number of new single chemical entities introduced by the pharmaceutical industry in comparison with the average of the five previous years.[4] Some have interpreted this as evidence of improvement in FDA procedures, but the numbers are still far below the average 1950-1962.

Some analysts have attributed the declining rate of pharmaceutical innovation to a kind of decreasing returns to research; that is, as in exploiting a natural resource where more costly mining or drilling must be undertaken as more ore or oil is obtained, the easy biological research opportunities are exploited first. The evidence for this thesis is not convincing.

Whether the industry has made testing more expensive than it could be, whether the FDA could do things more efficiently, and whether new drugs are naturally more costly to discover than they used to be, the 1962 regulations must be blamed for some of the slowdown in drug development. The outcome has been subjected to a cost-benefit analysis by Sam Peltzman.[5] The results of his investigation have been widely disseminated, so I will only briefly summarize them here. The costs are

1. Additional resources were used by the pharmaceutical companies and the FDA in testing and evaluating the results. This additional resource cost was excessive insofar as equally useful information might have been obtained at lower cost if the companies had been free to choose their own procedures. The FDA's costs were also increased, since the agency's work load was expanded. Peltzman estimates the additional cost to the FDA in 1970 as $15 million. He estimates that the companies' drug development costs were doubled by the 1962 regulations.

2. New chemical entities that otherwise would have appeared on the market did not appear, or their appearance was delayed. Most of the decrease in the number of new chemical entities approved was attributed by Peltzman to the 1962 amendments. The reduction in the demand for new drugs

(those derived from new chemical entities) occasioned by the decrease in approvals had (in 1970) a present value of $300 million to $400 million annually. Peltzman did not include in this estimate the loss from any reduction in the number of new drugs derived from already existing chemical entities, nor did he include the losses from deaths that might have been prevented and illnesses that might have been shortened had the flow of new drugs not been damped.

3. Old drugs commanded higher prices because of the reduced competition from new drugs. This loss is estimated at about $50 million.

On the benefit side is the reduction in ineffective drugs marketed. Peltzman believes this to be less than $100 million annually. Ineffective drugs did not survive the market test prior to 1962, and the FDA's screening did not significantly slow their disappearance. The estimated benefit assumes that harmful drugs would appear without the 1962 amendments but would not appear after 1962, and assigned expected values to their appearance.

A crude way of obtaining a similar loss estimate is to assume that the growth in drug demand depends on the number of new chemical entities introduced whether or not they have FDA approval and to assume that the regulations did not affect drug safety. The cost of complying with the regulations was about 5 percent of the retail value of drug sales, and the outcome is equivalent to imposing a tax of about 5 percent on the value of drugs purchased at retail, except that no one collects the tax. It is a deadweight loss.

Limitations on Drug Advertising and Promotion

A belief that has persisted since before the hearings of the Kefauver Subcommittee is that drug companies exploit their

> patent protection through expensive promotion campaigns in which extravagant claims for the effectiveness of the new drug were impressed upon doctors and (sometimes) patients. Since most doctors were thought to lack the pharmacological expertise necessary to evaluate new drugs, it was believed that they relied heavily on information supplied by the companies. . . . Moreover, they seemingly would have little incentive for a careful evaluation of drug company claims since prescription costs were borne by their patients.[6]

It was estimated that in 1968 the major drug companies spent approximately $600 million on promotion.[7] The amount spent on research and development in that same year was estimated by the National Science Foundation to be about $400 million, of which about 15 percent was classified as basic research.[8] Although the pharmaceutical industry has a high ratio of research and development expenditures to sales receipts, its ratio of promotional expenditure to sales is even higher.

The industry's promotional dollars are divided among several categories, with the largest share going to company detail men. One assumes that the companies would not spend money on detail men if they thought spending it in some other way would be more effective. According to studies conducted by M.K. Dresden, Jr., physicians indicated that detail men were by far their most valuable source of product information.[9] The belief in the influence of the detail men is also shared by the FDA. Again, I quote Dr. Crout:

> It has long been recognized that the industry-supported detailman is an important and influential source of drugs for practicing MD[s]. Drug labeling and drug advertising, which are closely regulated by FDA, also provide information.[10]

The magnitude of the industry's promotional expenditure and concern for the accuracy and reliability of the promotional claims have resulted in a growing number of regulations affecting the promotion of drug products. Most of the laws pertain to the content and presentation of drug advertisements. The Federal Trade Commission is charged with trying to assure that ads do not present false claims, but the pharmaceutical industry is subject to additional regulation by the Food and Drug Administration. The effect of the regulations is to make advertising somewhat more expensive than would otherwise be the case and perhaps to reduce the value of the brand name. Concern for the role played by the industry in providing drug information to the medical profession has generated proposals for further restraints on the activities of detail men. However, before describing what else might be in store, let us briefly indicate some of the requirements now in force.

Restrictions on Advertising

Any material distributed by a drug company about a drug, or in association with a drug, is subject to the labeling provisions of the Food, Drug, and Cosmetics Act. Presumably the FDA could require that the prescribing information—that which accompanies direct mailing, detailing, and advertising for the brand name— also accompany reprints from medical journals or monographs of any sort distributed by a drug company. The prescribing information must include "full disclosure," that is, it must reveal in its entirety the full content of the official labeling (the insert that accompanies every drug package). The regulations now in effect require that the promotion maintain "fair balance." If the advantages of a drug are indicated, the counterindications (what the drug may not be recommended for) must also be noted. The indications listed must be only those certified by the FDA.

The *label*—the printed material attached to, surrounding, or enclosed with a package; the *labeling*—any material (brochures, films, cassettes) prepared by the manufacturer that pertains to drug therapy and is seen by a physician; and *advertising*—printed promotional material that appears in a publication not prepared by the manufacturer—are subject to different regulations. Journal advertisements are, by regulation, allowed to use a condensed version of the full disclosure. However, the journal ads must usually run at least an extra page in length to include the required information. The FDA also requires that the generic name appear, on labels or advertisements, at least half as prominently as the brand name. The intent of this *generic-each-and-every-time regulation* is to reduce the value of the brand name.

A principal source of information to physicians is the *Physicians' Desk Reference,* a publication subsidized by the drug manufacturers in which drugs are classified according to use and the companies producing them. Its content is subject to FDA labeling regulations and must contain full statements about the drug. This manual is criticized because it does not contain all drugs and it does not contain price information.

Reactions of the Industry to the Constraints on Advertising

As one would expect, when one way of doing things is rendered less effective or more expensive, other ways that were previously less economic are used more intensively. The detail man becomes even more important, and the industry relies more on "professional education." This consists of such things as the sponsoring of conferences and seminars for doctors, dissemination of reprints of journal articles, and a host of activities classified as postgraduate education of medical practitioners. I cannot document the extent of this change, but the concern of some members of the regulatory fraternity over the effects of these activities suggests that the shift has been noticeable.

What More Is in Store?

The Detail Man. To critics of the drug industry, the notion that a prime source of information about drugs should be the detail man is abhorrent. It is akin to the fox being charged with guarding the geese. A staff member of Senator Nelson's Subcommittee (Ben Gordon, at a seminar given to the faculty of the College of Pharmacy, University of Minnesota, October 1975) has stated that the detail man should be eliminated and that information about drugs should be disseminated by a corps of personnel comparable to that employed by the

Agricultural Extension Service for the provision of information to farmers about agricultural technology.

The drug industry is not unique in using resources such as detail men to promote its products. Book salesmen visit college professors and tell them what their companies have in stock and are planning to publish. They also give free samples, as do (or did) the detail men, although professors may not pass them on to their "patients," as do the doctors. Producers of chemicals, machinery, aircraft, and other products employ chemists, engineers, and other personnel to describe their products to potential users. Neither the activities of these people, nor those of book salesmen, are attacked even though they are comparable to those of detail men.

The prohibition of detail men for drugs seems unlikely, in view of the repercussions that such a policy might have on other industries. However, that a governmentally supported corps of personnel will be available to provide drug data to physicians is not so improbable. It is likely that drug producers would devote less resources to detail men, since the productivity of detail men would probably decline. Also the value of a brand name would be less.

Drug Education. The virtually all-powerful influence of the drug industry is not confined to the educational effect of its advertising and promotion. It pervades the professional medical and dental journals and even the formal education of medical personnel. Let me again quote from Dr. Crout. The quotation is a long one, but Dr. Crout speaks more clearly for himself than I can speak for him.

> There is considerable evidence that the pharmaceutical industry plays a very important, perhaps a dominant, role in the post-graduate education of physicians, dentists, and other health professionals. This role of the pharmaceutical industry in supporting post-graduate medical education has increased rapidly in recent years and, in my opinion, is a problem deserving of national attention.
>
> Let me emphasize from the start that I do not consider this issue to be primarily a problem in drug regulation. While I will draw upon the experience of Bu[reau of] Drugs in citing a number of examples in this testimony, my remarks will also reflect views developed during two decades of personal experience as a student and a teacher of medicine before coming to FDA. I testify today as a concerned physician who believes that the growing influence of the pharmaceutical industry on medical education is a long-term threat to the integrity of my chosen profession. . . .
>
> From this point [the completion of his formal training] on, the physician is in large part left to his own devices to maintain and update his fund of knowledge. He can maintain his university contacts by joining a clinical teaching faculty. . . . He can also seek out any of a number of short courses sponsored by specialty societies and conducted in medical institutions.

He can also read the medical literature, attend medical meetings, and take advantage of a variety of audio-visual presentations, either in the privacy of his car, home, or office, or in staff meetings at his local hospital. . . .

It thus is not surprising that the drug industry is vitally interested in the educational materials the practicing physician receives. In view of the great financial resources available to the industry it should also not be surprising that it has come to support a large and growing proportion of such educational materials. . . .

It is less well recognized, however, that much of the written and audio-visual teaching material supplied to the MD on all medical subjects throughout his professional career is also supported by the pharmaceutical industry. This includes the vast majority of medical magazines which fill his mailbox, the clinical symposia that discuss specific drugs or general approaches to therapeutics, the audio-visual teaching systems he studies in his spare time, the films and closed circuit TV tapes he sees in his hospital conferences, and even the scientific exhibits and presentations by panels of experts he encounters at medical meetings.

This extensive underwriting of post-graduate medical education and communication by the drug industry has occurred primarily in the past decade, and is the problem I want to emphasize in this testimony. Let me note that while the drug industry has a natural interest in the post-graduate education of MDs, it is not alone in fostering this trend.

Pharmaceutical industry financing of such endeavors has been encouraged by medical institutions eager for attractive teaching materials, by respected investigators and clinicians eager to make their work and opinions more widely known, by practicing MDs under increasing pressure to participate in formal training to maintain licensure, and by medical societies facing growing demands to make such training available. These groups are well aware of the vast resources the industry has at its disposal, particularly in comparison with medical institutions and medical societies.

Make no mistake, modern educational materials are costly. There has been a growing sophistication in the techniques used to educate people, and the "old" methods—lectures, review articles, textbooks—are perceived by some as dull and tedious. Instead we now have "learning systems" generally involving films or videotapes accompanied by elaborate graphics and self-instruction materials. It may well be true that these newer kinds of materials can be prepared only with special subsidies (assuming their added value as educational instruments is worth the extra money).

There is a cost involved, however, in giving substantial control over that subsidy to the drug industry. That cost is the introduction of systematic bias. Without contending that industry-supported materials are regularly inaccurate, I believe that these sponsored materials are consistently tilted in the direction of therapeutic enthusiasm. There has been a rapid growth in expensive, slick audio-visual materials, conferences, symposia, and publications which have the appearance of independent, scholarly productions but which are in fact an integral part of the drug industry's overall promotional efforts, a more subtle part, of course, than straight-forward promotional materials like advertising.

Let me emphasize that the systematic bias I am describing does not arise because the medical authorities who contribute to these teaching programs present knowingly biased views because of pharmaceutical industry support. The problem is not that drug industry money corrupts medical experts, but rather that the industry sponsor can choose from among the many medical authorities on any given topic to support only those whose views already coincide with the interests of the sponsor. This ability of the pharmaceutical industry to select the medical author-ities it wishes to support is the basic cause of the biases we shall see. . . .

I also believe the growing proportion of medical communication that is supported by the drug industry threatens the integrity of the whole process of post-graduate medical education.[11]

Dr. Crout continues with examples from the medical literature—biased editorials, information on unproven uses of drugs, and support for brand name drugs. He discusses industry-sponsored seminars, videotapes, multimedia presentations, and scientific exhibits. He concludes with his observations on the role of regulation and proposed FDA guidelines. His recommendations are to exempt from the labeling requirements only material that passes the follow-ing five tests:

1. The material has been prepared solely for educational use and not with any intent that it be used for other purposes, such as sales to or distribution by the pharmaceutical industry.
2. The material is not promotional in nature taken as a whole and is in the form of balanced educational materials. For example, the material may not contain any significant emphasis on uses for drug products that are not approved by the FDA as safe and effective, that is, use for unapproved indi-cations or in derogation of required contrain-dications and warnings. Al-though the material may contain occasional references to such uses, such references may not be frequent or be given major consideration or impor-tance.
3. The material has been prepared independently, that is, the pharmaceutical industry has not participated in the preparation of the material and has not exercised editorial review over the content of any of the material.
4. The material covers a number of different drugs and does not support use of one particular drug or the drugs of a particular pharmaceutical company.
5. The material is not associated in any way with a promotional campaign for any drug product by the pharmaceutical firm supporting the exhibit. The material may contain reference to support by a pharmaceutical firm.[12]

Dr. Crout's solution to eliminating the influence of the drug companies on medical education seems to be to provide the medical schools with sufficient government funds so that they will disdain any support, direct or indirect, from other sources.

I cite Dr. Crout's views because they are not unique, and they are indicative of the kinds of new regulations that will be proposed.

The Economic Effects of Control over Drug Promotion

The typical large drug company engages in three more or less distinct activities: research and development, manufacture, and distribution. The effects of regulation on research and development have already been described. Its rate of return has been diminished, and the amount of it undertaken has been cut back. This outcome was desired by many people who believed that there was too much research on "me-too" products. The regulation of distribution activity will have a similar result, and it is one that many people also believe desirable. The view that it would be more efficient for only generic drugs to be produced, thereby eliminating "unnecessary" research and promotional activity, is a fairly common one. Research and promotion would be directed by the government. The drug companies would become manufacturers. In this view of regulation the outcome is desired for economic reasons even though it may be a by-product of achieving other ends.

The market can be viewed as an evaluator of methods of providing information, as well as a purveyor of information to buyers and sellers. If the information provided by the drug firms is useful and is not provided, obviously there will be a net social loss. Some of the substitute methods—the prescription drug extension service, for example—would, in effect, be a replacement of the companies' promotional activities by those of the government. Peltzman has viewed the 1962 amendments as a substitution of FDA information about drugs for some of the information obtained from the companies and the market, and he finds that the new information is at best no better than that previously obtainable and costs a good deal more.

I see no reason why the proposals to constrain drug promotion would not lead to an outcome similar to that from constraining the flow of new products. I assume that advertisers try to choose the most profitable level of such expenditure, although I am aware that measuring the effect of promotional activity is difficult. The value of advertising is in the information that it provides. If such information is useless, sales will be independent of the amount of it provided—or even inversely related to the amount provided if the advertising is misleading. Firms that did not advertise would be able to profitably sell their product, considered by consumers as a perfect substitute for the advertised one, at a lower price and drive the advertiser out of business.

The informational content of activities that are designed to be informative is clearly evaluated by the market. When *Consumer Reports* cuts its information about the quality of refrigerators and increases its reports on the sins of multinational corporations, it loses some subscriptions from people who want to know about refrigerators and gains some from those who want to hear more about the multinationals. The circulation of the *New York Times* is reputed to have grown less rapidly in recent years because its credibility as a news source fell. Drug promotion has an informational content. It is this feature that worries Dr. Crout. The informational content of cosmetic ads has always puzzled me, but my wife refused to use my mixture of vegetable fat and odorants that a consumer magazine assured me was the equivalent of a leading face cream, so I cannot say that the ads or the trademarks have no effect.

Assuming that the FDA or some other agency were put in charge of providing drug information *and* that the quality of such information was the same as that provided by present arrangements, would the government do it more efficiently? I cannot see that any great savings would result from having the *Physicians' Desk Reference* printed and distributed by the U.S. Government Printing Office or from having detail men paid by the County Pharmaceutical Extension Service instead of by the companies.

Drug Patents, Licensing, and Trade Secrets

Regulation of drug patents has definite economic objectives, and discussion of it does not properly fall within the scope of this paper. However, the effectiveness of many regulations designed to control prices depends on the rights associated with patents. The role of patent rights in encouraging discovery and development and what one could expect to happen as these rights are eroded is an interesting and important question. I will say a few things about patents even though I am not an expert in this area.

Patents as Property Rights

The granting of property rights to certain kinds of knowledge has long been recognized as a means for encouraging invention. A producer who held patent rights was assured that exact copies of his product could not be marketed without his consent, and his consent could be granted at some price. Economists have been troubled by the fact that—given the existence of the knowledge—patent rights discouraged producing that amount of the product that would make marginal production cost equal to the product price. If the value of the patent is to be greater than zero, and sale of the product is the only channel for covering all costs, sales receipts must exceed production costs. An obvious alternative is to finance invention from a source other than sales and recover only production costs through sales receipts. However, the other source is tax collections, and it can be shown that under certain conditions an optimal tax pattern would result in the same pattern of prices to consumers as would be obtained from a perfectly discriminating monopolist maximizing his profit subject to the same production and "collection" costs.[13] From this it has been inferred that pharmaceutical manufacturers may be pricing more nearly optimally than would a regulatory authority.

Under present U.S. law a patent expires seventeen years after it has been granted, and there has been much discussion about changing the length of life of the patent. Obviously, shortening a patent's life would not increase its value, nor would lengthening the life decrease the value. I do not propose to discuss optimal patent lives except to conjecture that legal problems of determining what property rights exist and that enforcing these rights makes for a finite life. If licenses to use a certain patent must be granted by the patent owner (compulsory licensing) at terms less favorable to the owner than those at which he would voluntarily grant this right, the value of the right must diminish. One cannot say much more about the effects of compulsory licensing without knowing by how much the value of a patent will be decreased.

The Effect of Patent Expiration in the Drug Industry

To briefly summarize, the past experience seems to suggest the validity of the following two hypotheses:

1. When the patent of a market leader expired, market share and price usually remained stable provided that
    a. There was not present a superior new single chemical entity of the same generic class.
    b. There was not present a molecularly different but therapeutically similar entry.
    c. The initial holder of the patent had not granted marketing license to other manufacturers.

2. When a new single chemical entity or a molecularly different but therapeutically similar competitive product was introduced, price competition and significant changes in market shares and leadership often occurred whether before or after patent expiration.

These observations are based on an analysis conducted by Chien of eleven drugs that had patent protection and his knowledge of the prescription drug business. They suggest that drug manufacturers have not had much reason to believe that patent expiration alone would necessarily result in a marked change in the demand for a brand name drug. In these cases investment in drug research and development could be made with a reasonable expectation that the stream of income generated by a drug in the years immediately following patent expiration would not end abruptly. However, they also suggest that competition through price or innovation had already existed and that this kind of competition seemed to have been workable.[14]

Even if a patent has expired, there may be no other reliable source. And even if one or more generic equivalents are available, a doctor may continue to prescribe a brand name drug. The antisubstitution laws prevent the pharmacist from substituting, so that these laws would have to be repealed in order for MAC to have significant impact outside the purchases made by government. And the strength of the brand name has to be diminished by the pressure of governmental purchasing power in order for the pharmacist to change his behavior on substitution. This also helps to explain the generic-each-and-every-time regulation with respect to advertising and labeling.

Dissemination of Trade Secrets

Related to the diminution in the value of a patent or a trade name is the move to more widely disseminate what might be generally termed trade secrets. These include the data relating to the safety and efficacy of a drug that are submitted in support of an NDA and the knowledge with respect to manufacture that has been accumulated by particular firms. Such information is not patentable. At the present time the applicant for an NDA may label certain portions of the application as trade secrets, and the FDA may not release such information, in spite of the Freedom of Information Act. The FDA is determined to increase public confidence in the integrity of the drug review process and is expected to try to make public as much information on its operations and relations with the drug industry as it can.

I do not know what price an NDA applicant would place on his application, that is, what he would charge to reveal its content. If the price is high, and the content is disclosed without his collecting the fee, the incentive to conduct the research required to develop and market a new drug is further diminished.

I believe that the Freedom of Information Act was designed with governmental decisions in mind. I do not believe its objective was to reveal the secrets that have been passed by one brewmaster to another for generations or the tricks employed by one manufacturer to make his costs lower than those of another. Making NDA applications public would be a move in this direction.

Notes

1. Robert B. Helms, ed., *Drug Development and Marketing* (Washington,

D.C.: American Enterprise Institute for Public Policy Research, 1975), p. 197.

2. Harold A. Clymer, "The Economics of Drug Innovation," in *The Development and Control of New Drug Products,* ed. M. Pernarowski and M. Darrach (Vancouver: University of British Columbia, 1972); David Schwartzman, "Pharmaceutical R and D Expenditures and Rates of Return," in Helms, *Drug Development,* pp. 63-79.

3. See, for example, William M. Wardell and Louis Lasagna, *Regulation and Drug Development* (Washington, D.C.: American Enterprise Institute for Public Policy Research, 1975).

4. Nineteen new single chemical entries were introduced in 1973 and eighteen in 1974, in comparison with a total of fifty-one during the previous five years. The number of new products introduced did not show any significant increase.

5. See, for example, Sam Peltzman, *Regulation of Pharmaceutical Innovation* (Washington, D.C.: American Enterprise Institute for Public Policy Research, 1974).

6. Ibid., p. 7.

7. *Task Force on Prescription Drugs: Second Interim Report and Recommendations,* HEW, August 30, 1968, p. 31.

8. National Science Foundation, *Research and Development in Industry, 1973* (Washington, D.C.: U.S. Government Printing Office, October 1975).

9. Mickey C. Smith, *Principles of Pharmaceutical Marketing* (Philadelphia: Lea and Febiger, 1975), p. 310.

10. *Competitive Problems in the Drug Industry,* Hearings Before the Subcommittee on Monopoly of the Select Committee on Small Business, United States Senate, Ninety-fourth Congress, Second Session on present Status of Competition in the Pharmaceutical Industry, part 30, pages 13918 and 14069.

11. Ibid., pp. 13915ff.

12. Dr. Crout's prepared statement, pp. 14069-14103.

13. See, for example, Mark A. Schankerman, "Common Costs in Pharmaceutical Research and Development: Implications for Direct Price Regulation," in *Impact of Public Policy on Drug Innovation and Pricing,* ed. Samuel A. Mitchell and Emery A. Link Proceedings of the Third Seminar on Pharmaceutical Public Policy Issues (Washington, D.C.: American University, 1976), pp. 3-26; also George Teeling-Smith, *The Canberra Hypothesis: The Economics of the Prescription Medicine Market* (England: Office of Health Economics, 1975).

14. For an interesting explanation, see Teeling-Smith, *Canberra Hypothesis;* David Schwartzman, *Innovation in the Pharmaceutical Industry* (Baltimore, Md.: Johns Hopkins University Press, 1976), pp. 251-299.

14 The Effect of National Health Insurance on the Economics of the Drug Industry

Robert I. Chien

Overview: *A relatively conservative yet flexible version of national health insurance similar to the Long-Ribicoff proposal is likely to be passed by Congress initially. Such a plan might easily be converted into a complete government-financed system during subsequent election years by gradually liberalizing limitations on deductibles, copayments, and coverage such as outpatient prescription drugs. Drug consumption will increase when this occurs, but the amount of increase will be moderate because aggregate drug demand is relatively insensitive to both price and income. Furthermore this increased demand will be completed in a few years.*

National health insurance will accelerate the dependence of both private business and the states on the federal government and further increase the pressure for cost containment of all services including drugs. Successful new drug development over the past fifty years through incentives for competitive innovation would be replaced by a monolithic administrative system unless the public is made fully aware of these implications.

Health Care as a Political Issue

A number of national problems have recently emerged that were previously not known to exist because problems that had been solved by the market have been converted into political ones. Few people have talked about a shortage of automobiles, since—except for a period during and immediately following World War II—the prices for cars have been free to adjust to clear the market. The petroleum shortage vanished when refinery product prices were permitted to rise so that people did not have to stand in line to buy gasoline or fuel oil. Similarly there was not a doctor shortage nor a national health care cost crisis

This paper was originally prepared by O.H. Brownlee, University of Minnesota, and Robert I. Chien as a part of a privately financed report on the future of the U.S. drug industry. It has been revised by Chien for this volume. The original paper also included comments on the effects of maximum allowable cost, antisubstitution repeal, volume purchase plans, and third-party payment programs.

229

until it was decided that everyone should have a "reasonable level of health care," regardless of where he resided, what the care cost, or what his own preferences might be. Historically some people have been in poor health because they were too poor to pay for drugs, doctors, and hospitals. Charitable agencies attempted to provide care for such persons, but it was not considered the duty of government to care for the nation's health. Families and individuals purchased health care according to the same principles that guided them in purchasing houses, repairing leaky roofs, or buying food.

The expanded role of the government in redistributing income has resulted in mixing the objectives of providing a minimum level of income for everyone, regardless of his own resources, and providing "adequate" amounts of so-called merit goods to everyone. The list of merit goods is an arbitrary one, but food, shelter, education, and health care are usually included, although transportation and petroleum have been added recently to some lists. Food stamps, rent subsidies, Medicare, Medicaid, and a national scholarship program already exist and may well be supplemented by bus stamps and gasoline and fuel oil coupons if some politicians' preferences are met.

The provision of particular goods and services rather than money to "needy" families or individuals incorporates the belief that these people are incapable of determining what is best for themselves. That children and feeble-minded persons should not be permitted to choose for themselves has been an accepted social principle, but that choices for children should be made by social workers rather than parents is a relatively recent phenomenon.

Health care has become a political problem because it has been included in the list of things that everyone should have, although what kind of care and how much is undefined. Because the amount of health care that would be chosen if its price were zero is far in excess of that which the society is willing to provide measures that reduce the price to individuals must be accompanied by measures for rationing available services by other means. Also ways of providing services at lower costs will be sought even though it means lower quality. Nearly all parts of the health care delivery system are under attack for their failure to "deliver adequate care at reasonable costs" even though most concepts of adequate care and reasonable costs are incompatible.

It is in this framework that one must consider the environment in which the health care industries, including the drug industry, will be operating during the next decade or so. Whether national health insurance will be adopted and whether its form will be decided politically, it is certain that this decision will have greater equality of income as a prime objective and that channeling a larger percentage of the national income through government acts as a depressant on that income itself.

The outlook is for continued confrontation between Congress, the administration agencies, and the producers of health care services. Quality of service and cost—of which profits are believed by politicians to be an important.

component—will be the issues. Price and profit controls will be among the tools government seeks to apply in the name and interest of the common people and, perhaps, just more votes to come their way.

Examples of National Health Insurance Proposals

There is little doubt that some form of national health insurance (NHI) will be enacted in the future. The nature of such insurance is less certain. The various forms of NHI suggested so far run the gamut from the fairly conservative (in that it would add least to federal expenditures) Long-Ribicoff bill, to the proposal of the American Hospital Association, all the way to the broad Kennedy-Corman bill.[1] There are at least twenty-one NHI bills before Congress, but I will attempt to summarize only three of these proposals.

The Long-Ribicoff Plan

The Long-Ribicoff Catastrophic Health Insurance and Medical Assistance Reform Plan consists of a catastrophic illness plan covering all those who pay Social Security taxes as well as a federal assistance plan for the poor and medically indigent, both administered through Medicare with private carriers handling claims. It also includes provisions for further encouraging private health insurance. The catastrophic portion of the bill would cover hospital costs after the first sixty days with about a 25 percent copayment by the patient. Eighty percent of physicians' fees in excess of $2000 per annum would be covered, with a maximum annual payment by the patient of $3000—the first $2000 plus not more than $1000 of 20 percent of the cost in excess of $2000. This portion of the bill would be financed through the payroll tax at a rate of 0.3 percent during the first three years, 0.35 percent for the next five years and 0.4 percent thereafter.

The second part of this plan would replace Medicaid and would be open to those whose annual family income falls below a specific amount depending on family size. Benefits would include hospital care, physicians' services, and other medical services. Those covered under this plan would contribute nominal amounts toward their medical costs. The first sixty days of hospitalization would be free, and thereafter expenses would be paid under the catastrophic portion of the bill. Physicians' fees would be fully covered with no limit on amount, except for a small charge for the first ten visits to a physician. This second part would be financed by federal and state general revenues.

The third part of the Long-Ribicoff proposal would try to stimulate the issuance and sale of private insurance to cover the deductible amounts for those covered under the catastrophic expense portion of the plan. It would ask private carriers to set up insurance plans covering the first sixty days of hospitalization and at least the first $2000 of medical expenses per person per year (with a maximum deductible of $100 per person and total cost sharing not to exceed 10 percent of total expenses).

The Long-Ribicoff bill is the least expensive of all the major plans and would provide the smallest amount of additional services. The most recent HEW study places the extra tab at $7.9 billion over the current program in 1980.

The National Health Care Service Plan

The plan introduced by the American Hospital Association proposes coverage of the entire population, including a provision for mandatory private insurance for employees to be paid for by their employers. It would cover hospitalization for ninety days, with little copayment, and physicians' fees for up to ten visits per year. This plan also contains a catastrophic illness provision, and the federal government would provide coverage for low-income families and the aged who are not eligible for an employee plan, thus superseding both Medicare and most of Medicaid. It would establish a health care corporation with regional offices that would furnish and coordinate health services. The coverage includes prescription drugs for specified conditions with a $1 copayment per prescription. Financing includes a mixture of contributions from the employer, the employee, the individual participant, federal general revenue, and the portion of payroll taxes assigned to the present Medicare program. The most recent HEW study places the extra tab at $20.2 billion over the current program in 1980. Because this plan covers a full range of outpatient services to be provided by the institutions to the public, it is believed to be even more expensive than the Kennedy plan in this respect.

The Kennedy-Corman Bill

The Kennedy-Corman bill would provide fairly sweeping medical coverage to the population with small deductions and copayments and would be administered by a new social service administration. It, too, would supersede both Medicare and Medicaid and would be financed by special payroll taxes and income taxes. According to the most recent HEW study, the extra cost of this Kennedy plan over the current program was estimated at $20.0 billion in 1980, with an increase of $130.1 billion in the federal outlays. It is probably the most expensive of all the proposals in increased federal expenditures, except for the previous Kennedy-Griffith bill. It would cover prescription drugs for specified chronic illnesses.

Outlook on Enactment

It has been generally believed that the NHI bill most likely to be passed will be similar to the Long-Ribicoff bill. There are four primary reasons to support this belief. First, such a program would require a lower level of government expenditure than most of the other proposed plans and could be financed with only a small increase in the tax rates. It would be relatively less inflationary than other proposed programs. Second, this sort of bill would not disrupt the present structure of the insurance industry. Third, it would be more in accord with the intuitive meaning of insurance; that is, it would provide protection against large outlays that could cause severe economic hardship rather than paying, for example, the cost of a low-cost prescription. Fourth, this type of NHI is very flexible in that its fundamental character can be altered without major administrative overhaul. For example, such a plan might easily be converted into a complete government-financed system over a number of national elections for vote-getting purposes simply by having the premium payment for part III of the bill covered by the federal government. Similarly outpatient prescription drug coverage may be added at a later date, and the amount of copayment may be gradually reduced.

**Impact on the Demand
for Health Care Services and Drugs**

The part of national health insurance that consists of replacement of private health insurance by government health insurance will have little impact on the quantities demanded for various components of the health care package. Similarly, if current forms of government payment (Medicare and Medicaid) are replaced by others, there should be little change in the services demanded by persons whose care is financed by the present government programs—providing that the terms of payment are unchanged. Since 90 percent of hospital charges were covered by third-party payments in 1975, the demand for such services is unlikely to be altered significantly if any of the various proposals are adopted. About 65 percent of physicians' fees were covered by third-party payments in 1975, so some expansion in the demand for the services of physicians should result if the effective prices for these services are further reduced. Since only 15 percent of costs of drugs and drug sundries were covered by third-party payments in 1975, complete coverage of prescription fees should make some difference in the volume of prescription drugs demanded.

The responses of drug purchases to changes in the prices of drugs have not been observed in a manner such that reliable estimates of such responses can be made. Available data are highly aggregated; that is, expenditures on all drugs or on very board classes are available, but data relating to the purchases of specific drugs—the characteristics of the buyers, the amounts they used and the prices they paid—are not usually available. It is to be expected that usage of drugs employed for treating chronic ailments, such as high blood pressure or diabetes, would be relatively insensitive to price. Furthermore, since chronic ailments characterize the bulk of those for which treatment by drugs has been prescribed for the aged (those sixty-five years of age or older), one might expect the demand for drugs by the aged who have access to health care to be relatively independent of the price of drugs.

We shall review (1) the expansion in the demand for health care in the United States that has accompanied expanded private health insurance, Medicare, and Medicaid, particularly the part of the increase that can be attributed to a reduction in the cost of care to those persons receiving it and (2) the estimated relationship between expenditures for prescription drugs as a group and the costs to the users for the United States. The U.S. estimates include some of those made by other persons working in the field of health economics, as well as some relatively crude ones we have made based on observations of drug purchases with varying costs to the users for selected populations in the United States.

*The Demand for Services of Doctors
and Hospitals in the United States*

There is general agreement that the expansion of third-party payment plans, such as Medicare, Medicaid, and others, has increased the quantities demanded in all health care categories: The plans lower both the user's costs of additional hospitalization and the cost of additional visits to doctors, encouraging health care consumption. Estimates of the amount of increase, however, vary substantially.

Because data representing the quantities of hospital services (the number of persons admitted and the average length of stay) and of physicians' services (the number of visits to a physician and the number of house calls) and the costs per unit of service to the users are available, several studies in which the quantities of services are related to the costs to the users have been made. Such studies observe variations in the out-of-pocket costs to patients—because of differences in amounts of coinsurance, for example—and relate these variations to the variation in the amount of service used, trying to take into consideration other factors that may influence demand, such as income, age, and sex, for example. Few of the studies have obtained observations on the behavior of individual patients. Most of the analyses relied on observations of state or other geographic area averages or of averages for a particular group at different points in time. If, however, there are differences among states in the average cost to patients, or if such costs vary over time, estimates of demand relations can be obtained from the "price" and "quantity" data.

Although he has not made a formal econometric analysis, a consultant to the Department of Health, Education, and Welfare whose estimates have been used by the department to forecast the costs of various national health insurance plans believes that if 50 percent of doctors' fees and hospitalization were covered by insurance (50 percent "coinsurance"), expenditure would expand by 25 percent; if all such costs were covered (100 percent "coinsurance"), expenditure would expand by about 50 percent. If only one of the two services were covered, expenditure on that service would expand by 1 percent for each 1 percent of the cost covered by insurance.

Estimates by Richard N. Rosett and Lien-fu Huang and by Martin S. Feldstein based on data for years prior to the initiation of Medicare and Medicaid are consistent with these numbers.[2] Rosett and Huang find that the demand for medical care will increase as the price falls and that the quantity demanded varies directly with the degree of coinsurance. This means that the expansion of demand for medical care depends heavily on the percentage of the tab that the insurance picks up. Derived estimates of the actual increase in demand range from 0.35 percent for a 1 percent reduction in cost, if insurance picks up 20 percent of the tab, to 1.5 percent for a 1 percent change in cost, if insurance picks up 80 percent of the tab. Our estimate, averaging these various studies, indicates a 25 percent increase in overall demand given zero user's cost, that is, a plan that picks up the whole tab.

These and other similar studies show, contrary to popular opinion, that the demand for health care is responsive to out-of-pocket cost and that consumption is not fixed: given lower costs, the resultant increase in the quantity demanded is substantial.[3] Other studies caution that much care is required in evaluating the expansion of any one category of health care expenditure (for example, prescription drugs) without considering other categories, because substitution of an inexpensive kind of health care service for a more expensive one does occur. All the health care markets are interrelated and must be approached with an eye to the "big picture."

These studies are not a random sample of the studies that have been made. They constitute those that we believe are most reliable. Some investigations report that quantities demanded vary directly with price, probably because the economic models on which the statistical estimates were based were improperly specified: the results may have characterized the responses of the suppliers of services to the prices they received rather than the responses of patients to the costs incurred.

The Relationship between the Cost to the User and the Quantity of Prescription Drugs Demanded

Because many factors influence the demand for prescription drugs, it is extremely difficult to estimate the influence of the out-of-pocket cost per unit on the quantity demanded. There are only a few instances in which price variation over time or price variation among different consumers at a given point in time has been observed *and* the relevant drug quantities purchased have been recorded. In addition, the amount paid by the user to the pharmacist is but one of the costs of getting the drug. A prescription must be obtained from a physician and a trip must be made to the pharmacy. The visit to the physician involves an expenditure of both money and time, and the trip to the pharmacist requires time. The higher the income level, the higher the value placed on time and thus the less sensitive the demand for a drug to the out-of-pocket payment made to the pharmacist. Also drug demand appears to vary with age and sex, with the severity of the illness, and with the expected efficacy and safety of the drug, but these latter features have not been studied in any of the sets of quantitative data that have come to our attention.

One consultant to the U.S. Department of Health, Education, and Welfare, whose estimates have been used by HEW in its projections of the costs of various national health insurance plans, believes that the sensitivity of the response of drug demand to the out-of-pocket cost is less than that of hospital or physicians' services. He believes that if the insurer paid half the bill, the expenditure on drugs would increase by about 12.5 percent and would increase by about 25 percent if there were no out-of-pocket cost to the consumer.

Samuel Mitchell estimates that drug consumption would increase 10 percent to 15 percent if there were national health insurance. Mitchell assumes that the out-of-pocket cost to users will be negligible and bases his estimate on the relative insensitivity of drug demand to increased income.[4]

I believe that if prescription drugs were to be provided with zero copayment, the quantity demanded would be only 10 percent to 15 percent larger than if current practice continued. If the coverage of drugs were to be phased in gradually over a period of five years, the growth rate in demand would be only about two to three percentage points per year more during each of these five years than if no change were made in the financing of drug purchases.

Such a range of increase in the growth rate is small relative to the rate of increase that the industry has been experiencing. Furthermore, after the program has been phased in, the growth rate will no longer be affected by the change in the method of financing.

Impact on Drug Prices and Profit

The foregoing paragraphs have discussed the potential impact of national health insurance on the unit demand for prescription drugs. Because the demand for prescription drugs is relatively inelastic, we do not foresee a bonanza for greatly increased drug production, particularly if outpatient drug coverage is likely to be gradual. On the other hand, the Department of Health, Education, and

Welfare has repeatedly defined the maximum allowable cost program on the
ground that although little savings can be accomplished at present, the program must be put into effect in anticipation of drug benefits under national
health insurance. Suggestions about an allowance for research and development
costs for inclusion in calculating the maximum allowable cost have been resisted
by the federal government based on the reasoning that rewards from the patent
system should cover those expenses even though the patent system itself has
been under attack and the effective patent life has been shortened because of
problems associated with the "drug lag." With the increasing control of the
federal government over pharmaceutical research and development through the
INDA-NDA process, and the prospect of the federal government's becoming a
monopsonist in drug purchases (and the purchase of many other health care
products and services), drug industry profits are under even more stress than
ever before. Given these trends, it is not unlikely that its past record of crea-
tive contributions will be replaced by a federally directed and financed pharmaceutical research and development program. The proven success based on private
initiative and competition through innovation will likely be replaced by a non-
competitive monolithic administrative system.

Conclusion

The enactment of additional national health insurance programs beyond Medicare and Medicaid is likely to take place by 1980 or 1984 with further amendments or "reforms" in the years following. This will mean eventual federal
control of all private health care activities and transfer of controls from the
state governments to Washington. This will probably help to push the federal
budget over the 50 percent mark of U.S. national income by the year 2000
and accelerate the dependence of both private businesses and the states on
Washington. The private health care providers will become government con-
tractors or vendors rather than enterprises with sufficient financial resources
to decide what and how much research is to be done. Others will become
salaried employees or grant applicants rather than small, independent business-
men. The drug industry will probably be no exception under this political
environment unless the public is made fully aware of these ominous implications and their potential dangers to the survival of the type of productive
society based on private initiative which many have known and cherished.

Notes

1. See Karen Davis, *National Health Insurance. Benefits, Costs and
Consequences* (The Brookings Institution: Washington, D.C., 1975) and

American Enterprise Institute, *National Health Insurance Proposals* (American Enterprise Institute for Public Policy Research: Washington, D.C., 1974).

2. Richard N. Rosett and Lien-fu Huang, "The Effect of Health Insurance on the Demand for Medical Care," *Journal of Political Economy,* March/April 1973; Martin Feldstein, "Hospital Cost Inflation: A Study of Nonprofit Price Dynamics," *American Economic Review,* December 1971.

3. Anne A. Scitovsky and Nelda M. Snyder, "Effect of Coinsurance on Use of Physician Services," *Social Security Bulletin,* June 1972; and Charles Phelps and Joseph P. Newhouse, "Effects of Coinsurance: A Multivariate Analysis," *Social Secuity Bulletin,* June 1972.

4. *Research from Washington,* "The Importance of Financial Constraints as a Determinant of Utilization of Health Care Services," Report 10-75, July 15, 1975.

Selected Bibliography

American Enterprise Institute for Public Policy Research. *National Health Insurance Proposals: Legislative Analysis.* Washington, D.C.: American Enterprise Institute for Public Policy Research, 1974.

_____. *New Drugs: Pending Legislation.* Washington, D.C.: American Enterprise Institute for Public Policy Research, 1976.

Ayanian, Robert. "Advertising and Rate of Return." Ph.D. dissertation, University of California at Los Angeles, 1974.

_____. "Investment in Intangibles and Rates of Return in the Drug Industry." Paper given at American Enterprise Institute for Public Policy Research Conference on Drug Development and Marketing, July, 1974.

_____. "The Profit Rates and Economic Performance of Drug Firms." In *Drug Development and Marketing,* edited by Robert B. Helms, pp. 91-97 Washington, D.C.: American Enterprise Institute for Public Policy Research, 1975.

Baily, Martin N. "Research and Development Costs and Returns: The U.S. Pharmaceutical Industry." *Journal of Political Economy* (January/February 1972).

Bloch, Harry. "True Profitability Measures." In *Regulation, Economics, and Pharmaceutical Innovation: The Proceedings of the Second Seminar on Economics of Pharmaceutical Innovation,* edited by Joseph D. Cooper, pp. 147-160, Washington, D.C.: The American University, 1974.

Brownlee, Oswald. "Rates of Return to Investment in the Pharmaceutical Industry: A Survey and Critical Appraisal." Unpublished paper.

_____, and Chien, Robert I. "Why is the Drug Discovery System in Severe Stress?" *Medical Marketing and Media* (June 1976): 46-50.

Cady, E. *Restricted Advertising and Competition: The Case of Retail Drugs.* Washington, D.C.: American Enterprise Institute for Public Policy Research, 1976.

Caglarcan, Erol; Faust, Richard E.; and Schnee, Jerome E. "Resource Allocation in Pharmaceutical Research and Development." In *Impact of Public Policy on Drug Innovation and Pricing: Proceedings of the Third Seminar on Pharmaceutical Public Policy Issues,* edited by Samuel A. Mitchell and Emery A Link, pp. 331-353, Washington, D.C.: The American University, 1976.

Clymer, Harold A. "The Changing Costs and Risks of Pharmaceutical Innovation." Paper presented at the First Seminar on Economics of Pharmaceutical Innovation, Washington D.C.: American University, 1969.

_____. "The Economic and Regulatory Climate: U.S. and Overseas Trends." In *Drug Development and Marketing,* edited by Robert B. Helms, pp. 137-154,

Washington, D.C.: American Enterprise Institute for Public Policy Research, 1975.

Cocks, Douglas L. "Product Innovation and the Dynamic Elements of Competition in the Ethical Pharmaceutical Industry." In *Drug Development and Marketing*, edited by Robert B. Helms, pp. 225-254, Washington, D.C.: American Enterprise Institute for Public Policy Research, 1975.

_____, and Virts, John R. "Market Definition and Concentration in the Ethical Pharmaceutical Industry." Unpublished paper.

_____, and Virts, John R. "Pricing Behavior of the Ethical Pharmaceutical Industry." *Journal of Business* 47 (July 1974): 349-362.

Comanor, William S. "The Drug Industry and Medical Research: The Economics of The Kefauver Investigations." *Journal of Business* 39 (January 1969): 12-18.

_____. "Research and Competitive Product Differentiation in the Pharmaceutical Industry in the United States." *Economica* 31 (November 1964): 372-384.

_____. "Research and Technical Change in the Pharmaceutical Industry." *Review of Economics and Statistics* 47 (May 1965): 182-190.

_____, and Schankerman, Mark A. "Identical Bids and Cartel Behavior." *Bell Journal of Economics* (1976): 281-286.

Conrad, Gordon R., and Plotkin, Irving H. "Risk and Return in American Industry: An Econometric Analysis." Reprinted in U.S. Senate, Select Committee on Small Business, Subcommittee on Monopoly, Hearings on *Competitive Problems in the Drug Industry*, part 5, 90th Cong., 1st Sess., 1968, pp. 1746-1784.

Cooper, Michael H. *Prices and Profits in the Pharmaceutical Industry.* New York: Oxford, Pergamon Press, 1966.

Costello, P.M. "Economics of the Ethical Drug Industry: A Reply to Whitney." *Antitrust Bulletin* 14 (Summer 1969): 397-403.

_____. "The Tetracycline Conspiracy: Structure, Conduct and Performance in the Drug Industry." *Antitrust Law and Economic Review* 1 (Summer 1968): 13-44.

Crout, J. Richard. "New Drug Regulation and Its Impact on Innovation." In *Impact of Public Policy on Drug Innovation and Pricing: Proceedings of the Third Seminar on Pharmaceutical Public Policy Issues*, edited by Samuel A. Mitchell and Emery A. Link, pp. 241-275, Washington, D.C.: American University, 1976.

Davis, Karen. *National Health Insurance: Benefits, Costs, and Consequences.* Washington, D.C.: The Brookings Institute, 1975.

Duetsch, Larry L. "Research Performance in the Ethical Drug Industry." *Marquette Business Review* 17 (Fall 1973): 129-142.

Feldstein, Martin S. "Advertising, Research and Profits in the Drug Industry." *Southern Economic Journal* 35 (January 1969): 239-243.

Firestone, John M. *Trends in Prescription Drug Prices.* Washington, D.C.: American Enterprise Institute for Public Policy Research, 1970.

Friedman, Jesse J. & Associates. *Economic Aspects of R&D Intensity in the Pharmaceutical Industry: A Composite Profile of Six Major Companies.* Washington, D.C.: Jesse J. Friedman & Associates, 1973.

_____, and Friedman, Murray N. "Relative Profitability and Monopoly Power." *The Conference Board Record* 9 (December 1972): 49-58.

Grabowski, Henry G. "The Determinants of Industrial Research and Development: A Study of the Chemical, Drug, and Petroleum Industries." *Journal of Political Economy* 76 (March-April 1968): 292-305.

_____. *Drug Regulation and Innovation: Empirical Evidence and Policy Options.* Washington, D.C.: American Enterprise Institute for Public Policy Research, 1976.

_____, Vernon, John M., and Thomas, Lacy Glenn. "The Effects of Regulatory Policy on the Incentive to Innovate: An International Comparative Analysis." In *Impact of Public Policy on Drug Innovation and Pricing: Proceedings of the Third Seminar on Pharmaceutical Public Policy Issues,* edited by Samuel A. Mitchell and Emery A. Link, pp. 47-95, Washington, D.C.: The American University, 1976.

Green, James R. "The Welfare Effects of an Antisubstitution Law in Pharmacy on the State of Oklahoma." Ph.D. dissertation, Oklahoma State University, 1972.

Harvard Business School. "A Note on the U.S. Prescription Drug Industry," parts I and II. Distributed by the Intercollegiate Case Clearing House, Boston, Mass.

Hornbrook, Mark C. "Market Domination and Promotional Intensity in the Wholesale-Retail Sector of the U.S. Pharmaceutical Industry." Paper presented at the Western Economic Association Annual Conference, San Francisco, California, June 24-27, 1976.

_____. "Market Structure and Conduct in the Wholesale-Retail Sector of the Pharmaceutical Industry." Paper presented at the Pharmacy Session of the American Public Health Association Meetings, New Orleans, Louisiana, October 20, 1974.

Jadlow, Joseph M., Jr. "The Economic Effects of the 1962 Drug Amendments." Ph.D. dissertation, University of Virginia, 1970.

Jondrow, James M. "A Measure of the Monetary Benefits and Costs to Consumers of the Regulation of Prescription Drug Effectiveness." Ph.D. dissertation, University of Wisconsin, 1972.

Lee, Armistead M. "Comparative Approaches to Cost Constraints in Pharmaceutical Benefits Program." In *Impact of Public Policy on Drug Innovation and Pricing: Proceedings of the Third Seminar on Pharmaceutical Public Policy Issues.* edited by Samuel A. Mitchell and Emergy A. Link, pp. 115-

194, Washington, D.C.: American University, 1976.

Markham, Jesse W. "Economic Incentives and Progress in the Drug Industry."
In *Drugs in Our Society*, edited by Paul Talalay, Baltimore: Johns Hopkins
Press, 1964.

Measday, Walter. *Pharmaceutical Industry in the Structure of American Industry*,
edited by Walter Adams, New York: Macmillan, 1971.

Peltzman, Sam. *Regulation of Pharmaceutical Innovation, The 1962 Amendments.* Washington, D.C.: American Enterprise Institute for Public Policy
Research, 1974.

Polanyi, George, and Polanyi, Priscilla. *Competition, Risk and Profit in the
Pharmaceutical Industry.* Association of the British Pharmaceutical Industry,
1975.

Research from Washington, Inc. *The Establishment of a National Insurance
Program for Prescription Drugs: Outlook and Implications.* Washington,
D.C.: Research from Washington, Inc., January 14, 1974.

Schankerman, Mark A. "Common Costs in Pharmaceutical Research and
Development: Implications for Direct Price Regulation." In *Impact of
Public Policy on Drug Innovation and Pricing: Proceedings of the Third
Seminar on Pharmaceutical Public Policy Issues,* edited by Samuel A. Mitchell
and Emery A. Link, pp. 3-45, Washington, D.C.: American University, 1976.

Schifrin, Leonard G. "The Ethical Drug Industry: The Case for Compulsory
Patent Licensing." *Antitrust Bulletin* 12 (Fall 1967): 893-915

Schnee, Jerome E. "Research and Technological Change in the Ethical Pharmaceutical Industry." Ph.D. dissertation, University of Pennsylvania, 1970.

———, and Caglarcan, Erol. "The Changing Pharmaceutical R&D Environment."
Business Economics 11 (May 1976): 31-38.

Schwartzman, David. *The Expected Return From Pharmaceutical Research.*
Washington, D.C.: American Enterprise Institute for Public Policy Research,
1975.

———. "Pharmaceutical R&D Expenditures and Rates of Return." In *Drug
Development and Marketing,* edited by Robert B. Helms, pp. 63-80, Washington, D.C.: American Enterprise Institute for Public Policy Research,
1975.

Solomon, Ezra. "Alternative Rate of Return Concepts and Their Implications
for Utility Regulation." *Bell Journal of Economics and Management Science*
2 (Autumn 1971).

Stauffer, T.R. "Discovery Risk, Profitability Performance and Survival Risk in
a Pharmaceutical Firm." In *Regulation, Economics and Pharmaceutical
Innovation: The Proceedings of the Second Seminar on Economics of
Pharmaceutical Innovation,* edited by Joseph D. Cooper, pp. 93-123,
Washington, D.C.: American University, 1974.

———. "The Measurement of Corporate Rates of Return: A Generalized Formulation." *Bell Journal of Economics and Management Science* 2 (Autumn 1971): 434-469.

_____. "Profitability in a Discovery-Intensive Industry: Pharmaceuticals." Paper given at American Enterprise Institute for Public Policy Research, 1974.

_____. "Profitability Measures in the Pharmaceutical Industry." In *Drug Development and Marketing*, edited by Robert B. Helms, pp. 97-120, Washington, D.C.: American Enterprise Institute for Public Policy Research, 1975.

Steele, Henry. "Monopoly and Competition in the Ethical Drugs Market." *Journal of Law and Economics* 5 (October 1962): 131-163.

_____. "Patent Restrictions and Price Competition in the Ethical Drugs Industry." *Journal of Law and Economics* 12 (July 1964): 198-223.

Stone, Charles F., III. "Economic Effects of New Drug Regulation in the United States." Unpublished paper.

Teeling-Smith, George. *The Canberra Hypothesis: The Economics of the Prescription Medicine Market.* England: Office of Health Economics, 1975.

_____. "Comparative International Source of Innovation." In *Regulation, Economics and Pharmaceutical Innovation: The Proceedings of the Second Seminar on Economics of Pharmaceutical Innovation*, edited by Joseph D. Cooper, pp. 59-72, Washington, D.C.: American University, 1974.

Telser, Lester G. "The Supply Response to Shifting Demand in the Ethical Pharmaceutical Industry." In *Drug Development and Marketing*, edited by Robert B. Helms, pp. 207-224, Washington, D.C.: American Enterprise Institute for Public Policy Research, 1975.

_____, Best, William; Egan, John W.; and Higinbotham, Harlow. "The Theory of Supply with Applications to the Ethical Pharmaceutical Industry." *Journal of Law and Economics* 18 (October 1975): 449-478.

Vernon, John M. "Concentration, Promotion, and Market Share Stability in the Pharmaceutical Industry." *Journal of Industrial Economics* 19 (July 1971): 246-266.

_____, and Peter Gusen. "Technical Change and Firm Size: The Pharmaceutical Industry." *The Review of Economics and Statistics* 56 (August 1974): 294-302.

Walker, Hugh D. *Market Power and Price Levels in the Ethical Drug Industry.* Bloomington, Indiana: Indiana University Press, 1971.

Wardell, William M. "Drug Development, Regulation, and the Practice of Medicine." *Journal of the American Medical Association* 229 (September 9, 1974): 1457-1461.

_____. "The Impact of Regulation on New Drug Development." Unpublished paper.

_____. "Monitored Release and Postmarketing Surveillance: Foreign and

Proposed U.S. Systems." In *Impact of Public Policy on Drug Innovation and Pricing: Proceedings of the Third Seminar on Pharmaceutical Public Policy Issues,* edited by Samuel A. Mitchell and Emery A. Link, pp. 289-327, Washington, D.C.: The American University, 1976.

———, Hassar, Mohammed and Lasagna, Louis. "The Rate of New Drug Discovery: The Output, Flow, and Regulatory Disposition of New Chemical Entities Produced by the U.S. Pharmaceutical Industry since 1962." Unpublished paper.

———, and Lasagna, Louis. *Regulation and Drug Development.* Washington, D.C.: American Enterprise Institute for Public Policy Research, 1975.

Wesolowski, Jeremii W. and Wesolowski, Zdzislaw P. "The Economics of Research and Development in the Pharmaceutical Industry." *Marquette Business Review* 14 (Fall 1970): 158-173.

Whitney, Simon N. "Economics of the Ethical Drug Industry: A Reply to Critics." *Antitrust Bulletin,* 13 (Fall 1968): 803-849.

List of Contributors
and Commentators

Oswald H. Brownlee
Professor of Economics
University of Minnesota

Robert I. Chien
Associate Professor of Marketing
Roosevelt University
President, Institute of Health Economics and Social Studies

Kenneth W. Clarkson
Professor of Economics
University of Miami

Douglas L. Cocks
Staff Economist
Eli Lilly and Company

William S. Comanor
Professor of Economics
University of California, Santa Barbara

Henry G. Grabowski
Professor of Economics
Duke University

Ronald W. Hansen
Assistant Professor of Management
University of Rochester

Joseph M. Jadlow
Professor of Economics
Oklahoma State University

W. Duncan Reekie
Professor of Business Studies
University of Edinburgh

David Schwartzman
Professor Economics
New School for Social Research

Gail E. Updegraff
Senior Economist
JRB Associates, Inc.

John M. Vernon
Professor of Economics
Duke University

John R. Virts
Corporate Staff Economist
Eli Lilly and Company

William M. Wardell
Associated Professor of Pharmacology, Toxicology, and Medicine
Director of the Center for the Study of Drug Development
University of Rochester

Leonard W. Weiss
Professor of Economics
University of Wisconsin

J. Fred Weston
Professor of Business Economics and Finance
University of California, Los Angeles

About the Editor

Robert I. Chien is associate professor of marketing at Roosevelt University in Chicago, president of the Institute of Health Economics and Social Studies, a non-profit organization for public policy research and communications in the health care field, and also president of Robert I. Chien & Associates, Inc., a management consulting firm. Prior to 1974, he was economics advisor to the chief executive officer and divisional director of corporate business research and development of G.D. Searle & Co., original developer of the birth control pill and other new medicines.

Dr. Chien received the LL.B. from the National Southwest Associated University (China), the M.B.A. from the University of Denver, and the M.A. in statistics as well as the Ph.D. in economics with a concentration in marketing from the University of Minnesota. He has taught economics, marketing, and statistics at Roosevelt University, Wayne State University, and the University of Minnesota, and has published widely on the subjects of pharmaceutical marketing, finance, and economics. He has been active in many professional associations and is listed in *American Men of Science, World's Who's Who in Finance and Industry, Dictionary of International Biography,* and other biographies. In addition, he has participated in numerous graduate seminars conducted by leading universities.